About Pearson

Pearson is the world's learning company, with presence across 70 countries worldwide. Our unique insights and world-class expertise comes from a long history of working closely with renowned teachers, authors and thought leaders, as a result of which, we have emerged as the preferred choice for millions of teachers and learners across the world.

We believe learning opens up opportunities, creates fulfilling careers and hence better lives. We hence collaborate with the best of minds to deliver you class-leading products, spread across the Higher Education and Test Preparation spectrum.

Superior learning experience and improved outcomes are at the heart of everything we do. This product is the result of one such effort.

Your feedback plays a critical role in the evolution of our products and you can contact us – reachus@pearson.com. *We look forward to it.*

Python Programming with Design Patterns

James W. Cooper

Pearson

ISBN 978-93-615-9456-4

First Impression, 2024
Second Impression, 2025

Published by Pearson India Education Services Pvt. Ltd, CIN: U72200TN2005PTC057128.

Head Office: 1st Floor, Berger Tower, Plot No. C-001A/2, Sector 16B, Noida - 201 301, Uttar Pradesh, India.
Registered Office: Featherlite, 'The Address' 5th Floor, Survey No 203/10B, 200 Ft MMRD Road, Zamin Pallavaram, Chennai – 600 044.

Website: in.pearson.com; Email: companysecretary.india@pearson.com

Printed in India at Sai Printo Pack Pvt Ltd

Pearson's Commitment to Diversity, Equity, and Inclusion

Pearson is dedicated to creating bias-free content that reflects the diversity of all learners. We embrace the many dimensions of diversity, including but not limited to race, ethnicity, gender, socioeconomic status, ability, age, sexual orientation, and religious or political beliefs.

Education is a powerful force for equity and change in our world. It has the potential to deliver opportunities that improve lives and enable economic mobility. As we work with authors to create content for every product and service, we acknowledge our responsibility to demonstrate inclusivity and incorporate diverse scholarship so that everyone can achieve their potential through learning. As the world's leading learning company, we have a duty to help drive change and live up to our purpose to help more people create a better life for themselves and to create a better world.

Our ambition is to purposefully contribute to a world where:

- Everyone has an equitable and lifelong opportunity to succeed through learning.
- Our educational products and services are inclusive and represent the rich diversity of learners.
- Our educational content accurately reflects the histories and experiences of the learners we serve.
- Our educational content prompts deeper discussions with learners and motivates them to expand their own learning (and worldview).

While we work hard to present unbiased content, we want to hear from you about any concerns or needs with this Pearson product so that we can investigate and address them.

- Please contact us with concerns about any potential bias at https://www.pearson.com/report-bias.html.

To Vicki

Contents at a Glance

I: Introduction

1 Introduction to Objects **5**

2 Visual Programming in Python **17**

3 Visual Programming of Tables of Data **41**

4 What Are Design Patterns? **53**

II: Creational Patterns

5 The Factory Pattern **61**

6 The Factory Method Pattern **67**

7 The Abstract Factory Pattern **75**

8 The Singleton Pattern **79**

9 The Builder Pattern **83**

10 The Prototype Pattern **91**

11 Summary of Creational Patterns **95**

III: Structural Patterns

12 The Adapter Pattern **99**

13 The Bridge Pattern **105**

14 The Composite Pattern **111**

15 The Decorator Pattern **121**

16 The Façade Pattern **129**

17 The Flyweight Pattern **139**

18 The Proxy Pattern **145**

19 Summary of Structural Patterns **151**

IV: Behavioral Patterns

20 Chain of Responsibility Pattern 155

21 The Command Pattern 167

22 The Interpreter Pattern 177

23 The Iterator Pattern 187

24 The Mediator Pattern 195

25 The Memento Pattern 203

26 The Observer Pattern 211

27 The State Pattern 217

28 The Strategy Pattern 225

29 The Template Pattern 233

30 The Visitor Pattern 239

V: A Brief Introduction to Python

31 Variables and Syntax in Python 249

32 Making Decisions in Python 263

33 Development Environments 275

34 Python Collections and Files 279

35 Functions 291

A Running Python programs 295

Index 299

Table of Contents

I: Introduction 1

- The tkinter Library 2
- GitHub 2

1 Introduction to Objects 5

- The Class __init__ Method 6
- Variables Inside a Class 6
- Collections of Classes 7
- Inheritance 8
- Derived Classes Created with Revised Methods 8
- Multiple Inheritance 8
- Drawing a Rectangle and a Square 10
- Visibility of Variables 12
  - Properties 13
  - Local Variables 13
- Types in Python 13
- Summary 14
- Programs on GitHub 15

2 Visual Programming in Python 17

- Importing Fewer Names 19
- Creating an Object-Oriented Version 19
- Using Message Boxes 21
- Using File Dialogs 22
- Understanding Options for the Pack Layout Manager 23
- Using the ttk Libraries 24
- Responding to User Input 25
  - Adding Two Numbers 26
  - Catching the Error 26
- Applying Colors in tkinter 27
- Creating Radio Buttons 27
  - Using a Class-Level Variable 30
- Communicating Between Classes 30
- Using the Grid Layout 30
- Creating Checkbuttons 32
  - Disabling Check Boxes 34

Adding Menus to Windows 35
Using the LabelFrame 39
Moving On 40
Examples on GitHub 40

3 Visual Programming of Tables of Data 41
Creating a Listbox 42
Displaying the State Data 44
Using a Combobox 46
The Treeview Widget 47
Inserting Tree Nodes 50
Moving On 51
Example Code on GitHub 51

4 What Are Design Patterns? 53
Defining Design Patterns 54
The Learning Process 55
Notes on Object-Oriented Approaches 56
Python Design Patterns 57
References 57

II: Creational Patterns 59

5 The Factory Pattern 61
How a Factory Works 61
Sample Code 62
The Two Subclasses 62
Building the Simple Factory 63
Using the Factory 63
A Simple GUI 64
Factory Patterns in Math Computation 65
Programs on GitHub 65
Thought Questions 66

6 The Factory Method Pattern 67
The Swimmer Class 68
Thc Event Classes 69
Straight Seeding 70
Circle Seeding 71

Our Seeding Program 72
Other Factories 74
When to Use a Factory Method 74
Programs on GitHub 74

7 The Abstract Factory Pattern 75
A GardenMaker Factory 75
How the User Interface Works 77
Consequences of the Abstract Factory Pattern 77
Thought Questions 78
Code on GitHub 78

8 The Singleton Pattern 79
Throwing the Exception 80
Creating an Instance of the Class 80
Static Classes As Singleton Patterns 81
Finding the Singletons in a Large Program 81
Other Consequences of the Singleton Pattern 82
Sample Code on GitHub 82

9 The Builder Pattern 83
An Investment Tracker 84
Calling the Builders 86
The List Box Builder 87
The Checkbox Builder 88
Displaying the Selected Securities 89
Consequences of the Builder Pattern 89
Thought Questions 89
Sample Code on GitHub 89

10 The Prototype Pattern 91
Cloning in Python 91
Using the Prototype 92
Consequences of the Prototype Pattern 94
Sample Code on GitHub 94

11 Summary of Creational Patterns 95

III: Structural Patterns 97

12 The Adapter Pattern 99

Moving Data Between Lists 99

Making an Adapter 101

The Class Adapter 103

Two-Way Adapters 103

Pluggable Adapters 103

Programs on GitHub 103

13 The Bridge Pattern 105

Creating the User Interface 107

Extending the Bridge 108

Consequences of the Bridge Pattern 109

Programs on GitHub 110

14 The Composite Pattern 111

An Implementation of a Composite 112

Salary Computation 112

The Employee Classes 112

The Boss Class 113

Building the Employee Tree 114

Printing the Employee Tree 114

Creating a Treeview of the Composite 116

Using Doubly Linked Lists 117

Consequences of the Composite Pattern 118

A Simple Composite 119

Other Implementation Issues 119

Dealing with Recursive Calls 119

Ordering Components 120

Caching Results 120

Programs on GitHub 120

15 The Decorator Pattern 121

Decorating a Button 121

Using a Decorator 122

Using Nonvisual Decorators 123

Decorated Code 124

The dataclass Decorator 125
Using dataclass with Default Values 126
Decorators, Adapters, and Composites 126
Consequences of the Decorator Pattern 126
Programs on GitHub 127

16 The Façade Pattern 129
Building the Façade Classes 131
Creating Databases and Tables 135
Using the SQLite Version 136
Consequences of the Façade 137
Programs on GitHub 137
Notes on MySQL 137
Using SQLite 138
References 138

17 The Flyweight Pattern 139
What Are Flyweights? 139
Example Code 140
Selecting a Folder 142
Copy-on-Write Objects 143
Program on GitHub 143

18 The Proxy Pattern 145
Using the Pillow Image Library 145
Displaying an Image Using PIL 146
Using Threads to Handle Image Loading 146
Logging from Threads 149
Copy-on-Write 149
Comparing Related Patterns 149
Programs on GitHub 150

19 Summary of Structural Patterns 151

IV: Behavioral Patterns 153

20 Chain of Responsibility Pattern 155
When to Use the Chain 156
Sample Code 156

The Listboxes 159
Programming a Help System 160
Receiving the Help Command 161
The First Case 162
A Chain or a Tree? 163
Kinds of Requests 164
Consequences of the Chain of Responsibility 164
Programs on GitHub 165

21 The Command Pattern 167
When to Use the Command Pattern 167
Command Objects 168
A Keyboard Example 168
Calling the Command Objects 170
Building Command Objects 171
The Command Pattern 172
Consequences of the Command Pattern 172
Providing the Undo Function 172
Creating the Red and Blue Buttons 175
Undoing the Lines 175
Summary 176
References 176
Programs on GitHub 176

22 The Interpreter Pattern 177
When to Use an Interpreter 177
Where the Pattern Can Be Helpful 177
A Simple Report Example 178
Interpreting the Language 179
How Parsing Works 180
Sorting Using attrgetter() 181
The Print Verb 182
The Console Interface 182
The User Interface 183
Consequences of the Interpreter Pattern 184
Programs on GitHub 185

23 The Iterator Pattern 187
Why We Use Iterators 187
Iterators in Python 187
A Fibonacci Iterator 188
Getting the Iterator 189
Filtered Iterators 189
The Iterator Generator 191
A Fibonacci Iterator 191
Generators in Classes 192
Consequences of the Iterator Pattern 192
Programs on GitHub 193

24 The Mediator Pattern 195
An Example System 195
Interactions Between Controls 197
Sample Code 198
Mediators and Command Objects 199
Consequences of the Mediator Pattern 200
Single Interface Mediators 200
Programs on GitHub 201

25 The Memento Pattern 203
When to Use a Memento 203
Sample Code 204
Consequences of the Memento Pattern 209
Programs on GitHub 209

26 The Observer Pattern 211
Example Program for Watching Colors Change 212
The Message to the Media 215
Consequences of the Observer Pattern 215
Programs on GitHub 215

27 The State Pattern 217
Sample Code 217
Switching Between States 221
How the Mediator Interacts with the StateManager 222
Consequences of the State Pattern 224

State Transitions 224
Programs on GitHub 224

28 The Strategy Pattern 225
Why We Use the Strategy Pattern 225
Sample Code 226
The Context 227
The Program Commands 227
The Line and Bar Graph Strategies 228
Consequences of the Strategy Pattern 230
Programs on GitHub 231

29 The Template Pattern 233
Why We Use Template Patterns 233
Kinds of Methods in a Template Class 234
Sample Code 234
Drawing a Standard Triangle 235
Drawing an Isosceles Triangle 236
The Triangle Drawing Program 237
Templates and Callbacks 238
Summary and Consequences 238
Example Code on GitHub 238

30 The Visitor Pattern 239
When to Use the Visitor Pattern 239
Working with the Visitor Pattern 241
Sample Code 241
Visiting Each Class 242
Visiting Several Classes 242
Bosses Are Employees, Too 243
Double Dispatching 245
Traversing a Series of Classes 245
Consequences of the Visitor Pattern 245
Example Code on GitHub 245

V: A Brief Introduction to Python 247

31 Variables and Syntax in Python 249
Data Types 250
Numeric Constants 250
Strings 250
Character Constants 251
Variables 252
Complex Numbers 253
Integer Division 253
Multiple Equal Signs for Initialization 254
A Simple Python Program 254
Compiling and Running This Program 255
Arithmetic Operators 255
Bitwise Operators 255
Combined Arithmetic and Assignment Statements 256
Comparison Operators 256
The input Statement 257
PEP 8 Standards 258
Variable and Function Names 258
Constants 258
Class Names 258
Indentation and Spacing 259
Comments 259
Docstrings 259
String Methods 260
Examples on GitHub 261

32 Making Decisions in Python 263
elif is "else if" 263
Combining Conditions 264
The Most Common Mistake 264
Looping Statements in Python 265
The for Loop and Lists 265
Using range in if Statements 266
Using break and continue 266
The continue Statement 267
Python Line Length 267

The print Function 267
Formatting Numbers 268
C and Java Style Formatting 269
The format string Function 269
f-string Formatting 269
Comma-Separated Numbers 270
Strings 270
Formatting Dates 271
Using the Python match Function 271
Pattern Matching 272
Reference 273
Moving On 273
Sample Code on GitHub 273

33 Development Environments 275
IDLE 275
Thonny 275
PyCharm 276
Visual Studio 276
Other Development Environments 276
LiClipse 276
Jupyter Notebook 277
Google Colaboratory 277
Anaconda 277
Wing 278
Command-Line Execution 278
CPython, IPython, and Jython 278

34 Python Collections and Files 279
Slicing 279
Slicing Strings 280
Negative Indexes 281
String Prefix and Suffix Removal 281
Changing List Contents 281
Copying a List 282
Reading Files 282
Using the with Loop 283
Handling Exceptions 284

Using Dictionaries 284
Combining Dictionaries 286
Using Tuples 286
Using Sets 287
Using the map Function 287
Writing a Complete Program 288
Impenetrable Coding 288
Using List Comprehension 289
Sample Programs on GitHub 290

35 Functions 291
Returning a Tuple 292
Where Does the Program Start? 292
Summary 293
Programs on GitHub 293

A Running Python Programs 295
If You Have Python Installed 295
Shortcuts 295
Creating an Executable Python Program 296
Command-Line Arguments 297

Index 299

Preface

When I began studying Python, I was impressed by how simple coding was and how easy it was to get started writing basic programs. I tried several development environments, and in all cases, I was able to get simple programs running in moments.

The Python syntax was simple, and there were no brackets or semicolons to remember. Other than remembering to use the Tab key (to generate those four-space indentations), coding in Python was easy.

But it was only after I played with Python for a few weeks that I began to see how sophisticated the language really is and how much you can really do with it. Python is a fully object-oriented language, making it easy to create classes that hold their own data without a lot of syntactic fussing.

In fact, I started trying to write some programs that I had written years ago in Java, and I was amazed by how much simpler they were in Python. And with the powerful IDEs, it was hard to make many mistakes.

When I realized how much I could get done quickly in Python, I also realized that it was time to write a book about powerful programs you can write in Python. This led to my writing new, clean, readable versions of the 23 classic design patterns that I had originally coded some years before.

The result is this book, which illustrates the basics of object-oriented programming, visual programming, and how to use all of the classic patterns. You can find complete working code for all these programs on GitHub at https://github.com/jwcnmr/jameswcooper/tree/main/Pythonpatterns.

This book is designed to help Python programmers broaden their knowledge of object-oriented programming (OOP) and the accompanying design patterns.

- If you are new to Python but have experience in other languages, you will be able to charge ahead by reviewing Chapter 31 through Chapter 35 and then starting back at Chapter 1.
- If you are experienced in Python but want to learn about OOP and design patterns, start at Chapter 1. If you like, you can skip Chapter 2 and Chapter 3 and go right through the rest of the book.
- If you are new to programming in general, spend some time going over Chapter 31 through 35 to try some of the programs. Then start on Chapter 1 to learn about OOP and design patterns.

You will likely find that Python is the easiest language you ever learned, as well as the most effortless language for writing the objects you use in design patterns. You'll see what they are for and how to use them in your own work.

In any case, the object-oriented programming methods presented in these pages can help you write better, more reusable program code.

Book Organization

This book is organized into five parts.

Part I, "Introduction"

Design patterns essentially describe how objects can interact effectively. This book starts by introducing objects in Chapter 1, "Introduction to Objects," and providing graphical examples that clearly illustrate how the patterns work.

Chapter 2, "Visual Programming in Python," and Chapter 3, "Visual Programming of Tables of Data," introduce the Python tkinter library, which gives you a way to create windows, buttons, lists, tables, and more with minimal complexity.

Chapter 4, "What Are Design Patterns?", begins the discussion of design patterns by exploring exactly what they are.

Part II, "Creational Patterns"

Part II starts by outlining the first group of patterns that the "Gang of Four" named Creational Patterns.

Chapter 5, "The Factory Pattern," describes the basic Factory pattern, which serves as the simple basis of the three factory patterns that follow. In this chapter, you create a Factory class that decides which of several related classes to use, based on the data itself.

Chapter 6, "The Factory Method Pattern," explores the Factory method. In this pattern, no single class makes the decision as to which subclass to instantiate. Instead, the superclass defers the decision to each subclass.

Chapter 7, "The Abstract Factory Pattern," discusses the Abstract Factory pattern. You can use this pattern when you want to return one of several related classes of objects, each of which can return several different objects on request. In other words, the Abstract Factory is a factory object that returns one of several groups of classes.

Chapter 8, "The Singleton Pattern," looks at the Singleton pattern, which describes a class in which there can be no more than one instance. It provides a single global point of access to that instance. You don't use this pattern all that often, but it is helpful to know how to write it.

In Chapter 9, "The Builder Pattern," you see that the Builder pattern separates the construction of a complex object from its visual representation, so that several different representations can be created, depending on the needs of the program.

Chapter 10, "The Prototype Pattern," shows how to use the Prototype pattern when creating an instance of a class is time consuming or complex. Instead of creating more instances, you make copies of the original instance and modify them as appropriate.

Chapter 11, "Summary of Creational Patterns," just summarizes the patterns in Part II.

Part III, "Structural Patterns"

Part III begins with a short discussion of Structural Patterns.

Chapter 12, "The Adapter Pattern," examines the Adapter pattern, which is used to convert the programming interface of one class into that of another. Adapters are useful whenever you want unrelated classes to work together in a single program.

Chapter 13, "The Bridge Pattern," takes up the similar Bridge pattern, which is designed to separate a class's interface from its implementation. This enables you to vary or replace the implementation without changing the client code.

Chapter 14, "The Composite Pattern," delves into systems in which a component may be an individual object or may represent a collection of objects. The Composite pattern is designed to accommodate both cases, often in a treelike structure.

In Chapter 15, "The Decorator Pattern," we look at the Decorator pattern, which provides a way to modify the behavior of individual objects without having to create a new derived class. Although this can apply to visual objects such as buttons, the most common use in Python is to create a kind of macro that modifies the behavior of a single class instance.

In Chapter 16, "The Façade Pattern," we learn to use the Façade pattern to write a simplifying interface to code that otherwise might be unduly complex. This chapter deals with such an interface to a couple of different databases.

Chapter 17, "The Flyweight Pattern," describes the Flyweight pattern, which enables you to reduce the number of objects by moving some of the data outside the class. You can consider this approach when you have multiple instances of the same class.

Chapter 18, "The Proxy Pattern," looks at the Proxy pattern, which is used when you need to represent an object that is complex or time consuming to create, by a simpler one. If creating an object is expensive in time or computer resources, Proxy enables you to postpone creation until you need the actual object.

Chapter 19, "Summary of Structural Patterns," summarizes these Structural patterns.

Part IV, "Behavioral Patterns"

Part IV outlines the Behavioral Patterns.

Chapter 20, "Chain of Responsibility Pattern," looks at how the Chain of Responsibility pattern allows a decoupling between objects by passing a request from one object to the next in a chain until the request is recognized.

Chapter 21, "The Command Pattern," shows how the Command pattern uses simple objects to represent the execution of software commands. Additionally, this pattern enables you to support logging and undoable operations.

Chapter 22, "The Interpreter Pattern," looks at the Interpreter pattern, which provides a definition of how to create a little execution language and include it in a program.

In Chapter 23, "The Iterator Pattern," we explore the well-known Iterator pattern, which describes the formal ways you can move through a collection of data items.

Chapter 24, "The Mediator Pattern," takes up the important Mediator pattern. This pattern defines how communication between objects can be simplified by using a separate object to keep all objects from having to know about each other.

Chapter 25, "The Memento Pattern," saves the internal state of an object, so you can restore it later.

In Chapter 26, "The Observer Pattern," we look at the Observer pattern, which enables you to define the way a number of objects can be notified of a change in a program state.

Chapter 27, "The State Pattern," describes the State pattern, which allows an object to modify its behavior when its internal state changes.

Chapter 28, "The Strategy Pattern," describes the Strategy pattern, which, like the State pattern, switches easily between algorithms without any monolithic conditional statements. The difference between the State and Strategy patterns is that the user generally chooses which of several strategies to apply.

In Chapter 29, "The Template Pattern," we look at the Template pattern. This pattern formalizes the idea of defining an algorithm in a class but leaves some of the details to be implemented in subclasses. In other words, if your base class is an abstract class, as often happens in these design patterns, you are using a simple form of the Template pattern.

Chapter 30, "The Visitor Pattern," explores The Visitor pattern, which turns the tables on the object-oriented model and creates an external class to act on data in other classes. This is useful if there are a fair number of instances of a small number of classes and you want to perform some operation that involves all or most of them.

Part V, "A Brief Introduction to Python"

In this last section of the book, we provide a succinct summary of the Python language. If you are only passingly familiar with Python, this will get you up to speed. It is sufficiently thorough to instruct beginner as well.

In Chapter 31, "Variables and Syntax in Python," we review the basic Python variables and syntax, and in Chapter 32, "Making Decisions in Python," we illustrate the ways your programs can make decisions.

In Chapter 33, "Development Environments," we provide a short summary of the most common development environments, and in Chapter 34, "Python Collections and Files," we discuss arrays and files.

Finally in Chapter 35, "Functions," we take up how to use functions on Python.

Enjoy writing design patterns and learning the ins and outs of the powerful Python language!

Register Your Book

Register your copy of *Python Programming with Design Patterns* on the InformIT site for convenient access to updates and/or corrections as they become available. To start the registration process, go to informit.com/register and log in or create an account. Enter the product ISBN **9780137579938** and click Submit. Look on the Registered Products tab for an Access Bonus Content link next to this product, and follow that link to access any available bonus materials. If you would like to be notified of exclusive offers on new editions and updates, please check the box to receive email from us.

Acknowledgments

I must start by thanking the late John Vlissides, one of the original "Gang of Four," for his clear explanations of several points about these design patterns. He worked just a few doors down from me at IBM Research and didn't mind my dropping in for a chat about patterns from time to time.

I also really appreciated early supportive comments from Arianne Dee and Ausif Mahmood, as well as Vaughn Cooper.

Of course, my editor, Debra J. Williams, has been both supportive and creative in helping me bring this project to fruition, as have the reviewers, Nick Cohron and Regina R. Monaco. And from a development point of view, Chris Zahn has been terrific.

I hope you enjoy writing patterns in Python as much as I have.

James Cooper
Wilton, CT
July 2021

About the Author

James W. Cooper holds a PhD in chemistry and worked in academia, for the scientific instrument industry, and for IBM for 25 years, primarily as a computer scientist at IBM's Thomas J. Watson Research Center. Now retired, he is the author of 20 books, including 3 on design patterns in various languages. His most recent books are *Flameout: The Rise and Fall of IBM Instruments* (2019) and *Food Myths Debunked* (2014).

James holds 11 patents and has written 60 columns for *JavaPro Magazine*. He has also written nearly 1,000 columns for the now vanished Examiner.com on foods and chemistry, and he currently writes his own blog: FoodScienceInstitute.com. Recently, he has written columns on Python for Medium.com and Substack.

He is also involved in local theater groups and is the treasurer for Troupers Light Opera, where he performs regularly.

PART I

Introduction

Python is an easy-to-learn language developed primarily by Dutch computer scientist Guido van Rossum starting in 1989. van Rossum's objective was to create a simple scripting language without the complicated brackets and syntax that all the C-like languages (C, C++, Java, and C#, among others) require.

Python is seductively easy to read and learn because, without all the "syntactic sugar" of other languages, you can read the statements directly. You probably can figure out this first example just by reading it:

```
array = [2, 5, 7, 9]
for a in array:
   print (a/2)
```

The result follows:

```
1.0
2.5
3.5
4.5
```

Python was named after the popular BBC series *Monty Python's Flying Circus*, and references to the actors and some of the well-known sketches can be found within the language and some of its tools. For example, a simple development environment named IDLE ships with the current Python downloads.

van Rossum released the first version, version 0.90, in 1991 and then released version 1.0 in 1994. The project continued to grow with version 2.0, released in 2000, and version 3.0, released in 2008. Version 3 rectified some design flaws in earlier versions of the language and thus was not completely compatible with earlier releases. van Rossum stepped down as the overall project leader in 2008 but continues to contribute to the language.

At its heart, Python is an object-oriented language: Just about every Python component is actually an object. So, we introduce object-oriented programming in Chapter 1, "Introduction to Objects," and use it throughout many of the examples in the rest of the book.

The technical underpinnings of Python are much like Java, in that the language compiler translates the code into lower-level *byte codes*. Then the problem of implementing Python amounts to writing an interpreter for those byte codes. Python implementations have been created for Windows, Mac OSX, and Linux platforms. You can also find implementations for AIX, AS/400s, iOS, OS/390, Solaris, VMS, and HP-UX.

Now, when you think of a scripting language, you might imagine that it supports relatively simple programming concepts. And in fact, anyone with basic computer programming skills can easily learn Python. But Python is a full-fledged language that is both simple enough for a quick programming problem and sophisticated enough to allow object-oriented programming, inheritance, exception handling, and multithreading. In writing our example programs that make up a major part of this book, we found that the Python programs were clearer and more succinct than the ones we wrote in previous languages.

In the major part of the book (Chapter 5-30), we show you how you can easily write the 23 most common design patterns, which are fundamental to object-oriented programming. These are the tools you will be able to use in all your further programming. In addition to being clever ways to write object-oriented programs, they show you how objects can communicate while keeping classes independent from one another.

If the example code above is somewhat confusing, we provide a concise introduction to Python in Chapters 31-35. Then you can come back to the Design Patterns section that starts in Chapter 5.

Python is a growing language, with new versions released about once a year. So many Python libraries are available that no book can cover them all. If you want to find out how to do something unusual in Python, or if you have a programming problem you can't solve, the Internet is your friend. Resources such as stackoverflow.com are invaluable.

The tkinter Library

Many of the patterns make use of the tkinter user interface (GUI) library. In many cases, this is just to give you a graphical example so you can see what the pattern does. However, the Adapter, Bridge, Command, and Mediator use the GUI library to carry out their functions. Chapter 2, "Visual Programming in Python," summarizes tkinter.

GitHub

All the example programs in this book are available on GitHub: Look at `jwcnmr/jameswcooper/pythonpatterns`. (In case you are unfamiliar with GitHub, it is a free software repository managed by Microsoft for sharing code; anyone can use it.)

To get started, go to GitHub.com and click Sign Up. You will need to create a user ID and a password and submit an email address for verification. Then you can search for any code repository (such as `jameswcooper`) and download any code you want. There is also a complete manual on the website. The complete path to the examples in this book is https://github.com/jwcnmr/jameswcooper/tree/main/Pythonpatterns.

All the examples in this book were compiled using Python 3.9 and clipped from either the PyCharm or Thonny development environments.

On to objects and patterns!

1

Introduction to Objects

Classes are one of the most important parts of the Python language and also a major component of object-oriented programming. Some books put off classes until later chapters, but because nearly every component of Python is an object, we will take a look at them up right away. And don't skip ahead, because we'll be using them in every single chapter that follows!

Almost every component of Python is an object.

- Objects hold data and have methods to access and change that data.

For example, strings, lists, tuples, sets, and dictionaries are all objects, as are complex numbers. They all have functions associated with them called *methods* that enable you to get and change that data.

```
list1 = [5, 20, 15, 6, 123] # create a list
x = list1.pop()             # remove the last item, x =123
```

This is how you manipulate some common Python objects. But how do you make your own objects?

- Classes enable you to create new objects.

At first, a class might seem a bit like a function. But the important difference is that a class can have many different *instances,* each containing different data. Classes can contain a number of functions, and they each operate on the data associated with that instance of the class. Each instance of a class is commonly called an *object,* and each function is usually referred to as a *method.*

Very often, you use classes to represent real-world concepts such as stores, customers, and banks. You create objects by first defining a class that describes that object. Instead of dealing with cute `Dog` classes, let's instead get right to work with a useful class that describes an employee. Our `Employee` class here contains the employee's name, salary, benefits, and ID number.

```
class Employee():
    def __init__(self, frname, lname, salary):
        self.idnum: int         #place holder
        self.frname = frname    #save name
        self.lname = lname
        self._salary = salary   # and salary
```

```
        self.benefits = 1000  # and benefits

    def getSalary(self):         # get the salary
        return self._salary
```

Note that the values for each employee are set in the `_init_` method, which gets called automatically when we create each instance of the `Employee` class. The `self` prefix is used to show that you want to access the variables inside that class instance. Other instances of the class can have different values for those same variables. Within a class, you access all the variables (and all the methods) using a `self` prefix.

The Class __init__ Method

When you create an instance of a class, you simply create a variable and pass in any arguments:

```
fred = Employee('Fred', 'Smythe', 1200)
sam  = Employee('Sam', 'Snerd', 1300)
```

The variables `fred` and `sam` are *instances* of the `Employee` class, with specific values for the name, salary, and so forth. We can, of course, create any number of such instances of the `Employee` class, one for each person employed.

- There can be many instances of a class, each holding different values.
- Each instance can also be called an *object.*
- The functions inside a class are called *methods.*

Variables Inside a Class

Our `Employee` class contains variables for first name, last name, salary, benefits, and an ID number. We use the `getSalary` method, but why not just access it directly? In many similar languages, variables inside a class are private or hidden, so you need an *accessor method* to retrieve those values. However, Python lets you do whatever you want to do, and you really don't need to use `getSalary` or a property. Instead, you can just write

```
print(fred._salary)
```

and get the data directly. So why bother with accessor functions? It is partly to emphasize that the variables inside the class are private and the implementation might change, but the accessor function would remain the same. And, in some cases, the value that the accessor function returns might have to be calculated at that moment.

There is a Python convention that you name these private variables with a leading underscore, to emphasize that you aren't meant to access them directly. This makes them harder to type accidentally. Many development environments, such as PyCharm, don't even suggest the existence of such variables when you type

```
fred.
```

and look at the possible variables and methods that come up: The ones with a leading underscore are not shown. You can still access them directly if you insist; this is just a convention, not a syntactic requirement.

Collections of Classes

So now, let's consider where we are going to keep all those Employee classes. You might keep them in a database, but within a program, using some sort of collection seems like a good idea. We'll define an Employee class that keeps the employees in a dictionary, each with its own ID number as a key. It looks like this:

```
# Contains a dictionary of Employees, keyed by ID
# number
class Employees:
    def __init__(self):
        self.empDict = {}       # employee dictionary
        self.index = 101        # starting ID number

    def addEmployee(self, emp):
        emp.idnum = self.index  # set its ID
        self.index += 1         # go on to next ID
        self.empDict.update({emp.idnum: emp}) # add
```

In the above Employee class, we create an empty dictionary and a starting ID number. Every time we add an employee to the class, it increments that index value.

We create the classes in some simple outer class called HR:

```
# This creates a small group Employees
class HR():
    def __init__(self):
        self.empdata = Employees()
        self.empdata.addEmployee(
                  Employee('Sarah', 'Smythe', 2000))
        self.empdata.addEmployee(
                  Employee('Billy', 'Bob', 1000))
        self.empdata.addEmployee(
                  Employee('Edward', 'Elgar', 2200))

    def listEmployees(self):
        dict = self.empdata.empDict
        for key in dict:
            empl= dict[key] # get the instance
            # and print it out
            print (empl.frname, empl.lname,
                                   empl.salary)
```

- You can keep class instances inside other classes.

Inheritance

Inheritance is the other powerful tool introduced in object-oriented programming. Not only can you create different instances of a class, as we have seen above, but you can create *derived classes*. These new classes have all the properties of the parent class plus anything additional that you write. Note, however, that your `__init__` method must call the parent class's `__init__` method.

In a real company, we might have other kinds of employees as well, including temporary workers who are paid (the same or less) but do not get benefits. Instead of creating a completely new class, we can *derive* a new `TempEmployee` class from the `Employee` class. The new class has all the same methods, so you don't have to write that code over again. You just have to write the parts that are new.

```
# Temp employees get no benefits
class TempEmployee(Employee):
    def __init__(self, frname,lname, idnum):
        super().__init__(frname, lname, idnum)
        self.benefits = 0
```

Derived Classes Created with Revised Methods

One neat trick you can use in object-oriented programming is to create a derived class in which one or more methods do something slightly different. This is called *polymorphism*, which is a $50 word for changing the shape of that new class.

For example, we can create another class from that called `Intern`. Interns do not get benefits and have a low salary cap. So, we write a new derived class whose `setSalary` method checks the salary to make sure it isn't above the cap. (Of course, we don't really think this is a good idea economically.)

```
# Interns get no benefits and a smaller salary
class Intern(TempEmployee):
    def __init__(self, frname, lname, sal):
        super().__init__(frname, lname, sal)
        self.setSalary(sal) # cap salary

    # limit intern salary
    def setSalary(self, val):
        if val > 500:
            self._salary = 500
        else:
            self._salary = val
```

Multiple Inheritance

Unlike Java and C# (but like C++), Python enables you to create classes that inherit from more than one base class. This might seem confusing at first, but most people create a class hierarchy and then note that some of these classes might have a method or two in common with other sorts of classes. We will see later, in Chapter 21, "The Command Pattern," that we use the Command class this way from time to time.

Suppose that a few of our employees are good public speakers. We could create a separate class indicating that they can be invited to give talks, and can be rewarded for doing so.

```
# class representing public speakers
class Speaker():
    def inviteTalk(self):
        pass
    def giveTalk(self):
        pass
```

This example leaves out the implementation details for now, but we can then create a new Employee-derived class that is *also* derived from Speaker:

```
class PublicEmployee(Employee, Speaker):
    def __init__(self, frname, lname, salary):
        super().__init__(frname, lname, salary)
```

Now we can create a set of employees in each of these classes:

```
class HR():
    def __init__(self):
        self.empdata = Employees()
        self.empdata.addEmployee(
                    Employee('Sarah', 'Smythe',2000))
        self.empdata.addEmployee(
                    PublicEmployee('Fran', 'Alien',3000))
        self.empdata.addEmployee(
                    TempEmployee('Billy', 'Bob', 1000))
        self.empdata.addEmployee(
                    Intern('Arnold', 'Stang', 800))

    def listEmployees(self):
        dict = self.empdata.empDict
        for key in dict:
            empl= dict[key]
            print (empl.frname, empl.lname,
                        empl.getSalary())
```

Note that although three of these are derived classes, they are still Employee objects, and you can list them out as shown above.

- Derived classes let you create related classes with different properties or computations.

Drawing a Rectangle and a Square

Let's illustrate one last example of inheritance by using the functions of the Canvas class to draw a rectangle and a square. Canvas is one of several visual objects in the tkinter library that we'll deal with in the following chapter. But, for now, let's just use the Canvas `create_rectangle` method to draw a rectangle.

The `create_rectangle` method has the arguments (x1, y1, x2, y2), but we wanted to create a method that uses the arguments (x, y, w, h) so that the conversion is buried inside the `Rectangle` class:

```
# Rectangle draws on canvas
class Rectangle():
    def __init__(self, canvas):
        self.canvas = canvas  # copy canvas ref

    def draw(self, x, y, w, h):   # draw the rect
        # canvas rectangle uses x1,y1, x2,y2
        self.canvas.create_rectangle(x, y, x+w, y+h)
```

This results in Figure 1.1.

Figure 1.1 Drawing a rectangle on a Canvas

But suppose that we want to draw a square instead. We can derive a class from `Rectangle` that draws squares very easily:

```
# Square derived from Rectangle
class Square(Rectangle):
    def __init__(self, canvas):
        super().__init__(canvas)

    def draw(self, x, y, w):
        super().draw( x, y, w, w) # draw a square
```

Note that we simply pass the width of the square into `Rectangle` twice: once as the width and once as the height.

```
def main():
    root = Tk()                    # the graphics library
    canvas = Canvas(root)          # create a Canvas inst
    rect1 = Rectangle(canvas)      # and a Rectangle
    rect1.draw(30, 10, 120, 80) # draw a rectangle

    square = Square(canvas)        # create a Square
    square.draw(200, 50, 60)       # and draw a square
```

Figure 1.2 shows the result.

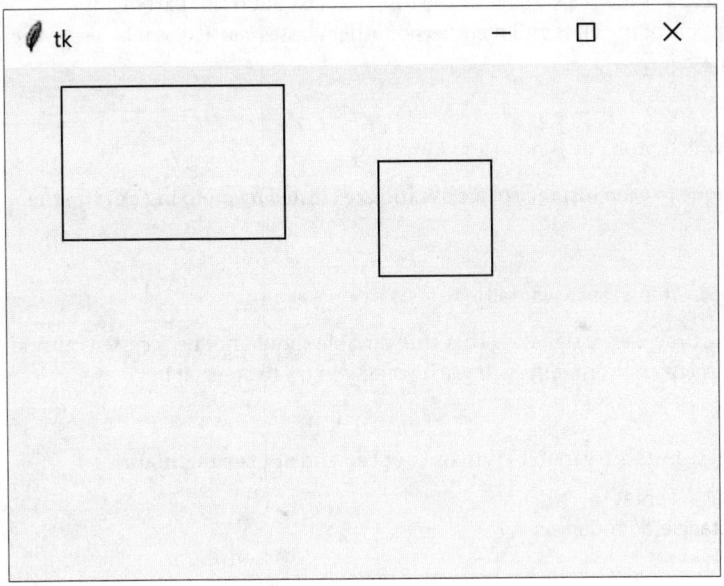

Figure 1.2 A rectangle and a square derived from that rectangle

Visibility of Variables

There are four levels of visibility of variables in a Python program:

- Global variables (ill-advised)
- Class variables inside a class
- Instance variables within class code
- Local variables only within a function (invisible elsewhere)

Consider the beginning of this simple program:

```
""" demonstrate variable access """
badidea = 2.77 # global variable

class ShowData():
    localidea = 3.56        # class variable

    def __init__(self):
        self._instvar = 5.55  # instance variable
```

The global variable `badidea` can be accessed by any function in any class and, worse, can be *changed* by any part of the program. People sometimes use global variables for constants, but using a class variable is more controlled and less prone to error.

In the previous example, `localidea` is a variable at the top of a class but is not part of any method in the class. Members of the class and members of other classes can access it by using the class name and variable name:

```
print(ShowData.localidea)
```

They can also change it, which probably is not a good practice.

Instance variables are unique to each instance of a class and are created by prefixing `self` to the variable name.

```
def __init__(self):
    self._instvar = 5.55  # instance variable
```

By creating a variable `_instvar` we are signaling that this variable should not be accessed outside the class. Various development environments will warn you if you try to access it by

```
print (ShowData._instvar)
```

The usual way to get at these instance variables is to use `getter` and `setter` methods:

```
    # return the instance variable
    def getInstvar(self):
         return self._instvar

    # set the value
    def setInstvar(self, x):
        self._instvar = x
```

Properties

You can also use the property decorator to fetch and store instance variables:

```
# getters and setters can protect
# use of instance variables
    @property
    def instvar(self):
        return self._instvar


    @instvar.setter
    def instvar(self, val):
        self._instvar = val
```

These decorators enable you to access or change that instance variable using methods that might protect the actual values if a value goes out of range.

```
print(sd.instvar)      # uses getter
sd.instvar = 123       # uses setter to change
```

Local Variables

Variables inside a function within a class exist only within that function. For example, both x and i are local only within that simple function and cannot be accessed outside of it:

```
def addnums(self):
    x = 0                   # i and x are local
    for i in range(0, 5):
        x += i
    return x
```

Types in Python

Variables in Python are typed dynamically at runtime, rather than because the types are declared in advance. Python deduces the type from the values you assign to the variable, which can sometimes lead to runtime problems when the types conflict. This approach is called duck typing, based on the old maxim, "If it looks like a duck and quacks like a duck, it's a duck."

In version 3.8, Python added *type hints* to tell the static type checking what to expect. Static type checking is not part of Python itself, but most development environments, such as PyCharm, carry it out automatically and highlight probable errors.

You can declare the type of every argument and return the type as follows:

```
class Summer():
    def addNums(self, x: float, y: float) ->float:
        return x + y
```

Even more impressive, you can have two or more functions that have the same name but different arguments:

```
def addNums(self, f: float, s: str)->float:
    fsum = f + float(s)
    return fsum
```

And Python will call the correct function, based on the arguments, whether you put in two floats or a float and a string:

```
sumr = Summer()
print(sumr.addNums(12.0, 2.3))
print(sumr.addNums(22.3, "13.5"))
```

then printing out:

```
14.3
35.8
```

This is called *polymorphism,* meaning essentially the capability to take different forms. Here, this means that you can have several methods with the same name but different arguments. Then you can call the method you need based on the arguments you select. This feature is commonly used all through Python.

However, if you make a call to `addNums(str, str)`, you will find that PyCharm and other type checkers flag this as an error because there is no such method. You then get the following error message:

```
Unexpected types (str, str)
```

Summary

This chapter covered all the basics of object-oriented programming, so here's a summary:

- You create classes by using the `class` keyword followed by a capitalized class name.
- Classes contain data, and each instance of a class can hold different data. This is called *encapsulation.*
- You can create classes derived from other classes. In parentheses after the class name, you indicate the name of the class the new one is derived from. This is called *inheritance.*
- You can create a derived class whose methods are in some way different than those of the base class. This is called *polymorphism.*
- You can also create classes that contain other classes. We'll see an example in the following chapter.

Programs on GitHub

Note that you can find all the examples on GitHub at jameswcooper/pythonpatterns.

- BasicHR.py: Contains `Employees` without derived classes
- HRclasses.py: Includes two derived classes
- Speaker.py: Includes the `Speaker` class
- Rectangle.py: Draws squares and rectangles
- Addnumstype.py: Shows a polymorphic function call

In case you are unfamiliar with GitHub, it is a free software repository for sharing code that anyone can use. To get started, go to GitHub.com and click Sign Up. You will need to create a user ID and a password and submit an email address for verification. Then you can search for any code repository (such as jameswcooper) and download the code you want. There is a complete manual available at that website as well.

After you have signed in, you can also access the examples directly at https://github.com/jwcnmr/jameswcooper/tree/main/Pythonpatterns.

2

Visual Programming in Python

You can make very nice visual interfaces using the tkinter toolkit provided with Python. It gives you tools for creating windows, buttons, radio buttons, check boxes, entry fields, list boxes, combo boxes and a number of other useful visual widgets.

To use the tkinter library, you must tell your program to import those tools:

```
import tkinter as tk
from tkinter import *
```

Then you set up the window like this:

```
# set up the window
root = tk.Tk()                    # get the window
```

You create a Hello button with:

```
# create Hello button
slogan = Button(root,
                text="Hello",
                command=disp_slogan)
```

Then you put in the layout:

```
slogan.pack()
```

The command argument refers to the function `write_slogan` that puts up a message box:

```
# write slogan out in a message box
def disp_slogan():
    messagebox.showinfo("our message",
                        "tkinter is easy to use")
```

Then, our other button is labeled Quit. You create it in the same way as the Hello button:

```
# create exit button with red letters
button = Button(root,
                text="QUIT",
                fg="red",
                command=quit)
button.pack()
```

The command argument in this button just calls Python's built-in `quit` function. Note that when you place a function name in a command argument, you *omit* the parentheses; otherwise, it would be called at once.

The `quit` function was added for ease of learning Python, but it does not always exit cleanly. You should use the call `sys.exit` instead.

The resulting display and message box for Hellobuttons.py are shown in Figure 2-1.

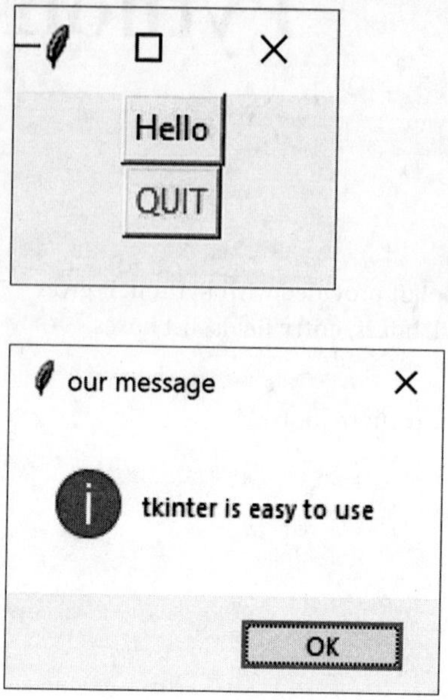

Figure 2-1 Two buttons and a message box window

The pack layout function can make this window much better looking if we make the window a bit bigger:

```
root.geometry("100x100+300+300")      # x, y window
                                      # size and position
```

To further enhance the window, you can put one button on the left and one on the right, and add 10 pixels of padding between the buttons:

```
slogan.pack(side=LEFT, padx=10)
button.pack(side=RIGHT, padx=10)
```

Then the window looks like Figure 2-2.

Figure 2-2 Two buttons side by side using the pack layout

Importing Fewer Names

The `import` statement imports all the names in the tkinter library.

```
from tkinter import *
```

However, your program might need only a few of these names. This could lead to you trying to create a variable with the same name as some other `tkinter` object. The `import` statement also loads your development environment with all the functions in the tkinter library. Understandably, you might want to only import the ones you plan to use:

```
from tkinter import Button, messagebox, LEFT, RIGHT
```

If you are using PyCharm, it can help you do this. Remove the `import *` statement and PyCharm will highlight the names it doesn't recognize. Click each of these names and PyCharm will suggest the name to import. This is very fast, because usually you only have to do this three or four times to import all the underlined names.

Creating an Object-Oriented Version

The idea of creating these two buttons, one of which calls an external function, seems inelegant and can be confusing. Instead, it would be better if the function the button click calls were part of the `Button` class. We do this in Derived2Buttons.py below.

In order to do this, we need to derive a new `Button` class that has the command method inside it. The easiest way to do this is to create a `DButton` class that inherits all the `Button` behaviors but also has a `comd` method.

```
#derived class from Button that contains empty comd function
class DButton(Button):
    def __init__(self, root, **kwargs):
        super().__init__(root, kwargs)
        super().config(command=self.comd)

    #abstract method to be called by children
    def comd(self):
        pass
```

The comd method is empty, but we will then derive the OK and Quit button classes from it. The `pass` keyword just means "Go on, but do nothing." Note, however that we pass

```
command=self.comd
```

on to the parent class. This is essentially an abstract method because it doesn't do anything, but the derived classes will fill it in. So, you can consider `DButton` as an *abstract class*.

The other thing that might be confusing is that the `__init__` method contains a reference to `**kwargs`. This is syntax borrowed from C and means a pointer to an array of name-value pairs, in dictionary form. That array of strings contains all the configuration arguments you can pass to the parent `Button` class. You use this exact same syntax in creating derived classes of any of the tkinter widgets.

Now, the actual `OKButton` class is derived from `DButton` and fills out the actual command method:

```
#derived from DButton with actual OK comd
class OKButton(DButton):
    def __init__(self, root):
        super().__init__(root, text="OK")

    def comd(self):
        messagebox.showinfo("our message",
                            "tkinter is easy to use")
```

What happens here is rather cool. The base `Button` class knows to call a function called comd, but that function is only filled in in the derived `OKButton` class; and it is this code that is called, even though `OKButton` has not told the parent class about it. The parent class's abstract comd method is replaced by the actual comd method in the `OKButton` class.

In a similar fashion, we can create the `QuitButton` class, also derived from `DButton`, with its own different comd method:

```
#derived from DButton calls Quit function
class QuitButton(DButton):
    def __init__(self, root):
        #also sets Quit to Red
        super().__init__(root, text="Quit", fg="red")

    #calls the quit function and the program exits
    def comd(self):
        quit()
```

This simplifies setting up the UI because most of the work is now done within the derived classes:

```
def buildUI():
    root = tk.Tk()  # get the window
    root.geometry("100x100+300+300")  # x, y window

    # create Hello button
    slogan = OKButton(root)
    slogan.pack(side=LEFT, padx=10)
```

```
    # create exit button with red letters
    button = QuitButton(root)
    button.pack(side=RIGHT, padx=10)

    # start running the tkinter loop
    root.mainloop()
```

Depending on your philosophical preferences, you can also move the two pack method calls into the derived classes and out of the buildUI function.

```
class OKButton(DButton):
    def __init__(self, root):
        super().__init__(root, text="OK")
        self.pack(side=LEFT, padx=10)
```

Using Message Boxes

There are several calls to the messagebox object that produce slightly different displays. The functions showwarning and showerror display distinctive icons of greater severity, as shown in Figure 2-3.

```
messagebox.showwarning("Warning", "file not found")
messagebox.showerror("Error", "Division by zero")
```

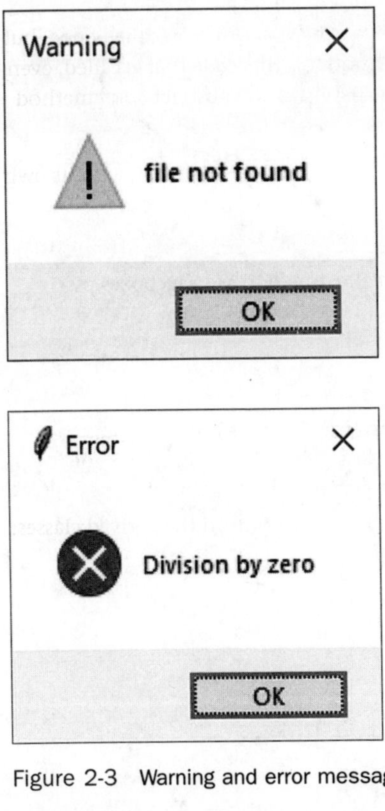

Figure 2-3 Warning and error message boxes

You can also ask questions with `askquestion`, `askyesnocancel`, `askretrycancel`, `askyesno`, and `askokcancel`. These functions return a subset of `True`, `False`, `None`, `OK`, `Yes`, or `No`, as shown in Figure 2-4.

```
result = messagebox.askokcancel("Continue", "Go on?")
result= messagebox.askyesnocancel("Really", "Want to go on?")
```

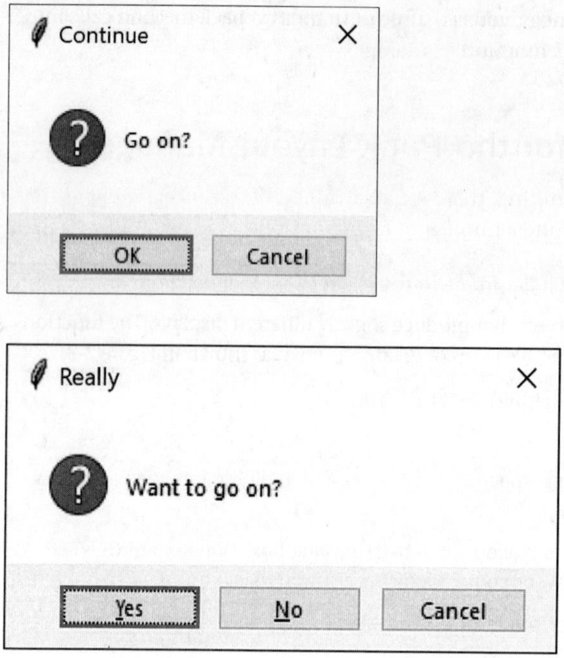

Figure 2-4 Message box askokcancel and askyesnocancel

All of these message boxes and the file dialogs that follow are illustrated in Messageboxes.py.

Using File Dialogs

If you want to open a file or files within your program, you can use `filedialog`.

```
from tkinter import filedialog
# open a single file
fname =filedialog.askopenfilename()
print(fname)
```

```
# select several files -returns a tuple
fnames =
   filedialog.askopenfilenames(
         defaultextension="*.py")
print(fnames)
```

The first dialog returns either the complete path to the file you select in the dialog or an empty string if you click Cancel. The second dialog returns a tuple of the files you select or an empty tuple. The analogous `asksaveasfile` opens a Save As dialog.

Understanding Options for the Pack Layout Manager

Although the pack layout is somewhat limiting, there are an awful lot of common problems that you can solve really nicely using `pack()` and a number of layout options:

`fill=X`
`fill=Y`
`fill=BOTH`
	Stretch widget to fill the frame in the X direction, Y direction, or both.

`side=LEFT` `side=RIGHT`	Position widget at left or right side of frame.
`expand=1`	Distribute remaining space in the frame among all widgets with a nonzero value for expand.
`anchor`	Where the widget is placed within the packing box. Options are CENTER (default), N, S, E, W, or contiguous combinations such as NE.
`padX=5,pady=5`	Add that number of pixels of border space.

The following simple example in packoptions.py illustrates how to use these layout options. Each of the two rows of widgets is set into its own frame.

Here is the first row:

```
frame1 = Frame()        # first row
frame1.pack(fill=X)     # fill all of X

lbl1 = Label(frame1, text="Name", width=7) # add a label
lbl1.pack(side=LEFT, padx=5, pady=5)    # on left
entry1 = Entry(frame1)                  # add aentry
entry1.pack(fill=X, padx=5, expand=True)
and here is the second row:
frame2 = Frame()        #second row
frame2.pack(fill=X)

lbl2 = Label(frame2, text="Address", width=7) #label
lbl2.pack(side=LEFT, padx=5, pady=5)
entry2 = Entry(frame2)                   # and entry
entry2.pack(fill=X, padx=5, expand=True)
```

Figure 2-5 shows the resulting window.

Figure 2-5 Pack layout using expand=TRUE, X filling, and padX=5

Using the ttk Libraries

The tkinter libraries interface directly to the underlying tk windowing toolkit that has been ported to most platforms. More recently, the tkinter.ttk toolkit has been added that gives somewhat better-looking widgets in some cases and has separated the graphics from the logical functions. The ttk toolkit includes rewritten code for Button, Checkbutton, Entry, Frame, Label, LabelFrame, Menubutton, PanedWindow, Radiobutton, Scale, and Scrollbar.

In addition, the ttk toolkit includes the additional widgets Combobox, Notebook, Progressbar, Separator, Sizegrip, and Treeview.

To use the older tkinter set, add this code to the top of your program:

```
import tkinter as tk
from tkinter import Button, messagebox, LEFT, RIGHT
```

To use the newer set of widgets, add this code instead:

```
import tkinter as tk
from tkinter import messagebox, LEFT, RIGHT
from tkinter.ttk import Button
```

This replaces the original tk widgets with the equivalent ttk widgets. If you want to use Combobox or Treeview, it is worth switching to the ttk toolkit. (We also found that the earlier pack example aligns slightly better using the ttk kit.)

Unfortunately, there are a couple of coding changes you have to make to use the ttk library. Most significant is that the `fg` or `foreground` (and `bg` or `background`) options are no longer part of the calling arguments to construct a new `Label` or `Button` class. Instead, you create an entry in the style table.

```
Style().configure("W.TButton", foreground="red")
super().__init__(root, text="Quit", style="W.TButton")
```

The name of the style is not random: For buttons, the suffix must be `TButton`; for labels, it must be `TLabel`. However, you can prefix the name with anything before the period.

Responding to User Input

In the introductory material in Chapter 31, "Variables and Syntax in Python," we use the `input` statement to get strings that you enter at the console. You can do much the same thing by using the `Entry` field in the tkinter GUI. This section shows those examples in simple tkinter windows.

Our first example was one where you enter your name and it says Hello back, giving homage to Heinlein in the process. The tkinter program does the same thing (see Figure 2-6).

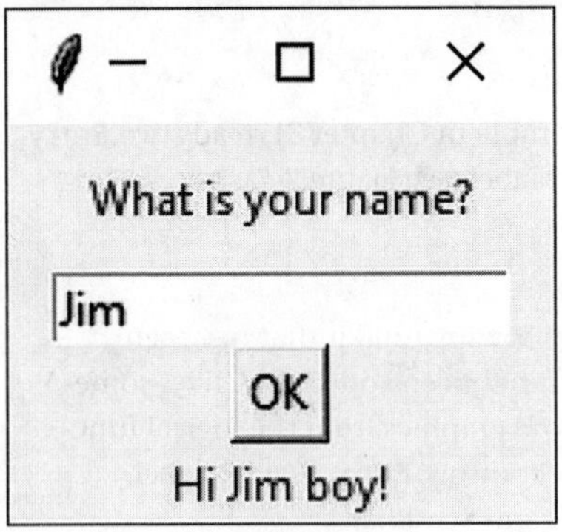

Figure 2-6 Hello name example

The code for this program, Yourname.py, creates the two labels, the Entry field, and the OK button:

```
def build(self):
    root = tk.Tk()
    # top label
    Label(root,
        text="""What is your name?""",
        justify=LEFT, fg='blue', pady=10, padx=20).pack()

    # create entry field
    self.nmEntry = Entry(root)
    self.nmEntry.pack()

    # OK button calls getName when clicked
    self.okButton = Button(root, text="OK", command=self.getName )
    self.okButton.pack()

    # This is the label whose text changes
    self.cLabel = Label(root, text='name', fg='blue')
    self.cLabel.pack()
    mainloop()
```

The OK button calls the `getName` method, which fetches the text from the entry field and inserts it into the bottom label text.

```
# gets the entry field text
# places it on the cLabel text field

def getName(self):
   newName = self.nmEntry.get()
   self.cLabel.configure(text="Hi "+newName+" boy!")
```

Adding Two Numbers

Our second example, Simplemath.py, rewritten from the example in Chapter 31, reads two Entry fields, converts them to floats, and puts the sum in the lower label (see Figure 2-7).

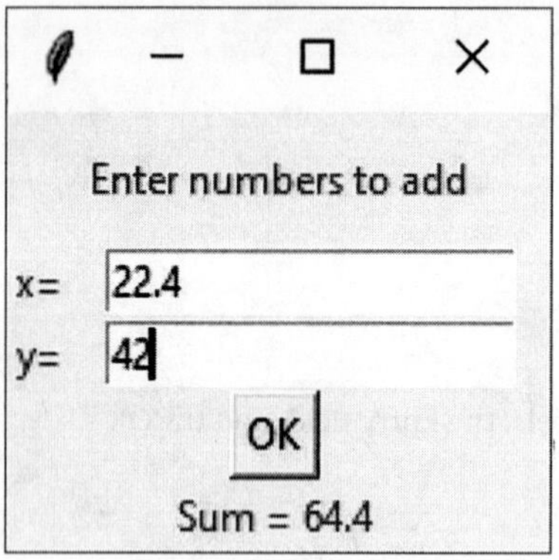

Figure 2-7 Adding two numbers

The code for this window is much the same, except that you fetch and add two numbers. Here is the function the OK button calls:

```
xval= float(self.xEntry.get())
yval = float(self.yEntry.get())
self.cLabel.configure(text="Sum = "+str(xval+yval))
```

Catching the Error

However, if you enter some illegal non-numeric value, you can catch the exception and issue a error message:

```
try:
    xval= float(self.xEntry.get())
    yval = float(self.yEntry.get())
    self.cLabel.configure(
        text="Sum = "+str(xval+yval))
```

```
except:
    messagebox.showerror("Conversion error",
                         "Not numbers")
```

Applying Colors in tkinter

The named colors in tkinter are white, black, red, green, blue, cyan, yellow, and magenta. You can also create any color you want by using hexadecimal values, which can be #RGB or #RRGGBB or longer 12- and 16-bit strings. So red would be #f00 and purple #c0f, for example. Each digit can be anywhere from 0 to f for the numbers between 0 and 15.

So, in the ttk toolkit, our Quit button with the red lettering is written like this:

```
class QuitButton(DButton):
    def __init__(self, root):
        # also sets Quit to Red
        Style().configure("W.TButton",
                          foreground="red")
        super().__init__(root,
                text="Quit",style="W.TButton")
        self.pack(side=RIGHT, padx=10)

    # calls the quit function and the program exits
    def comd(self):
        quit()
```

Creating Radio Buttons

The Radiobutton widget is named after the series of buttons on car radios. When they were actual, solid buttons, those five or six buttons enabled you to select different stations while you drove. But now that radio controls are more likely touch screens, the button design persists, with around six choices per screen, and some way to move on to other sets from other sources.

The idea of the radiobutton is to allow only one choice, so when you click on one button, any other button selection turns off. Figure 2-8 shows a simple example in radiobuttons.py.

When you click the Query button, the code looks to see which button is selected and goes on with the program. You can also set the argument *indicatoron* to 0 if you want to get actual buttons instead of the radio buttons.

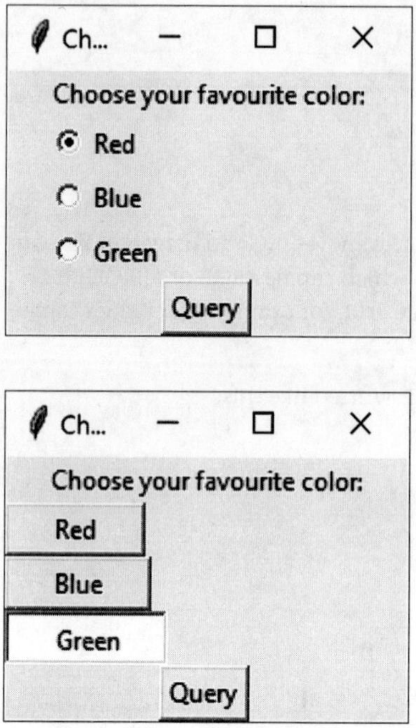

Figure 2-8 Radio buttons with indicatoron=1 (top) and indicatoron=0 (bottom)

When you create a set of radio buttons, you assign them all to the same group variable. This variable is of the type `IntVar`, a special type used to reach down into the Tk graphics toolkit. Each radio button is assigned an index value (such as 0, 1, or 2) when you create it. When you click one of the buttons, that index value is copied to the group variable. So, you can find out which button is selected by examining the value stored in the group variable. In the following code Radiobuts.py, the `ChoiceButton` class is derived from the `Radiobutton` class.

```
groupv = tk.IntVar()

ChoiceButton(root, 'Red', 0, groupv)
ChoiceButton(root, 'Blue', 1, groupv)
ChoiceButton(root, 'Green', 2, groupv)
```

You can also set which radio button is selected by setting the value of that group variable:

```
groupv.set(0)       # Red button selected
groupv.set(None)    # No buttons selected
```

Like the ordinary `Button` class, the `Radiobutton` class can receive commands when clicked. So, just as we did when we created `DButton`, we will derive the `ChoiceButton` class and include the command function inside it.

```
# ChoiceButton is derived from RadioButton
class ChoiceButton(tk.Radiobutton):
    def __init__(self, rt, color, index, gvar,
                                        clabel):
```

```
        super().__init__(rt, text=color,
                         padx=20, command=self.comd,
                         variable=gvar, value=index)

        self.pack(anchor=W)
        self.root = rt
        self.color = color
        self.index = index
        self.var = gvar
        self.clabel = clabel

# clicks are sent here
def comd(self):
    # change label text and label text color
    self.clabel.configure(fg=self.color,
                          text = self.color)
```

Figure 2-9 shows the original window and the name and color of the label text when you click a radio button.

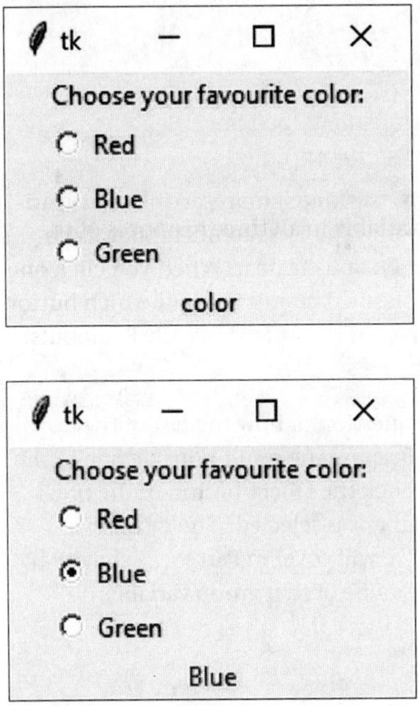

Figure 2-9 Original window (top) and window with a color name and color (bottom)

The comd method changes both the label text *and* the label color using the same color string. In this somewhat inelegant example, a reference to the group variable *gvar* is passed to *each* of the radio buttons, even though it is the same variable in all three cases. There is a better way to do this well with a class-level variable.

Using a Class-Level Variable

If all three ChoiceButton classes refer to the same variable, why not put it inside the class itself? This is a lot better than having it off in some random place in the main() routine. We'll declare gvar as a class-level variable, referring to it a ChoiceButton.gvar. There is one and only one such variable for all three classes, and all of them can examine its state.

```
class ChoiceButton(tk.Radiobutton):
    gvar = None  # the group var will go here

    def __init__(self, rt, color, index, cLabel):
        super().__init__(rt, text=color,
                         padx=20, command=self.comd,
                         variable=ChoiceButton.gvar,
                         value=index)
        self.pack(anchor=W)
        self.color = color    #button color name
        self.cLabel = cLabel #label to be colored
        self.index = index   # index of button
```

Next, we set it to None when we create the user interface:

```
# set the group variable inside the class
ChoiceButton.gvar = IntVar()
ChoiceButton.gvar.set(None)
ChoiceButton(root, 'Red',   0, cLabel)
ChoiceButton(root, 'Blue',  1, cLabel)
ChoiceButton(root, 'Green', 2, cLabel)
```

Everything else is the same; we don't have to pass the same variable to all three instances of the ChoiceButton class. This code is in Radioclassbuttons.py.

Communicating Between Classes

While it is pretty easy to respond to these clicks, there is the question of how the rest of the program receives these selections and how it handles them. Because the result is inside one of the ChoiceButton instances, this is a bit tricky. Likewise, if you click the Query button of the previous example, how do the button and the program find out what was selected? The most effective solution to this problem is the Mediator pattern, which we will cover in Part IV, "Behavioral Patterns."

Using the Grid Layout

The grid layout is even easier to use than the pack layout, which lets you arrange your widgets in a grid in your window. Grids are numbered rows and columns, and you can have any number of either. The grid is not drawn in your window, and any row or column that doesn't contain a widget is not shown.

For a simple illustration, let's redo the same example used previously for the pack layout:

```
root=Tk()
root.title("grid")


# create the first label and entry field
lbl1 = Label( text="Name")
lbl1.grid(row=0, column=0, padx=5, pady=5)
entry1 = Entry()
entry1.grid(row=0, column=1)

# and the second
lbl2 = Label( text="Address")
lbl2.grid(row=1, column=0, padx=5, pady=5)
entry2 = Entry()
entry2.grid(row=1, column=1, padx=5)

root.mainloop()
```

Note that this approach is a lot simpler than the code needed to create the same window using the pack layout. You don't have to create any frames: The grid accomplishes the same thing a bit more simply. The code is in gridoptions.py.

You can see a slight difference between the top window in Figure 2-10 and the one in Figure 2-5 (the pack example): the Name and Address labels are not left justified. This is where you can use the `sticky` modifier to the grid layout to indicate where in the grid cell you want to place the widget. By using these two grid method calls, you can place the label at the West side of the grid cell:

```
lbl1.grid(row=0, column=0, padx=5, pady=5, sticky=W)
lbl2.grid(row=1, column=0, padx=5, pady=5, sticky=W)
```

Figure 2-10 shows the result in the window on the right. (The other positions are, of course, N, S, and E, and you can combine them.)

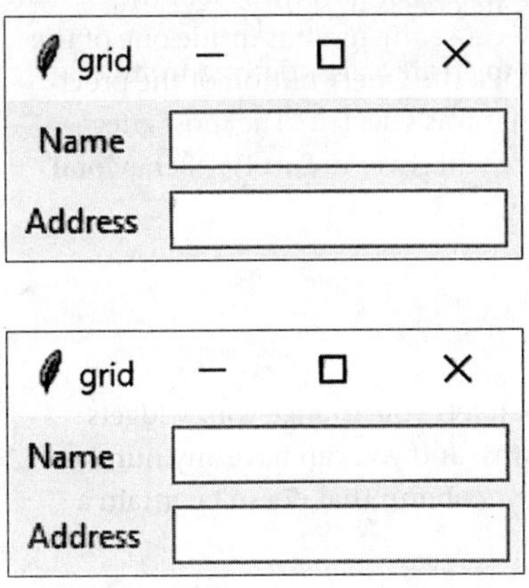

Figure 2-10 Grid layout without (top) and with sticky=W (bottom)

Creating Checkbuttons

In Python, the standard windowing UI check box is called a Checkbutton. Checkbuttons enable you to indicate the selections you want to give users, where they can select zero or more of the options. Let's create the ever-popular pizza topping selection menu using a series of checkbuttons and position them in a grid layout (see Figure 2-11).

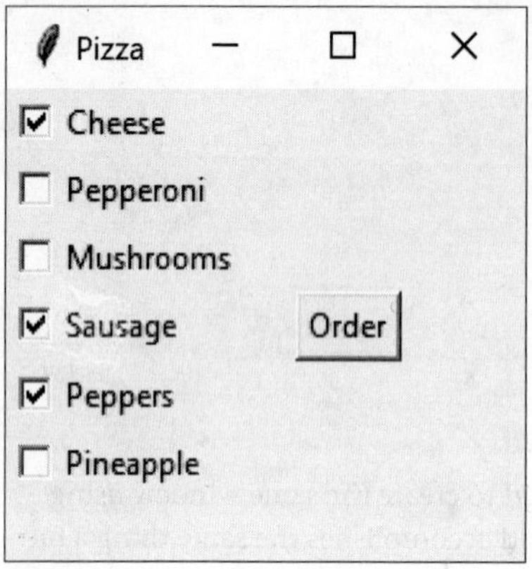

Figure 2-11 Checkbuttons in a grid.

Placing the checkbuttons in a grid is pretty simple: there are six rows and two columns, with row 4 of the second column containing the Order button.

But how to write the program? Once we create those boxes, how do we find out which are checked? Checkbuttons operate much as Radiobuttons do, with an `IntVar` object associated with each button. Unlike the Radiobutton, where a single button group refers to the same `IntVar`, you have to create an `IntVar` for *each* Checkbutton.

So how do we manage these buttons? With a List perhaps? Close, but how do we make the Order button aware of this list and how do we find out which ones are checked?

There are two steps to creating this program. The first step is to create a class derived from `Checkbutton`, that we'll just call `Checkbox`.

```
""" Checkbox class derived from Checkbutton
includes get methods to get the name var state"""
class Checkbox(Checkbutton):
    def __init__(self, root, btext, gvar):
        super().__init__(root, text=btext,
                         variable=gvar)
        self.text=btext
        self.var = gvar

    def getVar(self):
        return self.var.get()  # get value stored
```

This Checkbox class has two get methods: one to get the value contained in the associated IntVar and one to get the title string for the Checkbox. So, we can create the Checkbox classes and ask them whether the box is checked. But how to create them all?

You can do this most easily by creating a list of check box names and then looping through it to create the IntVar and Checkbox array. Here is the list of names:

```
self.names = ["Cheese","Pepperoni","Mushrooms",
              "Sausage","Peppers","Pineapple"]
```

Now, let's create the array of Checkboxes using these names. It's pretty simple, but we need to make sure we create a separate IntVar for each Checkbox:

```
boxes=[]            #list of check boxes stored here
r = 0
for name in self.names:
    var=IntVar()                    # create an IntVar
    cb = Checkbox(root, name, var) # create checkbox
    boxes.append(cb)                # add it to list
    cb.grid(column=0, row=r, sticky=W) # grid layout
    r += 1                              # row counter
```

The second and final step in building this program is to create the Order button. When we click it, we want to see a list of the toppings ordered. But, how does this button know about the orders? We subclass Button with an extra argument that passes that list of boxes to the button:

```
# Create the Order button and give it
# the list of boxes
OKButton(root, boxes).grid(column=1, row=3, padx=20)
```

The OK button stores the reference to the boxes list so that it can print the order when clicked. This derived button class, as with ones we've created earlier, has its own comd method that gets called when the button is clicked. It prints the check box label and tells whether the box is checked.

```
class OKButton(Button):
    def __init__(self, root, boxes):
        super().__init__(root, text="Order")
        super().config(command=self.comd)
        self.boxes= boxes      # save list
                               # of checkboxes
    # print out the list of ordered toppings
    def comd(self):
        for box in self.boxes:
            print (box.Text, box.getVar())
```

And here is the order list:

```
Cheese 1
Pepperoni 0
Mushrooms 0
Sausage 1
Peppers 1
Pineapple 0
```

Disabling Check Boxes

Sometimes you may want to keep people from clicking certain check boxes. Here, we duplicate the Internet joke about pineapple on pizza in the program checkboxes.py (see Figure 2-12).

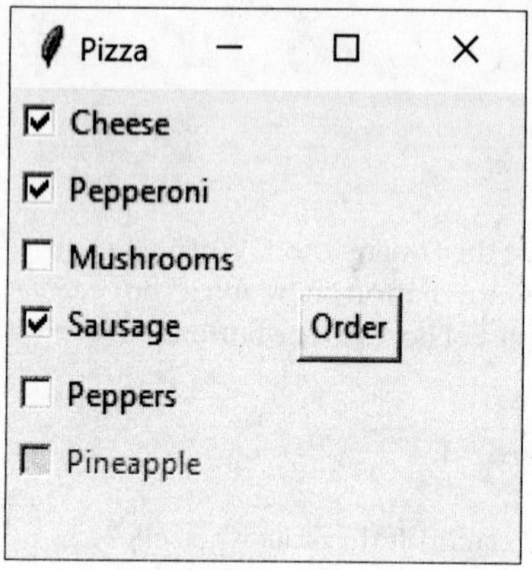

Figure 2-12 Check boxes, with one disabled

Note that Pineapple is grayed out in this display, so you can't click that check box. The code for doing this is part of the Checkbox class:

```
# Internet joke about Pineapple on pizza
if self.text == "Pineapple":
    #prevent Pineapple on pizza
    self.configure(state=DISABLED)
```

You can also use this form:

```
btn['state']=DISABLED
```

In either case, you can turn a button or other widget back on with either of the following:

```
btn['state'] = tk.NORMAL
btn.configure(state=NORMAL)
```

Adding Menus to Windows

As you begin to develop programs that have a number of options, you probably realize that menus would be just the thing. And menus in Python are superficially very simple to implement.

Suppose you want to create a couple of menus like these:

File	Draw
New	Circle
Open	Square
Exit	

The code for creating these menus can be as simple as this:

```
# create the menu bar
menubar = Menu(root)
root.config(menu=menubar)
root.title("Menu demo")
root.geometry("300x200")
filemenu = Menu(menubar, tearoff=0)
menubar.add_cascade(label="File", menu=filemenu)

filemenu.add_command(label="New", command=None)
filemenu.add_command(label="Open", command=None)
filemenu.add_separator()
filemenu.add_command(label="Exit", command=None)

drawmenu = Menu(menubar, tearoff=0)
menubar.add_cascade(label="Draw", menu=drawmenu)
drawmenu.add_command(label="Circle", command=None)
drawmenu.add_command(label="Square", command=None)
```

Figure 2-13 shows the resulting window from Menus.py, showing one of the menus.

Of course, this simple program skips over the commands that the menu items are meant to execute, and therein lies the complexity. If you have just two or three menu items, you can simply create the three functions that the three buttons are meant to call, and it won't clutter your program too much.

But if you have a dozen or more menu items, you begin to realize that this is not at all object-oriented programming. There shouldn't be all those functions at the top level in your program; they should be part of objects. And, each class should ideally handle one of those menu commands. This is the same problem discussed with buttons. Putting the command that the button executes into the `Button` class itself is a much better way to organize your program. These classes are quite general, so you can use them anywhere you want to make a menu.

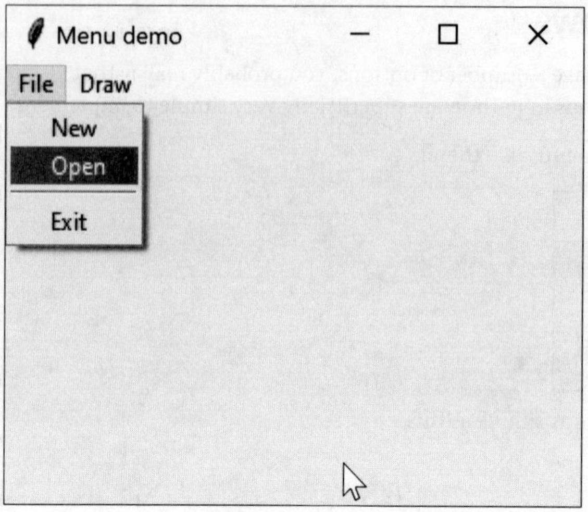

Figure 2-13 Menu display

So, what classes would we need here? At the very least we would need

- A `Menubar` class
- A `Topmenu` class that holds the name of that menu group
- A way to add menu commands to that menu
- Additionally, we create a basic `MenuCommand` class for each menu item.

Our `Menubar` class just subclasses `Menu` and adds one line of code:

```
# creates the menu bar
class Menubar(Menu):
    def __init__(self, root):
        super().__init__(root)
        root.config(menu=self)
```

The other main class, `Topmenu`, represents the top of each menu:

```
# this class represents the top menu item in each column
class TopMenu():
    def __init__(self, root, label, menubar):
        self.mb = menubar
        self.root = root
        self.fmenu = Menu(self.mb, tearoff=0)
        self.mb.add_cascade(label=label, menu=self.fmenu)
```

```
    def addMenuitem(self, mcomd):
        self.fmenu.add_command(label = mcomd.getLabel(),
                command = mcomd.comd)

    def addSeparator(self):
        self.fmenu.add_separator()
```

The rest of the code creates the class for each menu item. We'll begin with a base class and derive all the others from it:

```
# abstract base class for menu items
class Menucommand():
    def __init__(self, root, label):
        self.root = root
        self.label=label
    def getLabel(self):
        return self.label

    def comd(self): pass
```

The only thing we have to do is write the comd method into the derived classes, and most of those are pretty simple. For example:

```
# exits from the program
class Quitcommand(Menucommand):
    def __init__(self, root,  label):
        super().__init__(root,  label)

    def comd(self):
        sys.exit()
```

We use the sys.exit() method here because it is recommended in production code; it ensures that everything is closed before exiting.

The File | Open menu command is a little more complicated. We don't really have any need to open any files in this little program, but we strip off the path and save only the filename, which we display in the title bar:

```
# menu item that calls the file open dialog
class Opencommand(Menucommand):
    def __init__(self, root, label):
        super().__init__(root, label)

 def comd(self):
      fname= filedialog.askopenfilename(
              title="Select file")

      # check for nonzero string length
      if len(fname.strip()) > 0:
          nameparts = fname.split("/")
```

```
    # find the base file name without the path
            k = len(nameparts)
            if k>0 :
                fname = nameparts[k-1]
                   self.root.title(fname)
```

To draw the circle and square, we have to pass the Canvas object to those menu items:

```
# draws a circle
class Drawcircle(Menucommand):
    def __init__(self, root,  canvas, label):
        super().__init__(root,  label)
        self.canvas = canvas

    def comd(self):
        self.canvas.create_oval(130, 40,
                200, 110, fill="red")
```

That's really it. We create the menu command items and add them to the Topmenu and we have the whole program in object-oriented form:

```
menubar = Menubar(root)

#create the File menu and its children
filemenu = TopMenu(root, "File", menubar)
filemenu.addMenuitem(Menucommand(root, "New"))
filemenu.addMenuitem(Opencommand(root, "Open"))

filemenu.addSeparator()
filemenu.addMenuitem(Quitcommand(root, "Quit"))


# create the Draw menu and its children
drawmenu= TopMenu(root, "Draw", menubar)
drawmenu.addMenuitem(Drawcircle(root, canvas,
                    "Circle"))

drawmenu.addMenuitem(Drawsquare(root, canvas,
                    "Square"))
```

Figure 2-14 shows the result of ObjMenus.py.

Note that when we created the File|New menu item, we used the base MenuCommand class, which has an empty comd() method. We did this because we didn't plan to execute the New method, as it is beyond the scope of this example.

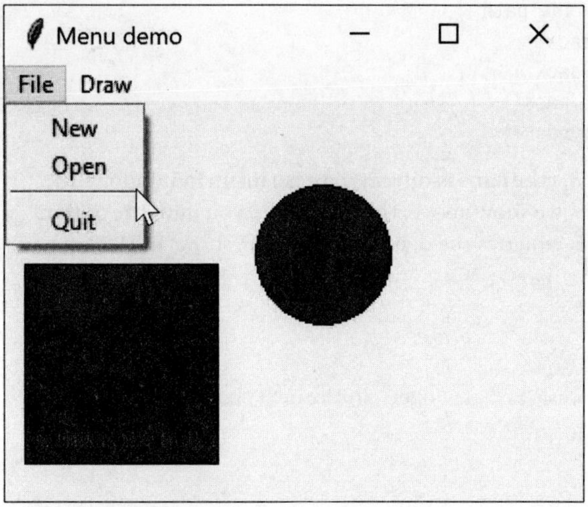

Figure 2-14 Menu bar, menu, and two graphics elements drawn in the canvas

Using the LabelFrame

The `LabelFrame` widget is just like the `Frame` widget, except that you can add a label as part of the frame, as shown in labelframetest.py (see Figure 2-15).

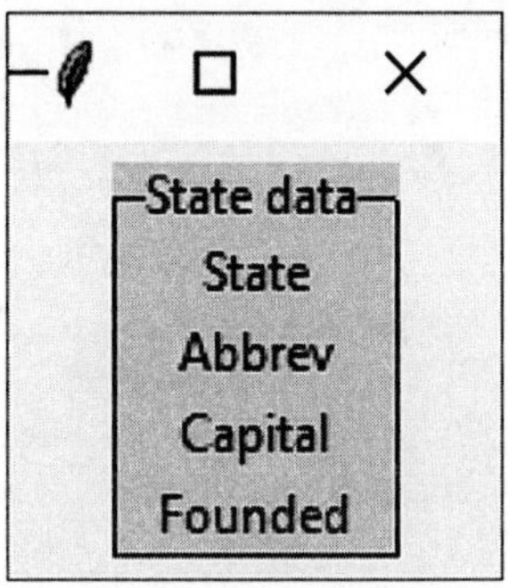

Figure 2-15 The LabelFrame with relief=RAISED and the "alt" theme.

```
# style required if used on Windows 10
    style = Style()
    style.theme_use('alt')

    # create LabelFrame
    labelframe = LabelFrame(root, text="State data",
                            borderwidth=7, relief=RAISED)
    labelframe.pack(pady=5)
```

```
# add 4 labels
Label(labelframe, text="State").pack()
Label(labelframe, text="Abbrev").pack()
Label(labelframe, text="Capital").pack()
Label(labelframe, text="Founded").pack()
```

Because of a bug in Python 3.6, 3.7, and 3.8, the frame is displayed only faintly in Windows 10 unless you include the "alt" style statement we show above. For the border, you have the option of `GROOVE`, `FLAT`, `RAISED`, or `RIDGEGROOVE`, which is the default; Figure 2-15 shows `RAISED`.

Moving On

In this chapter, we've covered most of the basic visual widgets. In the next chapter we'll look at displaying lists of data.

Examples on GitHub

- Hellobuttons.py: The first button example
- Derived2buttons.py: Subclassed buttons
- Messageboxes.py: Message boxes and file window examples
- Yourname.py: Entering and displaying your name
- Simplemath.py: Entering two numbers and adding them
- Packoptions.py: Using the pack method
- Radiobuts.py: Radio button examples
- Radioclassbuttons.py: Using a class variable
- Gridoptions.py: Using the grid
- Checkboxes.py: Extension of `Checkbuttons`
- Menus.py: Menu example
- Objmenus.py: Object-oriented menu example
- LabelFrameTest.py: `Labelframe` example
- Disable.py: Enabling and disabling buttons

3

Visual Programming of Tables of Data

In this chapter, we'll look at a few ways to represent lists of data. We'll start by writing code to read in a list of states, along with some of their data. Then we use these entries as examples for display, to easily find tables of all the U.S. states and their capitals and population data. When writing this book, we extracted the data from a table on Wikipedia and used Word to convert them to a comma-separated list. Here's how some of that data looks:

```
Alabama, AL, 1819, Montgomery
Alaska, AK, 1960, Juneau
Arizona, AZ, 1912, Phoenix
Arkansas, AR, 1836, Little Rock
California, CA, 1850, Sacramento
```

The full file contains 50 lines of comma-separated data. You can either read them in one at a time or just read them all into an array at once. Let's use the second approach:

```
class StateList():
    def __init__(self, stateFile):

        # read all lines into the contents
        with open(stateFile) as self.fobj:
            self.contents = self.fobj.readlines()
```

The `contents` variable now contains an array of strings. We can parse them one by one and create a `state` object for each one:

```
self._states = []              #create empty list
for st in self.contents:
    if len(st)>0:
        self.state = State(st)  #create State object
        self._states.append(self.state) #add to list
```

The rest of the work is done in the State class, which parses those strings, breaking them apart at the commas and storing each in an internal variable:

```
class State():
    def __init__(self, stateString):
        # split the string into tokens

        self._tokens = stateString.split(",")
           self._statename = "" # default if empty
        if len(self._tokens) > 3:
            self._statename = self._tokens[0]
            self._abbrev = self._tokens[1]
            self._founded = self._tokens[2]
            self._capital = self._tokens[3] # cap
```

Other than the accessor functions for the State variables, this is the bulk of the program. In essence, the StateList class creates a list (array) of state objects.

The rest of the program finds a way to display the data.

Creating a Listbox

The Listbox is much like ones you have seen in most applications: It is just a list of strings that you can click on to select one. For our list of states, we can quickly create such a Listbox like this:

```
class BuildUI():
    def __init__(self, root, slist):
        self.states= slist
        self.listbox = Listbox(root, selectmode=SINGLE)
        self.listbox.grid(column=0, row=0, rowspan=4, padx=10)
        for state in self.states:
            self.listbox.insert(END, state.getStateName())
```

This listbox is inserted in column 1 of a grid and spans several rows, as shown. The slist variable contains the list of State objects. What we insert in the listbox is just the name string from each state. The selection mode can be SINGLE, BROWSE, MULTIPLE, or EXTENDED. The most common choice is SINGLE. BROWSE enables you to move your selection with the mouse. MULTIPLE allows you to select multiple elements. With EXTENDED, you can select several groups using the Shift and Control keys. Figure 3-1 shows the basic list for this example.

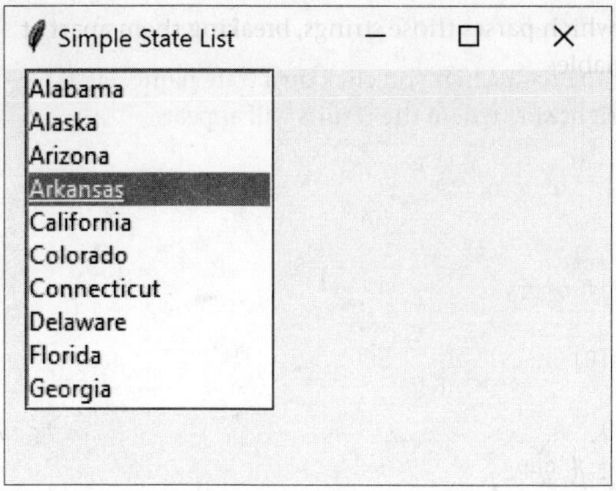

Figure 3-1 List of states in a Listbox, with the selectmode= SINGLE

Although the basic list does not contain a scrollbar, you can easily scroll through the contents with the mouse. But it isn't all that tricky to add in a scrollbar as you can see in Figure 3-2.

```
# set up the scroll bar
scrollBar = Scrollbar(root)
# connect to listbox
scrollBar.config(command=self.listbox.yview)

# stretch to top and bottom
scrollBar.grid(row=0, column=1, rowspan=4,
               sticky="NS")
# connect scrollbar y movement to listbox
self.listbox.config(yscrollcommand=scrollBar.set)
```

Figure 3-2 illustrates your completed scrollbar.

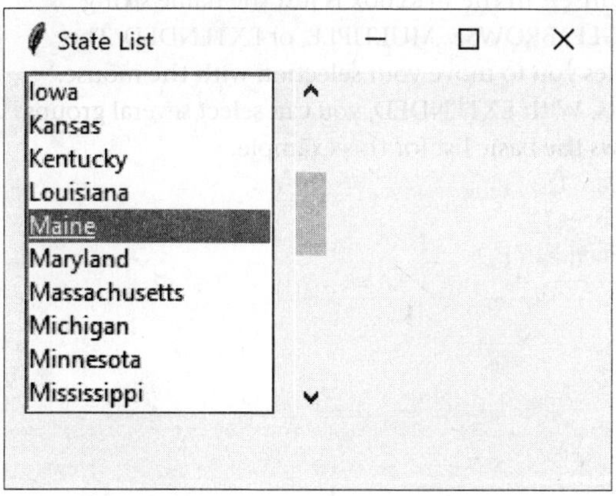

Figure 3-2 Listbox with a scrollbar attached

Displaying the State Data

There are two things we need to add to display the data when you click on a state name. First, we have to create a series of label fields along the right side where the results will appear:

```
# create 4 labels on right
self.lbstate = Label("")
# one red one
self.lbabbrev = Label(root, text="",
             foreground="red")

self.lbcapital = Label("")
self.lbfounded = Label("")

self.lbstate.grid(column=2, row=0, sticky=W) #left
self.lbabbrev.grid(column=2, row=1, sticky=W)
self.lbcapital.grid(column=2, row=2, sticky=W)
self.lbfounded.grid(column=2, row=3, sticky=W)
```

Next, we have to intercept the click event from the `Listbox` and send it to a callback function that can be activated when the click occurs. This takes place within the `BuildUI` class, which avoids any awkward global variables.

```
self.listbox.bind('<<ListboxSelect>>', self.lbselect)
```

You can bind any event to a callback function. The online Python documentation lists all the events that can occur on each widget. Here we bind the selection event to the `lbselect` method.

Then, the `lbselect` method simply finds the index of the list element you clicked, looks up that state object, and pulls out these values. Finally, it copies the state names into the label text (see Figure 3-3).

```
def lbselect(self, evt):
    index = self.listbox.curselection()  # tuple
    i= int(index[0])          # this is the actual index
    state = self.states[i]    # get state from list
    self.loadLabels(state)

def loadLabels(self,state):
    # fill in the labels from that state
    self.lbstate.config(text=state.getStateName())
    self.lbcapital.config(text=state.getCapital())
    self.lbabbrev.config(text=state.getAbbrev())
    self.lbfounded.config(text=state.getFounded())
```

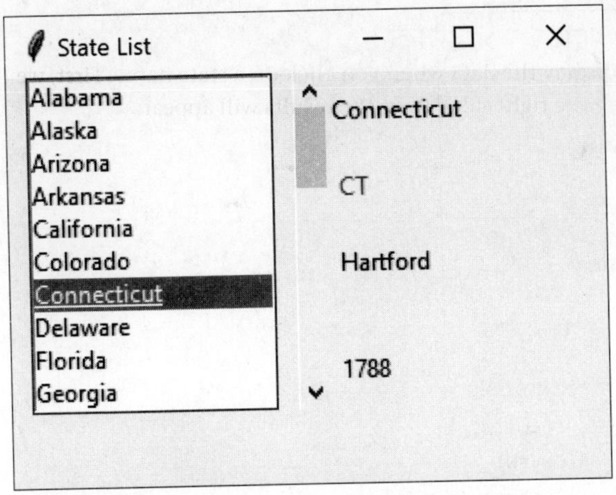

Figure 3-3 Listbox and scrollbar, with details displayed for the selected state

It might be nice to have a way to jump down in the alphabetical list without having to scroll. If we add an entry field, we can use it to find the first state that begins with that letter.

```
self.entry=Entry(root)        # create entry field
self.entry.grid(column=0, row=4, pady=4)
self.entry.focus_set()        # set the focus to it
# bind a keypress to lbselect
self.entry.bind("<Key>", self.keyPress)
```

The keypress method fetches the character from the event field, converts it to uppercase, and scans the state list for the first match. If it finds a match, it sets the listbox index to that row, as Figure 3-4 shows.

```
def keyPress(self, evt):
    char = evt.char.upper()
    i=0
    found= False
    # search for state starting with char
    while (not found) and (i< len(self.states)):
        found =self.states[i].getStateName().startswith(char)
        if not found:
            i = i+1
    if found:
        state = self.states[i]        # get the state
        self.listbox.select_clear(0, END)   # clear
        self.listbox.select_set(i)  # set selection
        self.listbox.see(i)         # make visible
        self.loadLabels(state)      # load labels
```

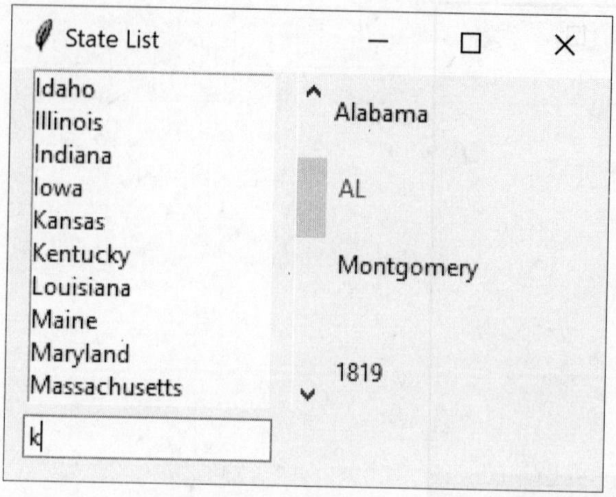

Figure 3-4 Listbox and Entry field that lets you skip ahead to any selected alphabetic position

Using a Combobox

The Combobox is a combination of an entry field and a drop-down list. You can type into the entry field or select an entry from the list. In either case, the method `combo.get()` returns the selected string.

Loading the `Combobox` is simpler than loading the `listbox`; you just pass it an array of names:

```
names=[]
for s in self.states:
    names.append(s.getStateName())

#add list to combo box
self.combo = Combobox(root, values=names)
self.combo.current(0)
self.combo.bind('<<ComboboxSelected>>',
                          self.onselect)
self.combo.grid(column=0, row=0, rowspan=8, padx=10)
```

Clicking a state calls the `onselect` method, which loads the state data:

```
def onselect(self, evt):
    index = self.combo.current()
    state = self.states[index]
    self.loadLabels(state)
```

If you set `combo.current` to `0` or a number greater than zero, that line in the `Combobox` is selected, and that line is copied into the entry field. If you set that value to `None`, then the entry box is empty (see Figure 3-5).

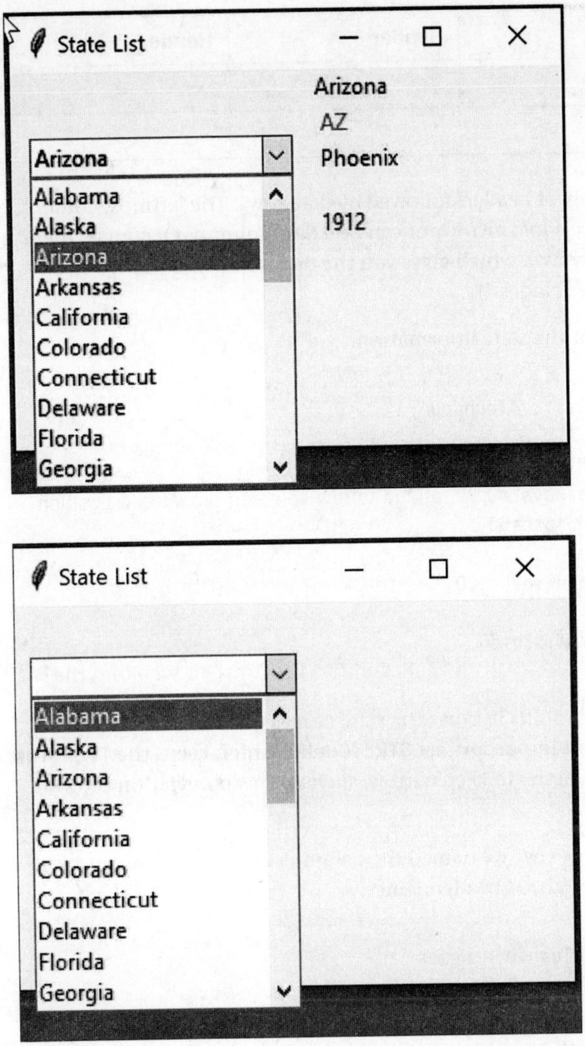

Figure 3-5 Combobox with current set to less than 0 (top) and equal to 0 (bottom)

The Treeview Widget

You can use the `Treeview` widget to view nested data or just use it to view tables of data. It does a great job either way. For some reason, the Python documentation on `Treeview` is pretty much impenetrable, though. The simple summary in this section should get you up to speed more easily.

Header #0	Header	Header	Header
Labels			
or text col			

The Treeview table consists of a top row of headers followed by data rows. The leftmost column, which is always named "#0", can be labels for the rows or can be a data column. Of course, there can also be rows that are children of any row, which gives you the opportunity to build a tree. (We'll show you this in the section "Tree Nodes.")

First, you need to create the columns for the state information:

```
# create columns
tree["columns"] = ("abbrev", "capital", "founded")

tree.column("#0", width=100, minwidth=100,
    stretch=NO) # left column is always #0
tree.column("abbrev", width=50, minwidth=50,
    stretch=NO)
tree.column("capital", width=100, minwidth=100,
    stretch=NO)
tree.column("founded", width=70, minwidth=60,
    stretch=NO)
```

Note that we only create three named columns because the state names go in the #0 column on the left. We define their widths and, most important, set STRETCH=NO, which keeps the Treeview from widening columns that you might prefer to keep narrow, such as the abbreviation column (this example keeps it at 50 pixels wide).

Then you create the actual headings. Note that we named the columns earlier; now we put headings in those named columns, using capitalized header names:

```
# create headings
tree.heading('#0', text='Name') # column 0 = names
tree.heading('abbrev', text='Abbrev')
tree.heading('capital', text='Capital')
tree.heading('founded', text='Founded')
```

Finally, we insert a couple of data rows:

```
tree.insert(node, rownum, text=col0txt, values=("one", "two", "three"))
```

If you are inserting at the main row, the node can be blank. The text for column 0 goes in text=. The remaining columns are in the list following values=. Here is an example:

```
tree.insert("", 1, text="California", values=("CA",
    "Sacramento", "1845"))
tree.insert("", 2, text="Kansas", values=( "KS",
    "Topeka", "1845"))
```

Figure 3-6 shows the result.

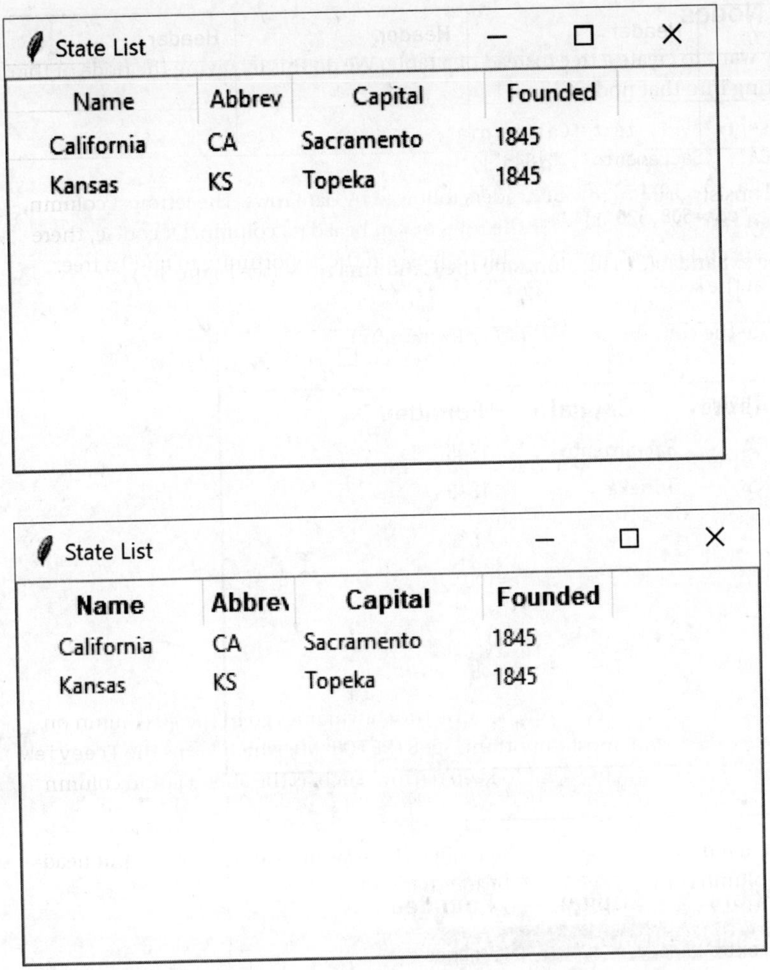

Figure 3-6 Treeview with normal (top) and boldface (bottom) headers

It is pretty common to put the header row in boldface. You can do this with a `Style` statement:

```
style = ttk.Style()
style.configure("Treeview.Heading",
        font=(None, 10, "bold"))
```

The trick in the `font` statement is that you set the size and bold, but you do not change the current font. Figure 3-6 shows the result.

Inserting Tree Nodes

Suppose we actually want to create a tree instead of a table. We do this by saving the node of that row and then inserting into that node:

```
folderCa= tree.insert("", 1, text="California",
      values=( "CA", "Sacramento", "1845"))
tree.insert(folderCa, 3, text="",
      values=(" ","pop=508,529"))
```

This gives you a little expandable mark alongside the California node (see Figure 3-7).

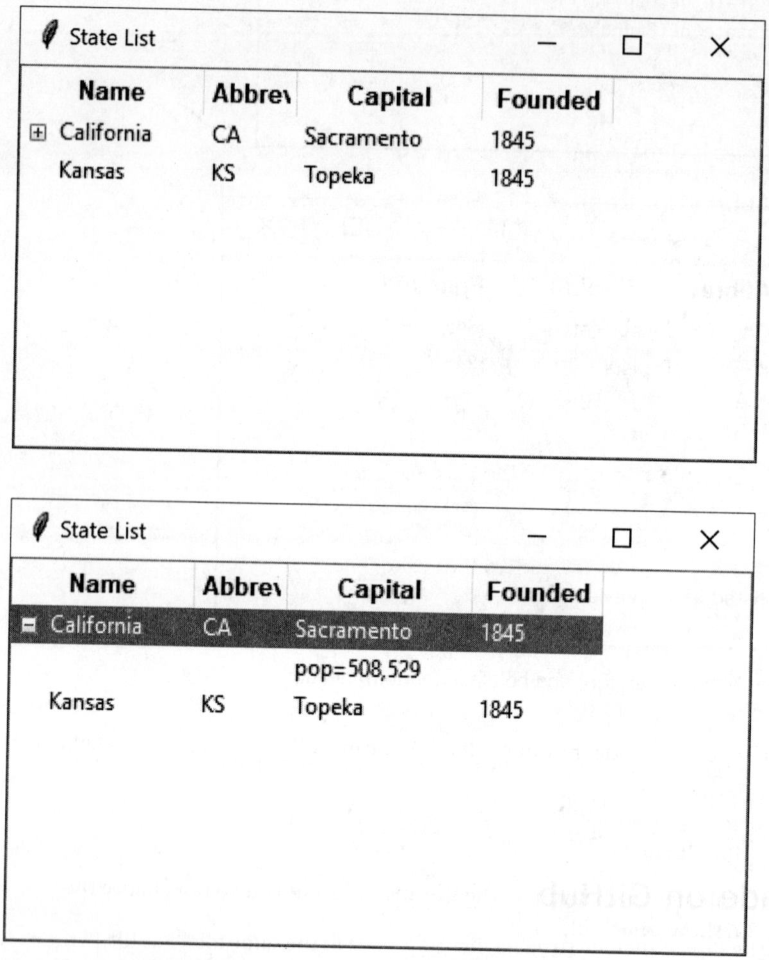

Figure 3-7 Treeview with collapsed (top) and expanded (bottom) leaf nodes

You can click that + sign to expand the tree. Note that we inserted under column 2, the Capital column, which shows the population in Figure 3-7.

You can display the entire list of states using the `States` array we developed in earlier examples; it is only four lines of code. Figure 3-8 shows the window.

```
i=1
for state in self.states:
    self.tree.insert("", i,
                     text=state.getStateName(),
                     values=( state.getAbbrev(),
                     state.getCapital(),
                     state.getFounded()))
    i += 1
```

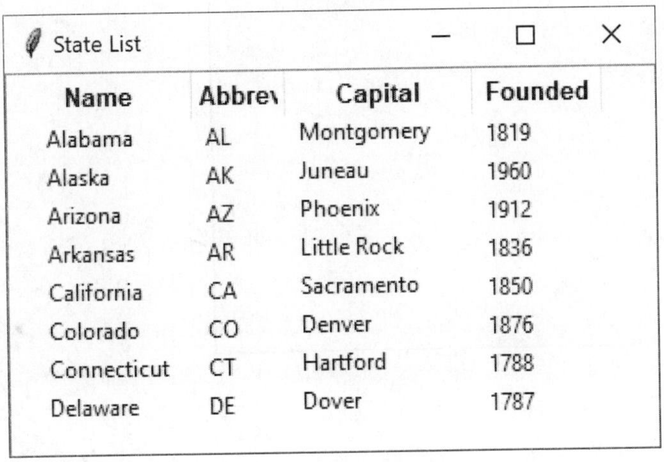

Figure 3-8 States listed as a Treeview table

Moving On

Now that we've laid the groundwork, we can dig into the actual design patterns which we begin discussing in Chapter 4, "What Are Design Patterns?"

Example Code on GitHub

In all these samples, be sure to include the data file (States.txt) in the same folder as the Python file. Also make sure all of these programs are part of the project in Vscode or PyCharm.

- States.txt: Data file for these list examples
- SimpleList.py: Basic listbox

- StateListScroll.py: Listbox with scrollbar
- StateListBox.py: Listbox with entry field
- StateDisplayCombo.py: Combobox display
- TreeTest.py: Tree with expandable node
- TreeStates.py: Tree of all states, capitals, and founding dates

4

What Are Design Patterns?

Sitting at your desk in front of your workstation, you stare into space, trying to figure out how to write a new program feature. You know intuitively what must be done, what data and what objects come into play, but you have this underlying feeling that there is a more elegant and general way to write this program.

In fact, you probably don't write any code until you can build a picture in your mind of what the code does and how the pieces of the code interact. The more you can picture this "organic whole," the more likely you are to feel comfortable that you have developed the best solution to the problem. If you don't grasp this whole right away, you might keep staring out the window for a time, even though the basic solution to the problem is quite obvious.

In one sense, you feel that the most elegant solution will be more reusable and more maintainable, but even if you are the sole likely programmer, you feel reassured when you have designed a solution that is relatively elegant and doesn't expose too many internal inelegancies.

One of the main reasons computer science researchers began to recognize design patterns is to satisfy this need for elegant but simple reusable solutions. The term *design patterns* sounds a bit formal to the uninitiated and can be somewhat off-putting when you first encounter it. But, in fact, design patterns are just convenient ways of reusing object-oriented code between projects and programmers. The idea behind design patterns is simple: to write down and catalog common interactions between objects that programmers have frequently found useful.

One frequently cited pattern from early literature on programming frameworks is the Model-View-Controller framework for Smalltalk (Krasner and Pope, 1988), which divided the user interface problem into three parts. The parts were referred to as a *data model*, containing the computational parts of the program; the *view*, which presents the user interface; and the *controller*, which interacts between the user and the view (see Figure 4-1).

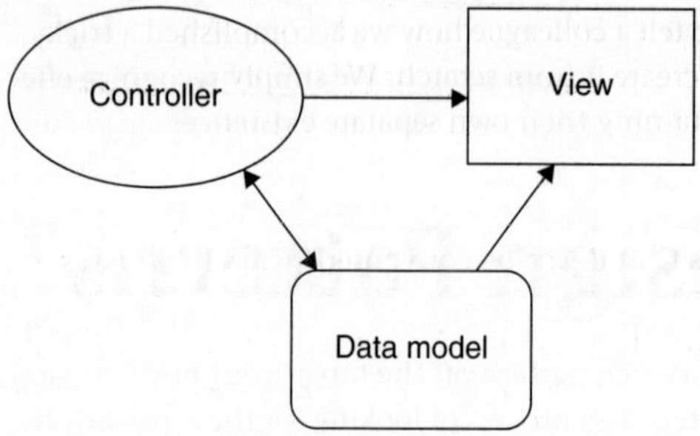

Figure 4-1 Model-View-Controller illustration

Each of these aspects of the problem is a separate object, and each has its own rules for managing its data. Communication among the user, the GUI, and the data should be carefully controlled, and this separation of functions accomplished that very nicely. Three objects talking to each other using this restrained set of connections is an example of a powerful design pattern.

In other words, design patterns describe how objects communicate without become entangled in each other's data models and methods. Keeping this separation has always been an objective of good OO programming. If you have been trying to keep objects minding their own business, you are probably already using some of the common design patterns.

Design patterns started to be recognized more formally in the early 1990s by Erich Gamma,[1] who described patterns incorporated in the GUI application framework ET++. The culmination of these discussions and a number of technical meetings was the book *Design Patterns: Elements of Reusable Software,* by Gamma, Helm, Johnson, and Vlissides.[2] This best-selling book, commonly referred to as the Gang of Four, or "GoF" book, has had a powerful impact on programmers seeking to understand how to use design patterns. It describes 23 commonly occurring and generally useful patterns and comments on how and when you might apply them. Throughout the following chapters, we refer to this groundbreaking book as *Design Patterns*.

Since the publication of the original *Design Patterns*, many other useful books have been published. These include our popular *Java Design Patterns: A Tutorial*[3] and an analogous book on C# design patterns.[4] Rhodes[5] maintains an interesting site describing how Python can make use of design patterns, as well.

Defining Design Patterns

We all talk about the way we do things in our everyday work, hobbies, and home life, and recognize repeating patterns all the time:

- Sticky buns are like dinner rolls, but I add brown sugar and nut filling to them.
- Her front garden is like mine, but in mine I use *astilbe*.
- This end table is constructed like that one, but in this one, the doors replace drawers.

We see the same thing in programming, when we tell a colleague how we accomplished a tricky bit of programming so that they don't have to re-create it from scratch. We simply recognize effective ways for objects to communicate while maintaining their own separate existences.

To summarize:

Design patterns are frequently used algorithms that describe convenient ways for classes to communicate.

It has become apparent that you don't just *write* a design pattern off the top of your head. In fact, most such patterns are *discovered* rather than written. The process of looking for these patterns is called *pattern mining* and is worthy of a book of its own.

The 23 design patterns selected for inclusion in the original *Design Patterns* book were patterns that had several known applications and were on a middle level of generality, where they could easily cross application areas and encompass several objects.

The authors divided these patterns into three types: creational, structural, and behavioral.

- *Creational patterns* create objects for you instead of having you instantiate objects directly. This gives your program more flexibility in deciding which objects need to be created for a given case.
- *Structural patterns* help you compose groups of objects into larger structures, such as complex user interfaces or accounting data.
- *Behavioral patterns* help you define the communication between objects in your system and control the flow in a complex program.

The Learning Process

We have found that learning design patterns is a multiple-step process:

1. Acceptance
2. Recognition
3. Internalization

First, you accept the premise that design patterns are important in your work. Then you recognize that you need to read about design patterns in order to determine when you might use them. Finally, you internalize the patterns in sufficient detail that you know which ones might help you solve a given design problem.

For some lucky people, design patterns are obvious tools, and they grasp their essential utility just by reading summaries of the patterns. For many of the rest of us, there is a slow induction period after we've read about a pattern, followed by the proverbial "Aha!" when we see how we can apply them in our work. These chapters help take you to that final stage of internalization by providing complete, working programs that you can try out for yourself.

The examples in *Design Patterns* are brief and are written in either C++ or, in some cases, Smalltalk. If you are working in another language, it is helpful to have the pattern examples in your language of choice. This part of the book attempts to fill that need for Python programmers.

Notes on Object-Oriented Approaches

The fundamental reason for using design patterns is to keep classes separated and prevent them from having to know too much about one another. Equally important, using these patterns helps you avoid reinventing the wheel and enables you to describe your programming approach succinctly in terms other programmers can easily understand.

There are a number of strategies that OO programmers use to achieve this separation, among them encapsulation and inheritance. Nearly all languages that have OO capabilities support inheritance. A class that inherits from a parent class has access to all the methods of that parent class. It also has access to all its variables. However, by starting your inheritance hierarchy with a complete, working class, you might be unduly restricting yourself as well as carrying along specific method implementation baggage. Instead, *Design Patterns* suggests that you always

Program to an interface and not to an implementation.

Putting this more succinctly, you should define the top of any class hierarchy with an *abstract* class or an *interface,* which implements no methods but simply defines the methods that class will support. Then in all your derived classes, you have more freedom to implement these methods as best suits your purposes.

Python does not directly support interfaces, but it does let you write abstract classes, where the methods have no implementation. Remember the `comd` interface to the `DButton` class:

```
class DButton(Button):
    def __init__(self, master, **kwargs):
        super().__init__(master, **kwargs)
        super().config(command=self.comd)

    # abstract method to be called by children
    def comd(self): pass
```

This is a good example of an abstract class. Here you fill in the code for the command method in the derived button classes. As you will see, it is also an example of the Command design pattern.

The other major concept you should recognize is *object composition.* We have already seen this approach in the `Statelist` examples. Object composition is simply the construction of objects that contain others—the encapsulation of several objects inside another one. Many beginning OO programmers tend to use inheritance to solve every problem, but as you begin to write more elaborate programs, the merits of object composition become apparent. Your new object can have the interface that works best for what you want to accomplish without having all the methods of the parent classes. Thus, the second major precept suggested by *Design Patterns* is

Favor object composition over inheritance.

At first this seems contrary to the customs of OO programming, but you will see any number of cases among the design patterns where we find that inclusion of one or more objects inside another is the preferred method.

Python Design Patterns

The following chapters discuss each of the 23 design patterns featured in the *Design Patterns* book, along with at least one working program example for that pattern. The programs have some sort of visual interface as well to make them more immediate to you.

Which design patterns are most useful? This depends on the individual programmer. The ones we use the most are Command, Factory, Decorator, Façade, and Mediator, but we have used nearly every one at some point.

References

1. Erich Gamma, *Object-Oriented Software Development based on ET++,* (in German) (Springer-Verlag, Berlin, 1992).
2. Erich Gamma, Richard Helm, Ralph Johnson, and John Vlissides, *Design Patterns, Elements of Reusable Object-Oriented Software* (Reading, MA: Addison-Wesley, 1995).
3. James Cooper, *Java Design Patterns: A Tutorial* (Boston: Addison-Wesley: 2000).
4. James Cooper, *C# Design Patterns: A Tutorial* (Boston: Addison-Wesley, 2003).
5. Brandon Rhodes, "Python Design Patterns," https://python-patterns.guide.

Creational Patterns

[illegible]

Singleton design pattern [illegible] instance [illegible]

[illegible]

However, [illegible] create [illegible]

[illegible] of the objects [illegible]

[illegible] your program [illegible]

- **The Factory pattern** [illegible]
- **The Abstract Factory method** [illegible] return [illegible] objects [illegible]
- **The Builder pattern** separates the [illegible] from its [illegible] can be created, depending on the needs of the [illegible]
- **The Prototype pattern** [illegible] of clones [illegible] rather than [illegible]
- **The Singleton pattern** [illegible] class that can [illegible] one instance. It provides a single global point of access to that instance.

PART II

Creational Patterns

All creational patterns deal with ways to create instances of objects. This is important because your program should not depend on how objects are created and arranged. In Python, of course, the simplest way to create an instance of an object is by creating a variable of that class type.

```
fred = Fred()          # instance of Fred class
```

However, this really amounts to hard coding, depending on how you create the object within your program. In many cases, the exact nature of the object that is created could vary with the needs of the program. Abstracting the creation process into a special “creator” class can make your program more flexible and general.

- **The Factory method** provides a simple decision-making class that returns one of several possible subclasses of an abstract base class, depending on the data provided.
- **The Abstract Factory method** provides an interface to create and return one of several families of related objects.
- **The Builder pattern** separates the construction of a complex object from its representation so that several different representations can be created, depending on the needs of the program.
- **The Prototype pattern** starts with an instantiated class and copies or clones it to make new instances. These instances can then be further tailored using their public methods.
- **The Singleton pattern** defines a class that can have no more than one instance. It provides a single global point of access to that instance.

5

The Factory Pattern

One type of pattern that we see again and again in OO programs is the Simple Factory pattern or class. A Simple Factory pattern returns an instance of one of several possible classes, depending on the data provided to it. Usually all the classes it returns have a common parent class and common methods, but each one performs a task differently and is optimized for different kinds of data. This Simple Factory is not one of the 23 GoF patterns, but it serves here as an introduction to the somewhat more subtle Factory Method GoF pattern we'll discuss shortly.

How a Factory Works

Let's consider a simple case where we could use a Factory class. Suppose we have an entry form and want to allow users to enter their names either as "firstname lastname" or as "lastname, first-name". To simplify this example, assume that we will always be able to decide the name order by whether there is a comma between the last and first name. Figure 5-1 shows a class diagram for this simple case.

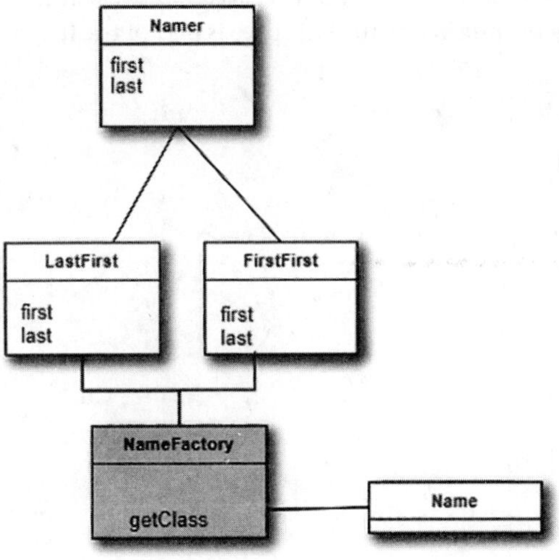

Figure 5-1 LastFirst and FirstFirst are derived from Namer. The NameFactory produces one or the other

In Figure 5-1, `Namer` is a base class and classes `LastFirst` and `FirstFirst` are derived from it. The `NameFactory` class decides which of these subclasses to return, depending on the arguments you give it. On the right, a `getClass` method is defined to be one that passes in some value *arg* and returns some instance of the class `Namer`. The programmer doesn't care which one it returns because they all have the same methods but different implementations. How it decides which one to return is entirely up to the factory. It could be a very complex function, but it is often quite simple.

Sample Code

Deciding on which of the two cases we just described is a pretty simple sort of decision to make; you could do so with a simple `if` statement in a single class. But let's use it here to illustrate how a factory works and what it can produce. We'll start by defining a simple base class that takes a string and splits it (somehow) into two names:

```
#base Namer class
class Namer():
    def __init__(self):
        self.last=""
        self.first=""
```

In this base class, we don't compute any names, as such, but we do provide place holders for the first and last names. We'll store the split first and last names in the Strings `first` and `last`, which the subclasses can then access. In this simple example, there is no need for getter and setter methods to access the class instance variables *`first`* and *`last`*.

The Two Subclasses

Now we can write two very simple subclasses that split the name into two parts in the constructor. In the `FirstFirst` class, we assume that everything before the last space is part of the first name:

```
#derived namer class for First <space> Last
class FirstFirst(Namer):
    def __init__(self, namestring):
        super().__init__()
        i = namestring.find(" ")    #find space
        if i > 0 :
            names = namestring.split()
            self.first = names[0]
            self.last = names[1]
        else:
            self.last = namestring
```

In the LastFirst class, we assume that a comma delimits the last name. In both classes, we also provide error recovery, in case the space or comma does not exist.

```
#derived Namer class for Last <comma> First
class LastFirst(Namer):
    def __init__(self, namestring):
        super().__init__()
        i = namestring.find(",")  # find comma
        if i > 0 :
            names = namestring.split(",")
            self.last = names[0]
            self.first = names[1]
        else:
            self.last = namestring
```

Building the Simple Factory

Now our simple Factory class is extremely simple. We just test for the existence of a comma and then return an instance of one class or the other:

```
class NamerFactory():
    def __init__(self, namestring):
        self.name = namestring
    def getNamer(self):
        i = self.name.find(",") #if it finds a comma
        if i>0:
            #get the LastFirst class
            return LastFirst(self.name)
        else:  # else get the FirstFirst
            return FirstFirst(self.name)
```

Using the Factory

Let's see how to put this together. In this example, we create a little program to ask for the name string and then ask the factory for the right Namer, right from the console.

```
class Builder:
    def compute(self):
        name = ""
        while name != 'quit':
            name = input("Enter name: ") # get entry
            # get the Namer Factory
            # and then the namer class
            namerFact = NamerFactory(name)
            # get namer
            namer = namerFact.getNamer()
```

```
            # print out split name
            print(namer.first, namer.last)

def main():
    bld = Builder()
    bld.compute()
```

And the actual program works just as expected, finding the comma or space and splitting into two names:

```
Enter name: Sandy Smith
 Sandy Smith
Enter name: Jones, Doug
 Doug Jones
Enter name: quit
 quit
```

You type in a name and then click the Compute button, and the divided name appears in the next line. The crux of this program is the `compute` method that fetches the text, obtains an instance of a `Namer` class, and prints the results.

A Simple GUI

We have also constructed a simple user interface using tkinter that enables you to enter the names in either order and see the two names separately displayed. You can see this program in Figure 5-2.

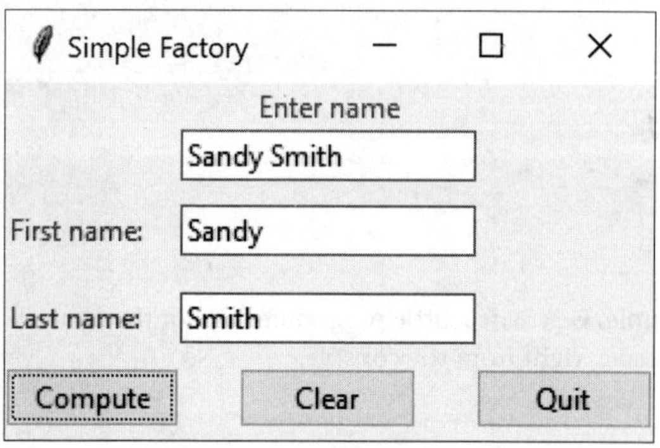

Figure 5-2 Simple name factory display

And that's the fundamental principle of the Simple Factory pattern. You create an abstraction that decides which of several possible classes to return and returns one. Then you call the methods of that class instance without ever knowing which subclass you are actually using. This approach keeps the issues of data dependence separated from the classes' useful methods.

Factory Patterns in Math Computation

Most people who use Factory patterns tend to think of them as tools for simplifying tangled programming classes. But it is perfectly possible to use them in programs that simply perform mathematical computations. For example, in the Fast Fourier Transform (FFT), you evaluate the following four equations repeatedly for a large number of point pairs over many passes through the array you are transforming. Because of the way the graphs of these computations are drawn, these equations constitute one instance of the FFT "butterfly." These are shown as Equations 1–4.

$$R_1' = R_1 + R_2 \cos(y) - I_2 \sin(y) \quad (1)$$

$$R_2' = R_1 - R_2 \cos(y) + I_2 \sin(y) \quad (2)$$

$$I_1' = I_1 + R_2 \sin(y) + I_2 \cos(y) \quad (3)$$

$$I_2' = I_1 - R_2 \sin(y) - I_2 \cos(y) \quad (4)$$

However, there are a number of times during each pass through the data, where the angle y is 0. In this case, your complex math evaluation reduces to Equations 5–8.

$$R_1' = R_1 + R_2 \quad (5)$$

$$R_2' = R_1 - R_2 \quad (6)$$

$$I_1' = I_1 + I_2 \quad (7)$$

$$I_2' = I_1 - I_2 \quad (8)$$

Then, we can make a simple factory class that decides which class instance to return. Since we are making Butterflies, we'll call our Factory a `Cocoon`:

```
class Cocoon():
    def getButterfly(self, y:float):
        if y !=0:
            return TrigButterfly(y)
        else:
            return AddButterfly(y)
```

Programs on GitHub

- NamerConsole.py: Console version of Namer factory
- NameUI.py: Illustrates the Namer factory with a UI
- Cocoon.py: Simple prototype of a Factory pattern

Thought Questions

1. Consider a personal checkbook management program such as Quicken. It manages several bank accounts and investments and can handle your bill paying. Where could you use a Factory pattern in designing a program like this?
2. Suppose you are writing a program to assist homeowners in designing additions to their houses. What objects might a Factory be used to produce?

6

The Factory Method Pattern

In Chapter 5, we saw a couple of examples of the simplest of factories. The factory concept recurs all throughout object-oriented programming. In such cases, a single class acts as a traffic cop and decides which subclass of a single hierarchy will be instantiated.

The Factory Method pattern is a clever but subtle extension of this idea, where no single class makes the decision as to which subclass to instantiate. Instead, the superclass defers the decision to each subclass. This pattern does not actually have a decision point where one subclass is directly selected over another class. Instead, programs written to this pattern define an abstract class that creates objects but lets each subclass decide which object to create.

We can draw a pretty simple example from the way swimmers are seeded into lanes in a swim meet. When swimmers compete in multiple heats in a given event, they are sorted to compete from slowest in the early heats to fastest in the last heat, and they are arranged within a heat with the fastest swimmers in the center lanes. This process is referred to as *straight seeding*.

When swimmers swim in championships, they frequently swim the event twice. During preliminaries, everyone competes. Then in the finals, the top 12 or 16 swimmers return to compete against each other. In order to make the preliminaries more equitable, the top heats are *circle* seeded: The fastest three swimmers are in the center lane in the fastest three heats, the second fastest three swimmers are in the lane next to the center in the top three heats, and so forth.

So, how do we build some objects to implement this seeding scheme and illustrate the Factory Method as shown in Figure 6-1? First, let's design an abstract `Event` class:

```
class Event():
    # place holders to be filled in actual classes
    def getSeeding(self): pass
    def isPrelim(self): pass
    def isFinal(self): pass
    def isTimedFinal(self): pass
```

Note the simplification of putting the `pass` statement on the same line, to avoid clutter.

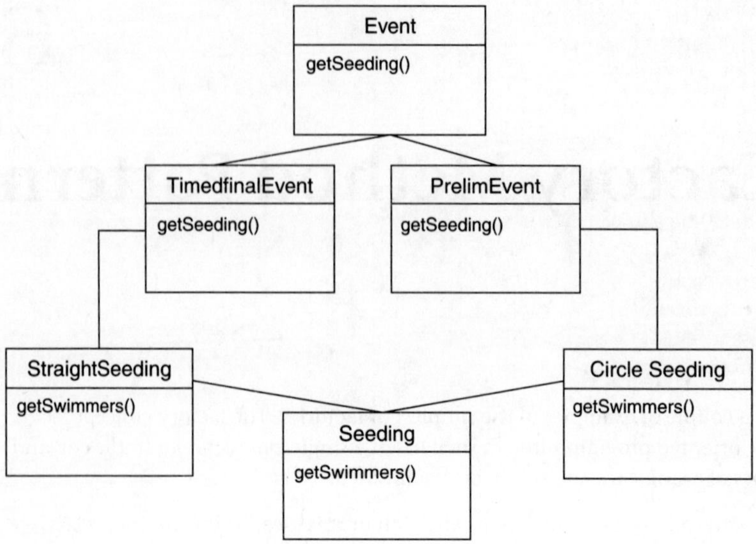

Figure 6-1 Factory Method pattern

This defines the methods simply, without any necessity of filling in the methods. Then we can derive concrete classes from the `Event` class, called `PrelimEvent` and `TimedFinalEvent`. The only difference between these classes is that one returns a certain kind of seeding, and the other returns a different kind of seeding.

We also define an abstract `Seeding` class having the following methods:

```
class Seeding:
    def getSwimmers(self): pass
```

We can then create two concrete seeding subclasses: `StraightSeeding` and `CircleSeeding`. The `PrelimEvent` class will return an instance of `CircleSeeding` and the `TimedFinalEvent` class will return an instance of `StraightSeeding`. Thus, we see that we have two hierarchies: one of Events and one of Seedings.

In the Event hierarchy, both derived `Event` classes contain a `getSeeding` method. One of them returns an instance of `StraightSeeding`, and the other returns an instance of `CircleSeeding`. As you see, there is no real factory decision point as we had in our simple example. Instead, the decision as to which `Event` class to instantiate is the one that determines which `Seeding` class will be instantiated.

Although it looks like there is a one-to-one correspondence between the two class hierarchies, this needn't be the case. There could be many kinds of Events and only a few kinds of Seeding that they use.

The Swimmer Class

We haven't said much about the `Swimmer` class, except that it contains a name, club age, seed time, and place to put the heat and lane after seeding. The `Event` class reads in the swimmers from some database (a file, in our example) and then passes that List to the Seeding class when you call the getSeeding method for that event.

Here it is in brief:

```
class Swimmer():
     def __init__(self, dataline):
          #read in a row and separate the columns
         sarray = dataline.split()
         self.frname=sarray[1]          #names
         self.lname=sarray[2]
         self.age=int(sarray[3])        #age
         self.club=sarray[4]            #club symbol
         self.seedtime=sarray[5]        #seed string
         self.time=0.0                  #set defaults
         self.lane=0 #seeded heats and lanes go here
         self.heat=0
    #Concatenate first and last names
     def getName(self):
          return self.frname+" "+self.lname #combine
```

The Event Classes

We have seen the abstract base Event class earlier. In actual use, we use it to read in the swimmer data (here from a file) and pass it on to instances of the Swimmer class to parse.

```
class Event():
    def __init__(self, filename, lanes):
        self.numLanes = lanes
        self.swimmers=[]          # array of swimmers
        # read in the data file for this event
        f = open(filename, "r")

        # the Swimmer class then parses each line
        for swstring in f:
            sw = Swimmer(swstring)
            self.swimmers.append(sw)
        f.close()
```

The PrelimEvent class just returns an instance of CircleSeeding:

```
class PrelimEvent (Event):
 # creates a preliminary event circle seeded
    def __init__(self, filename, lanes):
        super().__init__(filename, lanes)

    def  getSeeding(self):
        return CircleSeeding(self.swimmers, self.numLanes)
```

while the `TimedFinalEvent` returns an instance of `StraightSeeding`:

```
class TimedFinalEvent (Event):
# creates an event that will be straight seeded
    def __init__(self, filename,  lanes):
        super().__init__(filename, lanes)

    def getSeeding(self):
        return StraightSeeding(self.swimmers, self.numLanes)
```

Straight Seeding

In actually writing this program, we'll discover that most of the work is done in straight seeding. The changes for circle seeding are pretty minimal. So we instantiate our `StraightSeeding` class and copy in the `List` of swimmers and the number of lanes:

```
class StraightSeeding(Seeding):
    def __init__(self, sw, nlanes):
        self.swimmers = sw
        self.numLanes = nlanes
        self.count = len(sw)
        self.lanes = self.calcLaneOrder()
        self.seed()
```

Then, as part of the constructor, we do the basic seeding.

```
  def seed(self):
# loads the swmrs array and sorts it
    asw = self.sortUpwards()  # number in last heat
    self.lastHeat = self.count % self.numLanes
    if (self.lastHeat < 3):
        self.lastHeat = 3 # last heat has 3 or more

    lastLanes =self.count - self.lastHeat
    self.numHeats = self.count / self.numLanes

    if (lastLanes > 0):
        self.numHeats += 1 # compute total heats
    heats = self.numHeats

    # place heat and lane in each swimmer's object
    j = 0
      # load from fastest to slowest
      # so we start with last heat  # and work down
    for i in range(0, lastLanes) :
        sw = asw[i] # get each swimmer
        sw.setLane(self.lanes[j]) # copy in lane
        j += 1
```

```
            sw.setHeat(heats) # and heat
            if (j >= self.numLanes):
                heats -= 1 # next heat
                j=0

# Add in last partial heat
        if (j < self.numLanes):
            heats -= 1
            j = 0

        for i in range(lastLanes-1, self.count):
            sw = asw[i]
            sw.setLane(self.lanes[j])
            j += 1
            sw.setHeat(heats)

# copy from array back into list
        swimmers = []
        for i in range(0, self.count):
            swimmers.append(asw[i])
```

This makes the entire array of seeded swimmers available when you call the `getSwimmers` method.

Circle Seeding

The `CircleSeeding` class is derived from `StraightSeeding`, so it copies in the same data.

```
class CircleSeeding(StraightSeeding):
    def __init__(self, sw, nlanes):
        super().__init__(sw, nlanes)

    def seed(self):
        super().seed() # do straight seed as default
        if (self.numHeats >= 2):
            if (self.numHeats >= 3):
                circle = 3
            else:
                circle = 2
        i = 0

        for j in range(0, self.numLanes):
            for k in range(0, circle):
                self.swimmers[i].setLane(self.lanes[j])
                self.swimmers[i].setHeat(self.numHeats - k)
           i += 1
```

Because the constructor calls the parent class constructor, it copies the swimmer vector and lanes values. Then our call to `super.seed()` does the straight seeding. This simplifies programming because we will always need to seed the remaining heats by straight seeding. Then we seed the last two or three heats as shown above and we are done with that type of seeding as well.

Our Seeding Program

In this example, we took a list of swimmers who competed in the 500-yard freestyle and the 100-yard freestyle and used them to build our `TimeFinalEvent` and `PrelimEvent` classes.

The code for calling these two seedings is pretty simple. The console version enables you to enter 1 or 5 or 0 (to quit).

```
class Builder():

    def build(self):
        dist=1
        while dist > 0:
            dist = int(input(
          'Enter 1 for 100, 5 for 500 or 0 to quit: '))
            if dist==1 or dist ==5:
                self.evselect(dist)

    # seed selected event
    def evselect(self, dist):
        # there are only two swimmer files
        # We read in one or the other

        if dist == 5 :
            event = TimedFinalEvent(
               "500free.txt", 6)
        elif dist ==1:
            event = PrelimEvent("100free.txt", 6)

        seeding = event.getSeeding()    #factory
        swmrs= seeding.getSwimmers()    #do seedingr

        #print swimmer list in seeded order
        for sw in swmrs:
           print(f'{sw.heat:3}{sw.lane:3} {sw.getName():20}{sw.age:3}
                           {sw.seedtime:9}')

# -----main begins here----
def main():
    builder = Builder()
    builder.build()
```

You can see the results of these two seedings:

```
Enter 1 for 100, 5 for 500 or 0 to quit: 1
 13  3 Kelly Harrigan          14 54.13
 12  4 Torey Thelin            14 55.03
 11  2 Lindsay McKenna         13 55.10
 13  5 Jen Pittman             14 55.67
 12  1 Annie Goldstein         13 55.82
 11  6 Kyla Burruss            14 56.04
```

We also built a visual display, but you don't have to use it. Since both the console and the GUI versions use the same classes, we put them all in a separate file, SwimClasses.py, and told the main program to import the two class references it uses:

```
from SwimClasses import TimedFinalEvent, PrelimEvent
```

The files just need to be in the same directory.

In Figure 6-2, the Treeview widget makes an elegant-looking table.

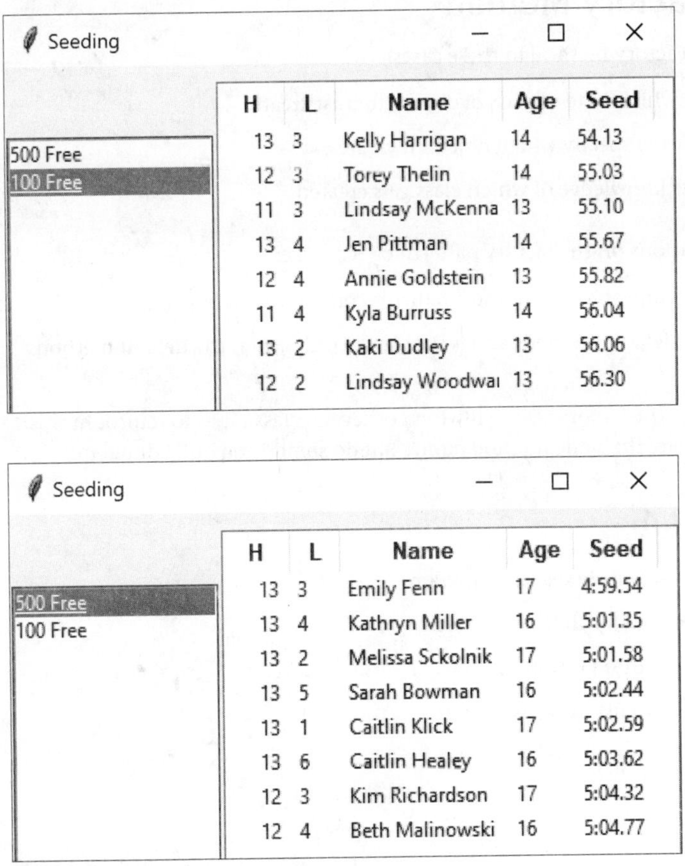

Figure 6-2 Straight seeding for 500 Free and circle seeding for 100 Free

Other Factories

One issue that we have skipped over is how the program that reads in the swimmer data decides which kind of event to generate. We finesse this here by simply calling the two constructors directly:

```
i = int(index[0])  # this is row number
# there are only two swimmer files
# We read in one or the other
if i <=0 :
    event = TimedFinalEvent("500free.txt",6)
else:
    event = PrelimEvent("100free.txt", 6)
```

Clearly, this is an instance where an `EventFactory` may be needed to decide which kind of event to generate. This revisits the simple factory we began the discussion with.

When to Use a Factory Method

You should consider using a Factory method in these cases:

- A class can't anticipate which kind of class of objects it must create.
- A class uses its subclasses to specify which objects it creates.
- You want to localize the knowledge of which class gets created.

There are several similar variations on the factory pattern to recognize:

1. The base class is abstract and the pattern must return a complete working class.
2. The base class contains default methods and is subclassed only when the default methods are insufficient.
3. Parameters are passed to the factory telling it which of several class types to return. In this case, the classes may share the same method names but do something quite different.

Programs on GitHub

- SwimFactoryConsole.py: Console seeding program
- SwimClasses.py: Classes used by all three versions
- SwimFactory.py: Puts a list into Listbox
- SwimFactoryTable.py: Puts a list into Treeview

7

The Abstract Factory Pattern

The Abstract Factory pattern is one level of abstraction higher than the Factory pattern. You use this pattern when you want to return one of several related classes of objects, each of which can return several different objects on request. In other words, the Abstract Factory is a factory object that returns one of several groups of classes. Determining which class from that group to use might even come from a Simple Factory.

One classic application of the abstract factory is the case where your system needs to support multiple "look-and-feel" user interfaces, such as Windows, Gnome, or OS/X. You tell the factory that you want your program to look like Windows, and it returns a GUI factory that returns Windows-like objects. Then when you request specific objects such as buttons, check boxes, and windows, the GUI factory returns Windows instances of these visual interface components.

A GardenMaker Factory

Let's consider a simple example of when you might want to use an abstract factory in your application.

Suppose you are writing a program to plan the layout of gardens. These could be annual gardens, vegetable gardens, or perennial gardens. No matter which kind of garden you are planning, you want to ask the same questions:

1. What are good border plants?
2. What are good center plants?
3. What plants do well in partial shade?

You probably have many other plant questions that we'll omit in this simple example.

We want a base `Garden` class that can answer these questions:

```
class Garden:
    def getShade(): pass
    def getCenter(): pass
    def getBorder(): pass
```

where our simple `Plant` object just contains and returns the plant name:

```
class Plant:
    def __init__(self, pname):
        self.name = pname     #save name
    def getName(self):
        return self.name
```

In a real system, each type of garden would probably consult an elaborate database of plant information. In our simple example, we'll return one kind of each plant. So, for example, for the vegetable garden we simply write

```
# one of three Garden subclasses
class VeggieGarden (Garden):
    def getShade(self):
        return Plant("Broccoli")
    def getCenter(self):
        return Plant("Corn")
    def getBorder(self):
        return Plant("Peas")
```

In a similar way, we can create `Garden` classes for `PerennialGarden` and `AnnualGarden`. Now we have a series of `Garden` objects, each of which returns one of several `Plant` objects. The factory is really just the three `ChoiceButtons`, derived from the `Radiobutton`.

```
ChoiceButton(lbframe, 'Vegetable', 0, VeggieGarden,
        self,  groupv)
ChoiceButton(lbframe, 'Annual', 1, AnnualGarden,
        self, groupv)
ChoiceButton(lbframe, 'Perennial', 2,
        PerennialGarden, self, groupv)
```

Each `ChoiceButton` has its own `comd` method that copies the correct instance of `Garden` into the main `Gardener` class:

```
# clicks are sent here
# The background is also cleared
def comd(self):
    self.gardener.setGarden(self.garden)
    self.gardener.clearCanvas()
```

Then when you click the Center, Border, or Shade buttons, that button writes the name of the current shade plant onto the canvas.

For example:

```
def setCenter(self):
    self.canv.create_text(100,120,
            text=self.garden.getCenter(self).getName())
```

This Simple Factory system can be used along with a more complex user interface to select the garden and begin planning it (see Figure 7-1).

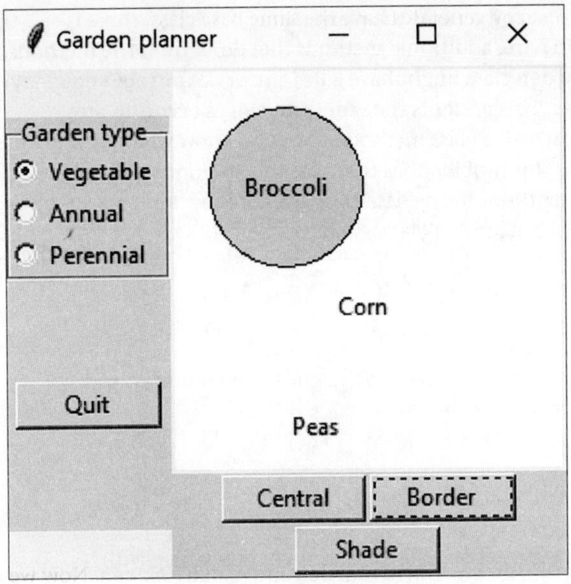

Figure 7-1 Garden planner interface

How the User Interface Works

This simple interface consists of two parts: On the left side, you select the garden type; on the right side, you select the plant category. When you click one of the garden types, this actuates the Abstract Factory and copies the correct garden into the `Gardener` class. Then when a user clicks one of the plant type buttons, the plant type is returned and the name of that plant is displayed.

One of the great strengths of the Abstract Factory is that you can easily add new subclasses. For example, if you needed a `GrassGarden` or a `WildFlowerGarden`, you can subclass `Garden` and produce these classes. The only real change you'd need to make in any existing code is to add some way to choose these new kinds of gardens.

Consequences of the Abstract Factory Pattern

One of the main purposes of the Abstract Factory is that it isolates the concrete classes that are generated. The actual class names of these classes are hidden in the factory and need not be known at the client level.

Because of this isolation of classes, you can freely change or interchange these product class families. Further, because you generate only one kind of concrete class, this system keeps you from inadvertently using classes from different families of products. However, adding new class families takes some effort because you need to define new, unambiguous conditions that cause such a new family of classes to be returned.

Although all the classes that the Abstract Factory generates have the same base class, there is nothing to prevent some subclasses from having additional methods that differ from the methods of other classes. For example, a `BonsaiGarden` class might have a `Height` or `WateringFrequency` method that does not exist in other classes. This presents the same problem as occurs in any subclasses: you don't know whether you can call a class method unless you know whether that subclass is one that allows those methods. This problem has the same two solutions as in any similar case: Either you can define all the methods in the base class, even if they don't always have an actual function, or you can test to see which kind of class you have.

Thought Questions

If you are writing a program to track investments, such as stocks, bonds, metal futures, and derivatives, how might you use an Abstract Factory?

Code on GitHub

The program Gardening.py launches the user interface shown in this chapter, along with exercises for the Abstract Factory and the various `Garden` classes.

8 The Singleton Pattern

The Singleton pattern is grouped with the other creational patterns, although, to some extent, it is a "noncreational" pattern. There are any number of cases in programming where you need to make sure that there can be one, and only one, instance of a class. For example, your system can have only one window manager or print spooler, as well as a single point of access to a database engine.

Python does not directly have a feature where a single static variable will be accessible from all class instances, so a simple flag won't work. Instead, this technique utilizes two subtle Python features you might not be aware of: the `static` method and the `__instance` variable.

Python has a Decorator that tells the compiler to make only a single static method within a class:

```
@staticmethod
```

This makes the method that follows static, rather than one that has a fresh copy for each instance of the class. The top of this class is written like this:

```
class Singleton:
    __instance = None

    # static method declared here
    @staticmethod
    def getInstance():
        if Singleton.__instance == None:
            Singleton()
        return Singleton.__instance
```

Basically, it says that if the `__instance` variable is `None`, create an instance of `Singleton`.

Because constructors do not return values, the problem is how to find out whether creating an instance was successful.

The best way, proposed on the tutorialspoint.com website, is to create a class that throws an `Exception` when it is instantiated more than once. Let's create our own `Exception` class for this case:

```
class SingletonException(Exception):
    def __init__(self, message):
        # Call the base class constructor
            # with the parameters it needs
        super().__init__(message)
```

Note that, other than calling its parent classes through the `super()` method, this new exception type doesn't do anything in particular. However, it is still convenient to have our own named exception type so that the compiler will warn us of the type of exception we must catch when we attempt to `create` an instance of `PrintSpooler` or anything else we create as a Singleton.

Throwing the Exception

The rest of the Singleton is just the `__init__` method, where the class is first created.

```
def __init__(self, name):
    if Singleton.__instance != None:
        raise SingletonException(
                "This class is a singleton!")
    else:
        Singleton.__instance = self
        self.name = name
        print("creating: "+ name)
```

If there is no instance of Singleton yet, it creates one and stores it in the `__instance` variable. If there already is an instance, we raise the `SingletonException`.

Creating an Instance of the Class

Now that we've created a simple Singleton pattern in the eponymous class, let's see how to use it. Remember that we must enclose every method that may throw an exception in a `try - except` block.

```
try:
    al = Singleton("Alan")
    bo = Singleton("Bob")
except SingletonException as e:
    print("two instances of a Singleton")
    details = e.args[0]
    print(details)
else:
    print (al.getName())
    print(bo.getName())
```

Then, if we execute this program, we get the following two messages:

```
creating: Alan
two instances of a Singleton
This class is a singleton!
```

where the last two lines indicate that an exception was thrown as expected. One message was generated to catch the exception, and the other message was provided by the Singleton itself.

One advantage of this approach is that you can restrict the singleton to a small number of instances bigger than 1 without extensive reprogramming (if you can think of a reason for that approach).

Static Classes As Singleton Patterns

There already is a kind of Singleton class in the standard Python class libraries: the `math` class. This class has all methods declared as `@staticmethod`, meaning that the class cannot be extended. The purpose of the `math` class is to wrap common mathematical functions, such as `sin` and `log`, in a class-like structure since the Python language does not support functions that are not methods in a class.

You can use the same approach to a Singleton Spooler pattern, giving it a static method. You can't create *any* instance of classes such as `math` or this Spooler, and can only call the static methods directly in the existing final class.

```
class Spooler:
    @staticmethod
    def printit(text):
        print(text) # simulate printing
name = "Fred"
Spooler.printit(name)
```

Note that we now invoke the Spooler `printit` method directly as `Spooler.printit`.

Finding the Singletons in a Large Program

In a large, complex program, it may not be simple to discover where in the code a Singleton has been instantiated.

One solution is to create such singletons at the beginning of the program and pass them as arguments to the major classes that might need to use them.

```
pr1 = iSpooler.Instance()
cust = Customers(pr1)
```

A more elaborate solution could be to create a registry of all the Singleton classes in the program and make the registry generally available. Each time a Singleton instantiates itself, it notes that in the registry. Then any part of the program can ask for the instance of any singleton using an identifying string and get back that instance variable.

The disadvantage of the registry approach is that type checking may be reduced, since the table of singletons in the registry probably keeps all the singletons as Objects (for example, in a `Hashtable` object). Of course, the registry itself is probably a singleton and must be passed to all parts of the program using the constructor or various set functions.

Other Consequences of the Singleton Pattern

Consequences of the Singleton pattern include the following:

1. It can be difficult to subclass a Singleton because this can work only if the base Singleton class has not yet been instantiated.
2. You can easily change a Singleton to allow a small number of instances in which this is allowable and meaningful.

Sample Code on GitHub

- Spooler.py: Prototype of Spooler
- Testlock.py: Creates a single instance of a Singleton

9

The Builder Pattern

We have already seen that the Factory pattern returns one of several different subclasses, depending on the data passed in arguments to the creation methods. But suppose we don't want just a computing algorithm, but a whole different user interface depending on the data we need to display. A typical example might be your email address book. You probably have both people and groups of people in your address book, and you would expect the display for the address book to change so that the People screen has places for first and last name, company, email address, and phone number.

On the other hand, if you display a group address page, you want to see the name of the group, its purpose, and a list of members and their email addresses. You click a person entry and get one display, and you click a group entry and get the other display. Let's assume that all email addresses are kept in an object called an Address and that people and groups are derived from this base class (see Figure 9-1).

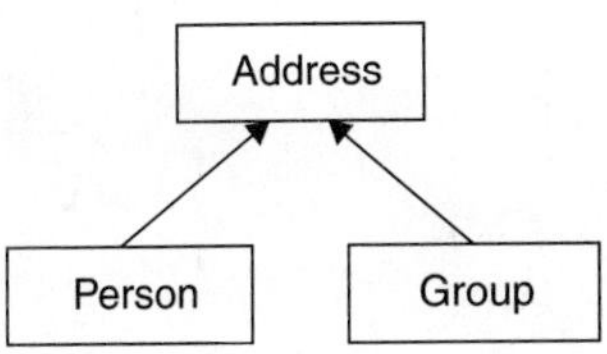

Figure 9-1 Simple address book that shows individuals or groups

Depending on which type of `Address` object we click, we'd want to see a somewhat different display of that object's properties. This is a little more than just a Factory pattern because we aren't returning objects that are simple descendants of a base display object, but totally different user interfaces made up of different combinations of display objects. The Builder pattern assembles a number of objects, such as display widgets, in various ways, depending on the data. Furthermore, since Python is one of the few languages where you can cleanly separate the data from the display methods into simple objects, Python is the ideal language to implement Builder patterns.

An Investment Tracker

Let's consider a somewhat simpler case in which you want to have a class build your UI. Suppose you are going to write a program to keep track of the performance of your investments. You might have stocks, bonds, and mutual funds. Let's say you want to display a list of your holdings in each category so that you can select one or more investments and plot their comparative performance.

Even though you can't predict in advance how many of each kind of investment you might own at any given time, you want a display that is easy to use for either a large number of funds (such as stocks) or a small number of funds (such as mutual funds). In each case, you want some sort of a multiple-choice display so that you can select one or more funds to plot. For a large number of funds, you can use a multichoice list box. For three or fewer funds, you can use a set of check boxes. Here you want your Builder class to generate an interface that depends on the number of items to be displayed, yet have the same methods for returning the results.

The next two figures show the displays. Figure 9-2 shows the first display, for a large number of stocks. Figure 9-3 shows the second display, for a small number of bonds.

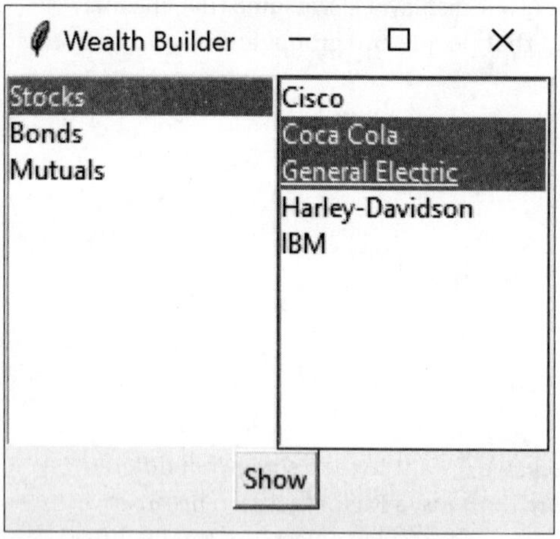

Figure 9-2 Wealth builder with a Stocks display

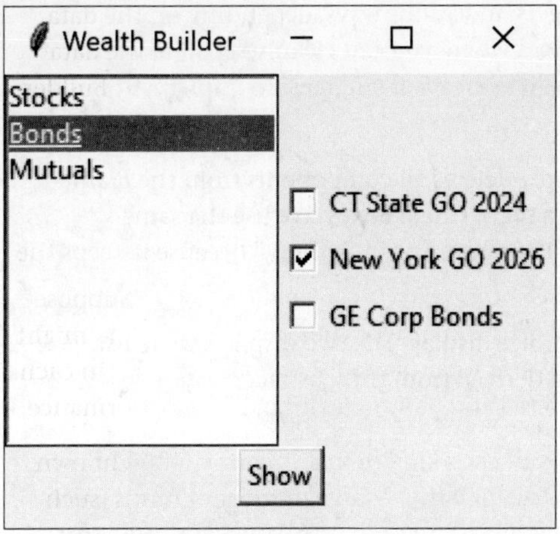

Figure 9-3 Wealth builder with a Bonds display

Then, by clicking the Show button, you can display which securities were selected, regardless of which type of display you have chosen (see Figure 9-4).

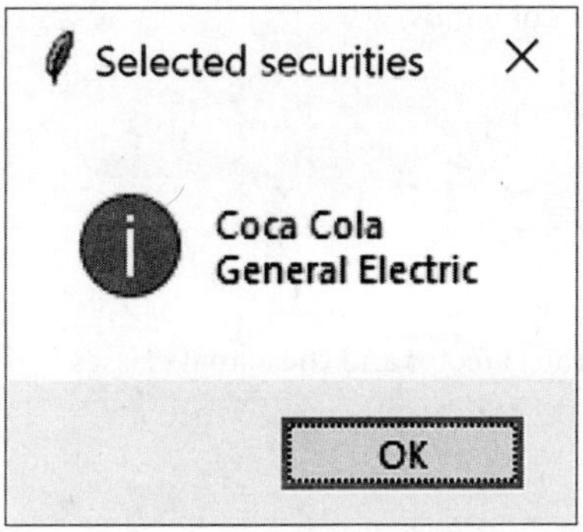

Figure 9-4 Display of selected securities

Now let's consider how to build the interface to carry out this variable display. We'll start with a `MultiChoice` abstract class that defines the methods we need to implement:

```
class MultiChoice:
    def __init__(self, frame, choiceList):
        self.choices = choiceList    #save list
        self.frame = frame

   #to be implemented in derived classes
    def makeUI(self): pass       #Frame of components
    def getSelected(self): pass  #get list of items
```

```
    #clears out the components of the frame
    def clearAll(self):
        for widget in self.frame.winfo_children():
            widget.destroy()
```

Note the clearAll method in the base class. It simply deletes all components from the Frame and works whether the frame contains a Listbox or a set of CheckBoxes. We use the same CheckBox class we developed in Chapter 2, "Visual Programming in Python," because it keeps the IntVal indicating whether the box is checked.

The makeUI method fills a Frame with a multiple-choice display. The two displays we're using here are a checkbox panel and a list box panel, both derived from this abstract class:

```
class ListboxChoice(MultiChoice):
```

or

```
class CheckboxChoice(MultiChoice):
```

Then you create a simple Factory class that decides which of these two classes to return:

```
class ChoiceFactory:
   """This class returns a Panel containing
   a set of choices displayed by one of
   several UI methods. """
   def getChoiceUI(self, choices, frame):
        if len(choices) <=3:
            #return a panel of checkboxes
            return CheckboxChoice(frame, choices)
        else:
            #return a multi-select list box panel
            return ListboxChoice(frame, choices)
```

In the language of *Design Patterns*, this factory class is called the Director and the actual classes derived from MultiChoice are each Builders.

Calling the Builders

We're going to need one or more builders, so we might have called the main class Architect or Contractor. However, we're dealing with lists of investments in this example, so we'll just call it WealthBuilder. In this main class, we create the user interface, consisting of a Frame with the center divided into a 1 × 2 grid layout (see Figures 9-2 and 9-3). The left part contains our list of investment types and the right part is an empty panel that we'll fill depending on which kind of investments are selected. The second grid row contains the Show button, which has a columnspan of 2.

```
class BuildUI():
    def __init__(self, root):
        self.root = root
        self.root.geometry("250x200")
        self.root.title("Wealth Builder")
        self.seclist=[] # start with empty list
```

In this simple program, we keep our three lists of investments in three instances of the Securities class, which has a name and a list of security names of that type. We load them with arbitrary values as part of program initialization:

```
def build(self):
    # create securities list
    self.stocks= Securities("Stocks",
         ["Cisco", "Coca Cola", "General Electric",
         "Harley-Davidson", "IBM"])
    self.seclist.append(self.stocks)
    self.bonds = Securities("Bonds",
       ["CT State GO 2024", "New York GO 2026",
            "GE Corp Bonds"] )
    self.seclist.append(self.bonds)
    self.mutuals = Securities("Mutuals",
       ["Fidelity Magellan", "T Rowe Price",
           "Vanguard Primecap", "Lindner"])
    self.seclist.append(self.mutuals)
```

In a real system, we'd probably read them in from a file or database. Then when the user clicks one of the three investment types in the left Listbox, we pass the equivalent Securities class to your Factory, which returns one of the Builders:

```
# callback when left list box is selected
def lbselect(self, evt):
    index = self.leftList.curselection()  # a tuple
    i = int(index[0])  # this is the actual index
    securities = self.seclist[i]
    cf = ChoiceFactory()
    self.cui = cf.getChoiceUI(securities.getList(),
                  self.rframe)
    self.cui.makeUI()
```

We do save the MultiChoice panel that the factory creates in the cui variable so that we can pass it to the Plot dialog.

The List Box Builder

The simpler of the two builders is the Listbox builder. It returns a panel containing a Listbox that shows the list of investments.

```
class ListboxChoice( MultiChoice):

    def  __init__(self, frame, choices):
        super().__init__(frame, choices)

    # creates and loads the listbox into the frame
    def makeUI(self):
       self.clearAll()
      #create a frame containing a list box
```

```
        self.list = Listbox(self.frame,
                    selectmode=MULTIPLE)    #list box
        self.list.pack()

    #add investments into list box
        for st in self.choices:
            self.list.insert(END, st)
```

The other important method in this class is the getSelected method. It returns a String array of the investments the user selects:

```
# returns a list of the selected elements
    def getSelected(self):
        sel = self.list.curselection()
        selist=[]
        for i in sel:
            st = self.list.get(i)
            selist.append(st)
        return selist
```

The Checkbox Builder

The Checkbox builder is even simpler. Here we need to find out how many elements are to be displayed and create a horizontal grid of that many divisions. Then we insert a check box in each grid line:

```
class CheckboxChoice(MultiChoice):
    def __init__(self, panel, choices):
        super().__init__(panel, choices)

    #creates the checkbox UI
    def makeUI(self):
        self.boxes = []  # list of check boxes
        self.clearAll()
        r = 0
        for name in self.choices:
            var = IntVar()  # create an IntVar
            # create a checkbox
            cb = Checkbox(self.frame, name, var)
            self.boxes.append(cb)  # add it to list
            cb.grid(column=0, row=r, sticky=W)
            r += 1

     # returns list of selected check boxes
    def getSelected(self):
        items=[]         #empty list
        for b in self.boxes:
            if b.getVar() > 0:
                items.append(b.getText())
        return items
```

Displaying the Selected Securities

When you click the Show button, the button asks the builder for the current UI and obtains a list of the selected securities, as shown earlier with the `lbselect` method. Note that this calls the `securities.getList()` method, which returns the list of those selected, regardless of which interface is being displayed, because both the `ListBoxChoice` and the `CheckBoxChoice` classes have that `getList` method.

Consequences of the Builder Pattern

The consequences of the Builder pattern include the following:

1. A Builder enables you to vary the internal representation of the product it builds. It also hides the details of how the product is assembled.
2. Each specific Builder is independent of the others and also of the rest of the program. This improves modularity and makes adding other builders relatively simple.
3. Because each Builder constructs the final product step by step, depending on the data, you have more control over each final product that it constructs.

A Builder pattern is somewhat like an Abstract Factory pattern, in that both return classes are made up of a number of methods and objects. The main difference is that whereas the Abstract Factory returns a family of related classes, the Builder constructs a complex object step by step, depending on the data presented to it.

Thought Questions

1. Some word processing and graphics programs construct menus dynamically based on the context of the data being displayed. How can you use a Builder effectively here?
2. Not all Builders must construct visual objects. What might you use a Builder to construct in the personal finance industry? Suppose you were scoring a track meet made up of five to six different events? Can you use a Builder there?

Sample Code on GitHub

- BuilderChoices.py: Creates the WealthBuilder display

10

The Prototype Pattern

The Prototype pattern is used when creating an instance of a class is very time consuming or complex in some way. Instead of creating more instances, you make copies of the original instance and modify the copies as appropriate.

Prototypes can also be used whenever you need classes that differ only in the type of processing they offer—for example, in parsing strings that represent numbers in different radixes.

Let's consider the case of an extensive database in which you need to make a number of queries to construct an answer. When you have this answer as a table or ResultSet, you might want to manipulate it to produce other answers without issuing additional queries.

In a case like one we have been working on, let's consider a database of a large number of swimmers in a league or statewide organization. Each swimmer swims several strokes and distances throughout a season. The best times for swimmers are tabulated by age group, and many swimmers have birthdays and move into new age groups within a single season. Thus, the query to determine which swimmers did the best in their age group that season is dependent on the date of each meet and on each swimmer's birthday. The computational cost of assembling this table of times is therefore fairly high.

Once we have a class containing this table, sorted by sex, we might want to examine this information sorted just by time or just by actual age instead of by age group. It would not be sensible to recompute these data, and we do not want to destroy the original data order. Instead, we want some sort of copy of the data.

Cloning in Python

Functions in the **lib** library include a `copy` function that you can access this way:

```
from Lib import copy
```

All the copy functions are *static:* No classes are involved. The two methods of interest are

```
newarray = copy.copy(array)
```

and

```
newarray = copy.deepcopy(array)
```

The first function makes a *shallow* copy of the array of objects. The second makes a deep copy, ensuring that all objects are copied and that any references stay separate from the original array of objects.

If you are copying simple lists or arrays of objects, the first function works fine. It is only if the objects contain references to other objects that you need to invoke the complexity and slower execution time of the deep copy.

Using the Prototype

Now let's write a simple program that reads data from a database and then clones the resulting object. In the example program, Proto, these data were merely read from a file, but the original data were derived from a large database (as we just discussed).

Then we create a class called `Swimmer` that holds one name, club name, sex, and time, just as we did earlier. We also create a class called `Swimmers` that maintains a list of the Swimmers we read in from the database.

In addition, we provide a `getSwimmer` method in the `SwimData` class and `getName` methods in the `Swimmer` class for accessing the age, sex, and times. After we've read the data into `SwimInfo`, we can display it in a listbox.

Then when the user clicks the Clone button, we'll clone this class and sort the data differently in the new class. Again, we clone the data because creating a new class instance would be much slower, and we want to keep the data in both forms.

In the original class, the names are sorted by sex and then by time. In the cloned class, they are sorted only by time. In Figure 10-1, you can see the simple user interface that enables you to display the original data on the left and the sorted data in the cloned class on the right.

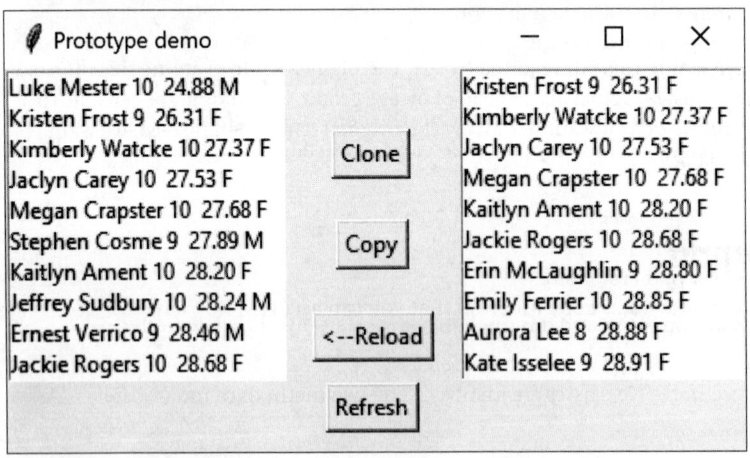

Figure 10-1 Original data on the left, sorted data on the right

The listbox on the left is loaded when the program starts and the listbox on the right is loaded when you click the **Copy** button. Now click the **Refresh** button to refresh the leftmost listbox from the original data array (see Figure 10-2).

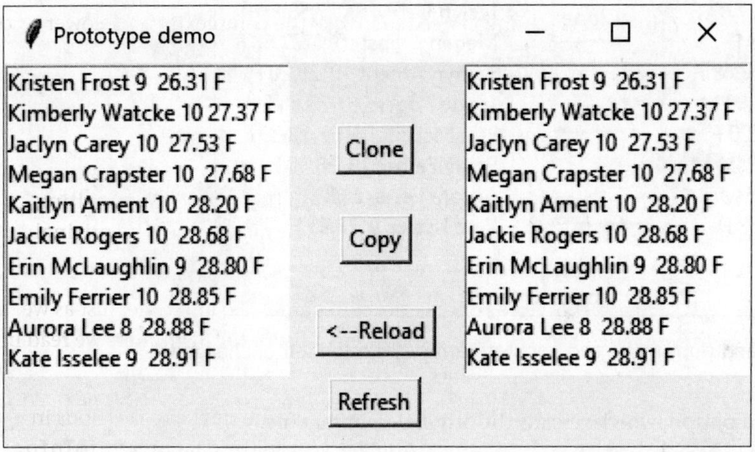

Figure 10-2 Original data on the left were also sorted because a shallow copy was used

Why were the names in the leftmost listbox also re-sorted? This occurs because we used a real shallow copy, just copying the original array into a new one.

```
def shallowCopy(self):
    swmrs = self.swmrs  # copies the pointers
    sw = self.sbySex(swmrs)
    self.fillList(self.rightlist, sw)
```

In other words, the references to the data objects are copies, but they refer to the same underlying data. Thus, any operation performed on the copied data also occurs on the original data in the Prototype class. This isn't what we want here.

Instead, you should click the Clone button, which calls the `copy.copy` function we described above, and you have a separate list of swimmers than can be sorted without affecting the original.

```
def clone(self):
    swmrs = copy.copy(self.swmrs)
    sw = self.sbySex(swmrs)
    self.fillList(self.rightlist, sw)
```

This gives you the display you want, and it is unchanged even after you click Refresh (see Figure 10-3).

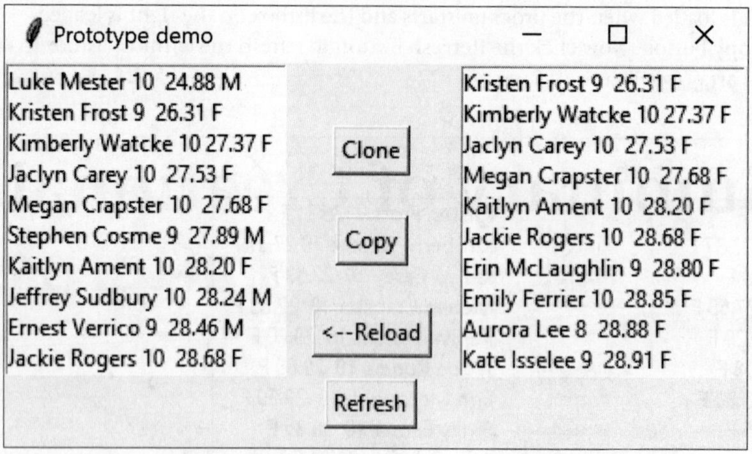

Figure 10-3 Clone and Copy make two separate arrays, with the left unchanged

We include the Reload button, which rereads the original swimmer file.

Consequences of the Prototype Pattern

Using the Prototype pattern, you can add and remove classes at runtime by cloning them as needed. You can revise the internal data representation of a class at runtime based on program conditions. You can also specify new objects at runtime without creating a proliferation of classes and inheritance structures.

As with the registry of Singletons discussed in in Chapter 8, "The Singleton Pattern," you can also create a registry of Prototype classes that can be cloned and ask the registry object for a list of possible prototypes. You may be able to clone an existing class instead of writing one from scratch.

Note that every class that you might use as a prototype must itself be instantiated (perhaps at some expense) for you to use a Prototype registry. This can be a performance drawback.

Finally, the idea of having prototype classes to copy implies that you have sufficient access to the data or methods in these classes to change them after cloning. This may require adding data access methods to these prototype classes so that you can modify the data after you have cloned the class.

Sample Code on GitHub

In all these samples, be sure to include the data file (swimmers.txt) in the same folder as the Python file. Also make sure they are part of the project in Vscode or PyCharm.

- Proto.py: Creates the Swimmers prototype demo in this chapter
- Swimmers.txt: Data file for Proto

11

Summary of Creational Patterns

- **The Factory pattern** is used to choose and return an instance of a class from a number of similar classes, based on data you provide to the factory.
- **The Abstract Factory pattern** is used to return one of several groups of classes. In some cases, it actually returns a factory for that group of classes.
- **The Builder pattern** assembles a number of objects to make a new object, based on the data with which it is presented. Frequently, the choice of which way the objects are assembled is achieved using a factory.
- **The Prototype pattern** copies or clones an existing class instead of creating a new instance when creating new instances is more expensive.
- **The Singleton pattern** is a pattern that ensures that there is only one instance of an object and that it is possible to obtain global access to that one instance.

Structur [illegible]
form lar [illegible]
patterns [illegible]
provide [illegible]
objects [illegible]
For exa [illegible]
used to [illegible]
easier [illegible]
combin [illegible]
instance [illegible]
either [illegible]
frequent [illegible]
that [illegible]
environ [illegible]

The Fly [illegible]
instanc [illegible]
allows [illegible]
are man [illegible]

The Fa [illegible]
subsyst [illegible]
its imple [illegible]
at the De [illegible]
objects [illegible]

You'll se [illegible]
some ove [illegible]
Patterns [illegible]
patterns.

PART III

Structural Patterns

Structural patterns describe how classes and objects can be combined to form larger structures. The difference between *class* patterns and *object* patterns is that class patterns describe how inheritance can be used to provide more useful program interfaces. *Object* patterns, on the other hand, describe how objects can be composed into larger structures using object composition, or the inclusion of objects within other objects.

For example, we'll see in this section that the Adapter pattern can be used to make one class interface match another, to make programming easier. We'll also look at a number of other structural patterns where we combine objects to provide new functionality. The Composite pattern, for instance, is exactly that: a composition of objects, each of which may be either a simple object or itself a composite object. The Proxy pattern is frequently a simple object that takes the place of a more complex object that can be invoked later, such as when the program runs in a network environment.

The Flyweight pattern is a pattern for sharing objects, where each instance does not contain its own state, but stores it externally. This allows efficient sharing of objects to save space, particularly when there are many instances but only a few different types.

The Façade pattern is used to make a single class represent an entire subsystem, and the Bridge pattern separates an object's interface from its implementation so that you can vary them separately. Finally, we'll look at the Decorator pattern, which can be used to add responsibilities to objects dynamically.

You'll see that there is some overlap among these patterns and even some overlap with the behavioral patterns in Part IV, "Behavioral Patterns." We'll summarize these similarities after we describe the patterns.

12

The Adapter Pattern

The Adapter pattern is used to convert the programming interface of one class into that of another. We use adapters whenever we want unrelated classes to work together in a single program. The concept of an adapter is thus pretty simple; we write a class that has the desired interface and then make it communicate with the class that has a different interface.

There are two ways to do this: by inheritance, and by object composition. With inheritance, we derive a new class from the nonconforming one and add the methods we need to make the new derived class match the desired interface. The other way is to include the original class inside the new one and create the methods to translate calls within the new class. These two approaches, termed class adapters and object adapters, are both fairly easy to implement in Python.

Moving Data Between Lists

Let's consider a simple Python program that enables you to enter student names into a list and then select some of those names to be transferred to another list. The initial list consists of a class roster. The second list contains students who will be doing advanced work, as shown in Figure 12-1.

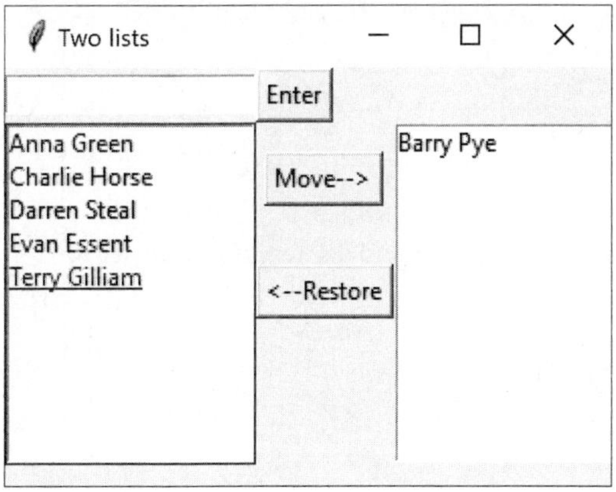

Figure 12-1 Student names app

In this simple program, you enter names into the top entry field and click Insert to move the names into the listbox on the left. To move a name to the listbox on the right, you click the name and then click Add. To remove a name from the listbox on the right, click the name and then click Remove; this moves the name back to the list on the left.

This is a very simple program to write in Python. It consists of a GUI creation constructor and three `DButtons`, each with their own `comd` method. Because you perform the same operations on the two listboxes, you create a derived `Listbox` class with those operations built in:

```
# Derived Listbox with 3 convenience methods
class DListbox(Listbox):
    def __init__(self, root):
        super().__init__(root)
     # Get the current selected text
    def getSelected(self):
        selection = self.curselection()
        selindex = selection[0]
        return self.get(selindex)
    # delete the selected row
    def deleteSelection(self):
        selection = self.curselection()
        selindex = selection[0]
        self.delete(selindex)
    # Insert at bottom of list
    def insertAtEnd(self, text):
        self.insert(END, text)
```

The Entry button copies the entry field into the bottom of the left list and then clears the entry field:

```
class EntryButton(DButton):
    def __init__(self, root, buildui, **kwargs):
        super().__init__(root, text="Enter")
        self.buildui = buildui
    # copies entry field into left list
    def comd(self):
        entry = self.buildui.getEntry()
        text = entry.get()
        leftList = self.buildui.getLeftList()
        leftList.insertAtEnd(text)
        entry.delete(0, END) # clears entry
```

The Move button copies the selected list item into the right list and deletes it from the left:

```
class MoveButton(DButton):
    def __init__(self, root, buildui, **kwargs):
        super().__init__(root, text="Move-->")
        self.buildui = buildui
```

```
# copies selected line into right list
    def comd(self):
        self.leftlist =self.buildui.getLeftList()
        self.seltext = self.leftlist.getSelected()
        self.rightlist = self.buildui.getRightList()
        self.rightlist.insertAtEnd(self.seltext)

# and deletes from left
        self.leftlist.deleteSelection()
```

This program is called addStudents.py and is on the website.

Making an Adapter

Suppose that we want a different display on the right side. Maybe we want a table of students that includes more data, such as their IQ or test scores. This is likely a job for a table. Fortunately, the Treeview widget can do what we want (see Figure 12-2).

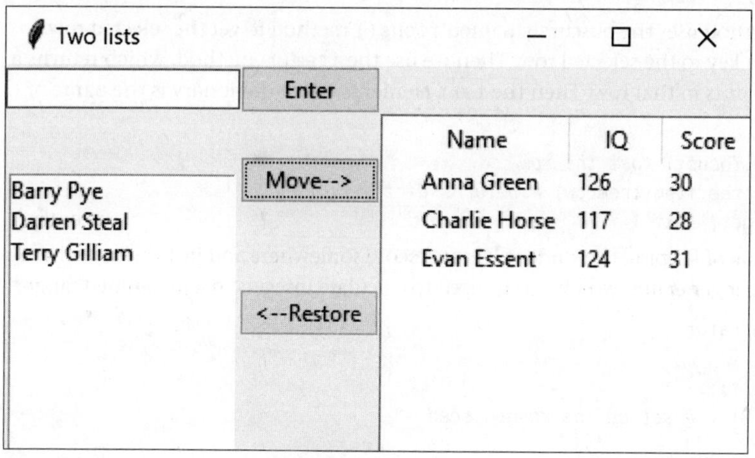

Figure 12-2 Student names with Treeview

We still have to create the Treeview columns in our UI builder class, but let's say we prefer not to change the listbox interfaces. To be more specific, we'd like to be able to use the same methods as we showed in the `DListbox` class illustrated at the beginning of this chapter.

So, we want to build an `Adapter` class that has those same methods but that interfaces with the Treeview widget.

```
class ListboxAdapter(DListbox):
    def __init__(self, root, tree):
        super().__init__(root)
        self.tree = tree
        self.index=1
```

```
# gets the text selected from the tree
def getSelected(self):
    treerow = self.tree.focus() #get the row
    row = self.tree.item(treerow) # returns dict
    return row.get('text')

# delete the line selected in the tree
def deleteSelection(self):
    treerow = self.tree.focus()
    self.tree.delete(treerow)

# insert a line at the bottom of the treelist
def insertAtEnd(self, name):
    # create random IQs and scores
    self.tree.insert("", self.index, text=name,
                    values=(Randint.getIQ(self),
                        Randint.getScore(self)) )

    self.index += 1
```

The getSelected method uses the obscurely named focus() method to get the selected row. That method returns a key to the selected row. Then we use the item() method, which returns a dictionary of the elements in that row. Then the text element of that dictionary is the name of the student:

```
treerow = self.tree.focus() #get the row
        row = self.tree.item(treerow) # returns dict
        return row.get('text')
```

We can finesse the issue of keeping the student IQs and score somewhere and just generate them using a random number generator, which can be used to calculate integers in a predefined range:

```
# Random number generator
class Randint():
    def __init__(self):
        seed(None, 2)   # set up the random seed

    # compute a random IQ between 115 and 145
    @staticmethod
    def getIQ(self):
        return randint(115,145)

    # compute a random score between 25 and 35
    @staticmethod
    def getScore(self):
        return randint(25,35)
```

The Class Adapter

The previous example is an *object* adapter that operates on an instance of the Treelist inside the adapter. By contrast, a class adapter derives a new class from the Treelist that has the methods you need. This is very simple to achieve, and the code differs very little between the two.

- The Class adapter
  - Doesn't work when you want to adapt a class and all its subclasses because you define the class it derives from when you create it
  - Lets the adapter change some of the adapted class's methods, but still allows the others to be used unchanged
- An Object adapter
  - Can allow subclasses to be adapted by simply passing them in as part of a constructor
  - Requires that you specifically bring to the surface any of the adapted object's methods that you want to make available

Two-Way Adapters

The two-way adapter is a clever concept that enables an object to be viewed by different classes as being of type Listbox or type Treelist. This is most easily carried out using a class adapter because all the methods of the base class are automatically available to the derived class. However, this works only if you do not override any of the base class's methods with ones that behave differently. As it happens, the `ListboxAdapter` class here is an ideal two-way adapter because the two classes have no methods in common.

Pluggable Adapters

A pluggable adapter is one that adapts dynamically to one of several classes. Of course, the adapter can adapt only to classes that it can recognize. Usually, the adapter decides which class it is adapting based on differing constructors or `setParameter` methods.

Programs on GitHub

- addStudents.py: Adds students to the left list and can move some to the right list.
- addStudentsAdapter.py: Adds students to the left list and can move some to the Treeview on the right using an Adapter.

13

The Bridge Pattern

At first sight, the Bridge pattern looks much like the Adapter pattern in that a class is used to convert one kind of interface to another. However, the intent of the Adapter pattern is to make one or more classes' interfaces look the same as the interface of a particular class. The Bridge pattern is designed to separate a class's interface from its implementation so that you can vary or replace the implementation without changing the client code.

Suppose that we have a program that displays a list of products in a window. The simplest interface for that display is a simple Listbox. But after a significant number of products have been sold, we may want to display the products in a table along with their sales figures.

We have just discussed the Adapter pattern, so you might think immediately of the class-based adapter, where we adapt the interface of the Listbox to our simpler needs in this display. In simple programs, this works fine, but as we'll see below, there are limits to that approach.

Let's further suppose that we need to produce two kinds of displays from our product data: a customer view, which is just the list of products we've already mentioned, and an executive view, which also shows the number of units shipped. We'll display the product list in an ordinary Listbox and display the executive view in a Treeview display (see Figure 13-1). These two displays are the implementations of the display classes.

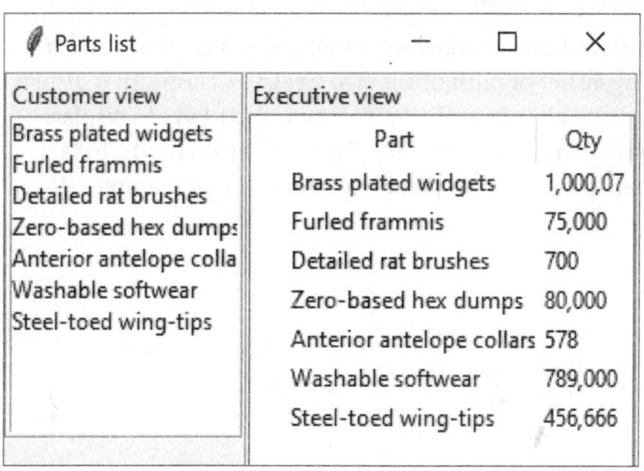

Figure 13-1   Parts list with Treeview

Now, we want to define a single simple interface that remains the same, regardless of the type and complexity of the actual implementation classes. We'll start by defining an abstract `Bridger` class:

```
class Bridger(Frame):
    def addData(self):pass
```

This class is so simple that it just receives a List of data and passes it on to the display classes.

On the other side of the bridge are the implementation classes, which usually have a more elaborate and somewhat lower-level interface. Here we'll have them add the data lines to the display one at a time.

```
class VisList():
    def addLines(self): pass
    def removeLine(self): pass
```

Implicit in the definition of these classes is some mechanism for determining which part of each string is the name of the product and which part is the quantity shipped. In this simple example, we separate the quantity from the name with two dashes and parse these apart in a `Product` class.

The Bridge between the interface on the left and the implementation on the right is the `ListBridge` class, which instantiates one or the other of the list display classes. Note that it extends the `Bridger` class for use of the application program.

```
# General bridge between data and any VisList class
class ListBridge(Bridger):
    def __init__(self, frame, vislist):
        self.list = vislist
        self.list.pack()

    # adds the list of Products into any VisList
    def addData(self, products):
        self.list.addLines( products)
```

In the current example, we use the `Bridge` class twice: once to display the Listbox on the left side and once to display the Treeview table on the right side.

The power and simplicity of the Bridge pattern becomes obvious when you realize that you can completely change the display by replacing either or both of the two `VisList` classes that display the data. You don't have to change the `Bridge` class code: Just give it new `VisLists` to display. Those classes can be anything, as long as they implement the simple `VisList` methods. In fact, we left the `removeLine` method empty here because it isn't really relevant to this example.

The `VisList` for Listbox is quite simple:

```
# Listbox visual list
class LbVisList(Listbox, VisList):
    def __init__(self, frame ):
        super().__init__(frame)

    def addLines(self, prodlist):
        for prod in prodlist:
            self.insert(END, prod.name)
```

The Treeview table on the right is equally simple, except for setting up the column names and dimensions:

```
# Treelist (table) visual list
class TbVisList(Treeview, VisList)      :
    def __init__(self, frame ):
        super().__init__(frame)
        # set up table columns
        self["columns"] = ("quantity")
        self.column("#0", width=150, minwidth=100, stretch=NO)
        self.column("quantity", width=50, minwidth=50, stretch=NO)
        self.heading('#0', text='Part')
        self.heading('quantity', text='Qty'
        self.index = 0       #row counter

        # adds the whole list of products to the table
    def addLines(self, prodlist):
        for prod in prodlist:
            self.insert("", self.index, text=prod.name,
                            values=(prod.count))
            self.index += 1
```

Creating the User Interface

Although all the usual grid and pack layout code still applies, creating the two frames inside a two-member grid is really easy. Coding involves creating the frame and the `VisList`, creating the Bridge, and adding the data:

```
self.vislist = LbVisList(self.lframe)
self.lbridge = ListBridge(self.lframe, self.vislist)
self.lbridge.addData(prod.getProducts())
```

Similarly, you create the Treeview version of a `VisList`, add it to another instance of the Bridge, and add the data:

```
self.rvislist = TbVisList(self.rframe)
self.rlb = ListBridge( self.rframe, self.rvislist)
self.rlb.addData(prod.getProducts())
```

Extending the Bridge

The power of the Bridge becomes apparent when we need to make some changes in the way these lists display the data. For example, you might want to have the products displayed in alphabetical order. You might think you'd need to either modify or subclass *both* the list and table classes. This can quickly get to be a maintenance nightmare, especially if more than two such displays eventually are needed. Instead, we simply make the changes in the extended interface class, creating a new sortBridge class from the parent listBridge class. However, you only need to create a new VisList that sorts the data and installs it instead of the original LbVislist class.

```
# Sorted listbox visual list
class SortVisList(Listbox, VisList):
    def __init__(self, frame ):
        super().__init__(frame)

    # sort into alphabetical order
    def addLines(self, prodlist):
        # sort array alphabetically
        self.prods = self.sortUpwards( prodlist)
        for prod in self.prods:
            self.insert(END, prod.name)
```

The sorting routine is the same one used in the Swimfactory example, so we won't repeat it here. Figure 13-2 shows the resulting sorted display.

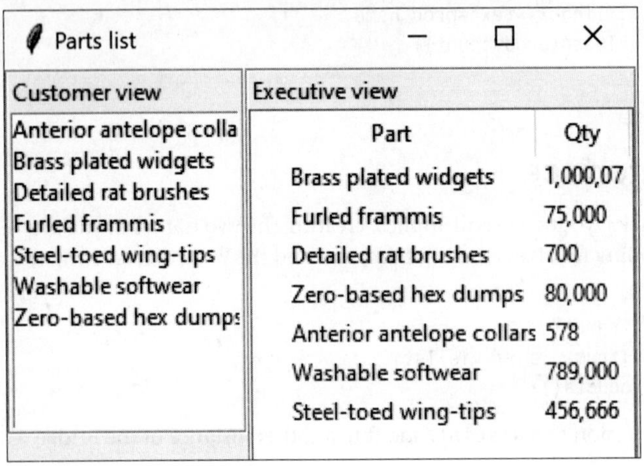

Figure 13-2 Sorted VisList

This clearly shows that you can vary the interface without changing the implementation. The converse is also true. For example, you can create another type of list display and replace one of the current list displays without any other program changes, as long as the new list also implements the visList interface.

In the next example, we have created a Treeview component that implements the visList interface and replaces the ordinary list without any change in the public interface to the classes in Figure 13-3.

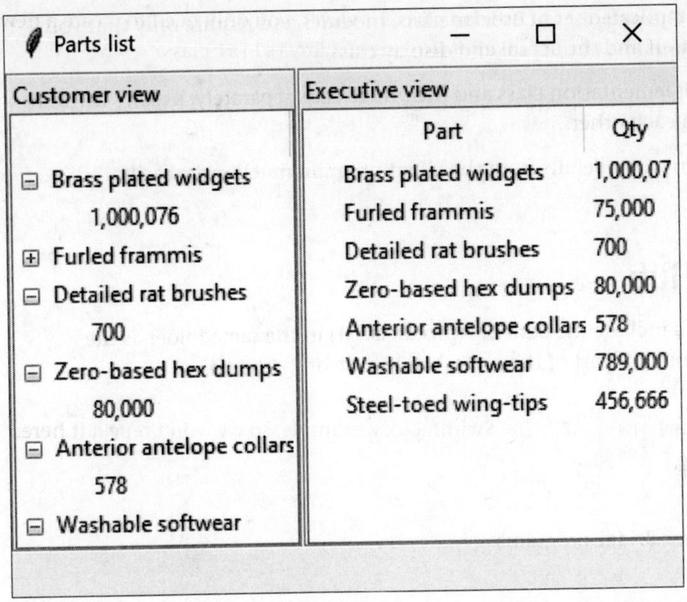

Figure 13-3 Treeview as left VisList

Note that this simple new `VisList` is the only change in the code:

```
#Tree VisList for left display
class TbexpVisList(Treeview, VisList)    :
    def __init__(self, frame ):
        super().__init__(frame)
        self.column("#0", width=150, minwidth=100,
                    stretch=NO)
        self.index = 0

    def addLines(self, prodlist):
        for prod in prodlist:
            fline = self.insert("", self.index,
                         text=prod.name)
            # add count as a leaf
            self.insert(fline, 'end',
                        text=prod.count )
            self.index += 1
```

Consequences of the Bridge Pattern

Consequences of the Bridge pattern include the following:

1. The Bridge pattern is intended to keep the interface to your client program constant while enabling you to change the actual kind of class you display or use. This can prevent you

from recompiling a complicated set of user interface modules and require only that you recompile the bridge itself and the actual end display class.

2. You can extend the implementation class and the bridge class separately, usually without much interaction with each other.
3. You can hide implementation details from the client program much more easily.

Programs on GitHub

In all these samples, be sure to include the data file (products.txt) in the same folder as the Python file. Also make sure they are part of the project in Vscode or PyCharm.

- BasicBridge.py
- SortBridge.py
- TreeBridge.py
- Products.txt: Data file for Bridge programs

14 The Composite Pattern

Programmers frequently develop systems in which a component may be an individual object, or it may represent a collection of objects. The Composite pattern is designed to accommodate both cases. You can use the Composite pattern to build part-whole hierarchies or to construct data representations of trees. In summary, a composite is a collection of objects, any one of which may be either a composite or just a primitive object. In tree nomenclature, some objects may be nodes with additional branches and some may be leaves.

The problem that develops is the dichotomy between having a single simple interface to access all the objects in a composite and having the capability to distinguish between nodes and leaves. Nodes have children and can have children added to them. Leaves, on the other hand, do not at the moment have children and, in some implementations, may be prevented from having children added to them.

In considering a tree of employees, some authors have suggested creating a separate interface for nodes and leaves, where a leaf could have these methods:

```
def getName(self):pass
def getSalary(self):pass
```

A node could have the additional methods:

```
def getSubordinates(self):pass
def add(self, e:Employee):pass
def getChild(self, name:str):
```

This leaves us with the programming problem of deciding which elements will be which when we construct the composite. However, *Design Patterns* suggests that each element should have the *same* interface, whether it is a composite or a primitive element. This is easier to accomplish, but we are left with the question of what the `getChild()` operation should accomplish when the object is actually a leaf.

Just as difficult is the issue of adding or removing leaves from elements of the composite. A nonleaf node can have child leaves added to it, but a leaf node cannot. However, here you want all components in the composite to have the same interface. Attempts to add children to a leaf node must not be allowed, and we might design the leaf node class to throw an exception if the program attempts to add to such a node.

An Implementation of a Composite

Let's consider a small company. Suppose that it started with a single person, the CEO, who got the business going. Then the CEO hired a couple of people to handle the marketing and manufacturing. Soon each of those people hired additional assistants to help with advertising, shipping, and so forth, and they became the company's first two vice presidents. As the company's success continued, the firm continued to grow until it had the organizational chart in Figure 14-1.

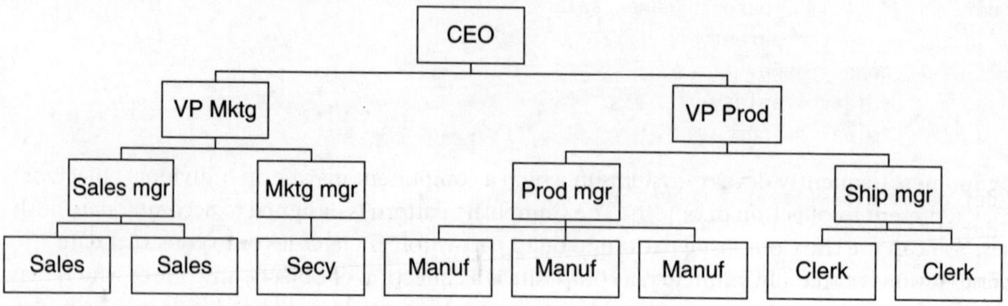

Figure 14-1 Org chart for a Composite

Salary Computation

Now, if the company is successful, each of these company members receives a salary, and at any time, we could ask for the cost of any employee to the company. Here we define the cost as the salary of that person and those of all his or her subordinates. This is an ideal example for a composite:

- The cost of an individual employee is simply his or her salary (and benefits).
- The cost of an employee who heads a department is his or her salary plus the salaries of all their subordinates.

We would want a single interface that produces the salary totals correctly, regardless of whether the employee has subordinates or not.

```
def getSalaries(self):pass
```

At this point, we realize that the idea of all Composites having the same standard method names in their interface is probably naïve. We'd prefer that the public methods be related to the kind of class we are actually developing. So instead of having generic methods such as `getValue()`, we use `getSalaries()`.

The Employee Classes

Now imagine representing the company as a Composite made up of nodes: managers and employees. It would be possible to use a single class to represent all employees, but because each level may have different properties, it might be more useful to define at least two classes: `Employees` and `Bosses`. `Employees` are leaf nodes and cannot have employees under them. `Bosses` are nodes that may have employee nodes under them.

Our concrete `Employee` class can store the name and salary of each employee and enables us to fetch them as needed.

```
# Employee is the base class
class Employee():
    def __init__(self, parent, name, salary:int):
        self.parent = parent
        self.name = name
        self.salary = salary
        self.isleaf = True

    def getSalaries(self):  return self.salary
    def getSubordinates(self): return None
```

The `Employee` class can have concrete implementations of the add, `getSubordinates`, and `getChild` methods. But because an `Employee` is a leaf, all of these could return some sort of error indication. For example, `getSubordinates` could return `None` as above, but because an `Employee` is always a leaf, you could avoid calling these methods on leaf nodes.

The Boss Class

The `Boss` class is a subclass of `Employee` and enables us to store subordinate employees as well. We'll store them in a List called *subordinates* and return them as a list or just enumerate through the list. Thus, if a particular `Boss` has temporarily run out of `Employees`, the List will just be empty.

```
class Boss(Employee):
    def __init__(self, name, salary:int):
        super().__init__(name, salary)
        self.subordinates = []
        self.isleaf = False

     def add(self, e:Employee):
        self.subordinates.append(e)
```

Similarly, you can use this same List to return a sum of salaries for any employee and his or her subordinates:

```
    # called recursively as it walks down the tree
    def getSalaries(self):
        self.sum = self.salary
        for e in self.subordinates:
            self.sum = self.sum + e.getSalaries()
        return self.sum
```

Note that this method starts with the salary of the current Employee and then calls the `getSalaries()` method on each subordinate. This, of course, is recursive; any employees who have subordinates will be included.

Building the Employee Tree

We start by creating a CEO Employee and then add his or her subordinates and then their subordinates, as follows:

```
#builds the employee tree
def build(self):
    seed(None, 2)          # initialize random seed
    boss = Boss("CEO", 200000)
# add VPs under Boss
    marketVP = Boss("Marketing_VP", 100000)
    boss.add(marketVP)
    prodVP = Boss("Production_VP", 100000)
    boss.add(prodVP)
    salesMgr = Boss("Sales_Mgr", 50000)
    marketVP.add(salesMgr)
    advMgr = Boss("Advt_Mgr", 50000)
    marketVP.add(advMgr)
    # add salesmen reporting to Sales Mgr
    for i in range(0, 6):
        salesMgr.add(Employee("Sales_" + str(i),
                int(30000.0 + random() * 10000)))

    advMgr.add(Employee("Secy", 20000))
    prodMgr = Boss("Prod_Mgr", 40000)
    prodVP.add(prodMgr)
    shipMgr = Boss("Ship_Mgr", 35000)
    prodVP.add(shipMgr)

    # Add manufacturing and shipping employees
    for i in range(0, 4):
        prodMgr.add(Employee("Manuf_"
        + str(i), int(25000 + random() * 5000))
    for i in range(0, 4):
        shipMgr.add(Employee("Ship_Clrk_"
         + str(i), int(20000 + random() * 5000)))
```

Printing the Employee Tree

You don't really need to create a graphic interface to print this tree. You just indent two spaces for each new sublevel. This simple recursive code walks down the tree and indents as needed.

```
# print employee tree recursively,
# walking down the tree
def addNodes(self,  emp:Employee ):
    if not emp.isleaf:       #Bosses are not Leaves
        empList = emp.getSubordinates()
        if empList != None: # must be a Boss
```

```
        for newEmp in empList:
            print(" "*self.indent, newEmp.name,
                                   newEmp.salary)
            self.indent += 2
            self.addNodes(newEmp)
            self.indent-=2
```

The resulting employee list follows:

```
CEO 200000
 Marketing_VP 100000
   Sales_Mgr 50000
     Sales_0 39023
     Sales_1 36485
     Sales_2 35844
     Sales_3 32353
     Sales_4 32080
     Sales_5 33285
   Advt_Mgr 50000
     Secy 20000
 Production_VP 100000
   Prod_Mgr 40000
     Manuf_0 26536
     Manuf_1 29837
     Manuf_2 28931
     Manuf_3 28509
   Ship_Mgr 35000
     Ship_Clrk_0 20856
     Ship_Clrk_1 20552
     Ship_Clrk_2 20476
     Ship_Clrk_3 21465
```

If you want to get the salary span for an employee, you can easily compute it using a `Salary` class:

```
#compute salaries under selected employee
class SalarySpan():
    def __init__(self, boss, name):
        self.boss = boss
        self.name = name
    # print sum of salaries
    # for employee and subordinates
    def print(self):
        #search for match
        if self.name == self.boss.name:
            print(self.name, self.boss.name)
            newEmp = self.boss
        else:
            newEmp = self.boss.getChild(self.name)
        sum = newEmp.getSalaries()  # sum salaries
        print('Salary span for '+self.name, sum)
```

We provide the simple question at the end of the tree printout:

```
Enter employee name for salary span (q for quit): Ship_Mgr
Salary span for Ship_Mgr 120963
```

Note that these values vary every time you run the program because some of the salaries are computed using a random number generator.

Creating a Treeview of the Composite

After we have constructed this Composite structure, we could also load a Treeview by starting at the top node and calling the `addNode()` method recursively until all the leaves in each node are accessed—much as we did above in the console version, but loading a Treeview element each time.

```
# builds Treeview recursively, walking down the tree
    def addNodes(self, pnode, emp:Employee ):
        if not emp.isleaf:     # Bosses are not Leaves
            empList = emp.subordinates
            if empList != None: # must be a Boss
               for newEmp in empList:
                    newnode = Tree.tree.insert(pnode,
                              Tree.index,
                              text = newEmp.name)
                    self.addNodes(newnode, newEmp)
```

Figure 14-2 shows the final program display.

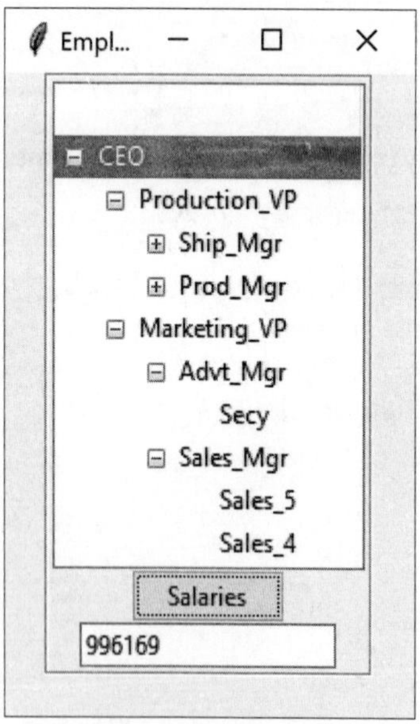

Figure 14-2 Final Employee tree

The Salaries button computes the sum of all the salaries for the CEO on down or from any Employee you click.

This simple computation calls the getChild() method recursively to obtain all the subordinates of that Employee. Note that we use the comma format string to insert the commas in the salary.

```
#click here to compute salaries for an employee
class SalaryButton(DButton):
    def __init__(self,  master, boss, entry,
                 **kwargs):

        super().__init__(master, text="Salaries")
        self.boss = boss
        self.entry = entry

    def comd(self):
        curitem = Tree.tree.focus() # get item
        dict= Tree.tree.item(curitem)
        name= dict["text"]          # get name

        # search for match
        if name == self.boss.name:
            print(name, self.boss.name)
            newEmp = self.boss
        else:
            newEmp = self.boss.getChild(name)
        sum = newEmp.getSalaries()

        # put salary sum in entry field
        self.entry.delete(0, "end")
        self.entry.insert(0, f'{sum:,}')
```

Using Doubly Linked Lists

In the previous implementation, we keep a reference to each subordinate in the List in each Boss class. This means that you can move down the chain from the president to any employee, but there is no way to move back up to find out who an employee's supervisor is. This is easily remedied by providing a constructor for each Employee subclass that includes a reference to the parent node:

```
class Employee():
    def __init__(self, parent, name, salary:int):
        self.parent = parent
        self.name = name
        self.salary = salary
        self.isleaf = True
```

Then you can quickly walk up the tree to produce a reporting chain:

```
emp = Tree.findMatch(self, self.boss)
quit = False
```

```
mesg = ""
while not quit:
    mesg += (emp.name +"\n")
    emp = emp.parent
    quit = emp.name == "CEO"
mesg += (emp.name +"\n")
messagebox.showinfo("Report chain", mesg)
```

as shown in Figure 14-3.

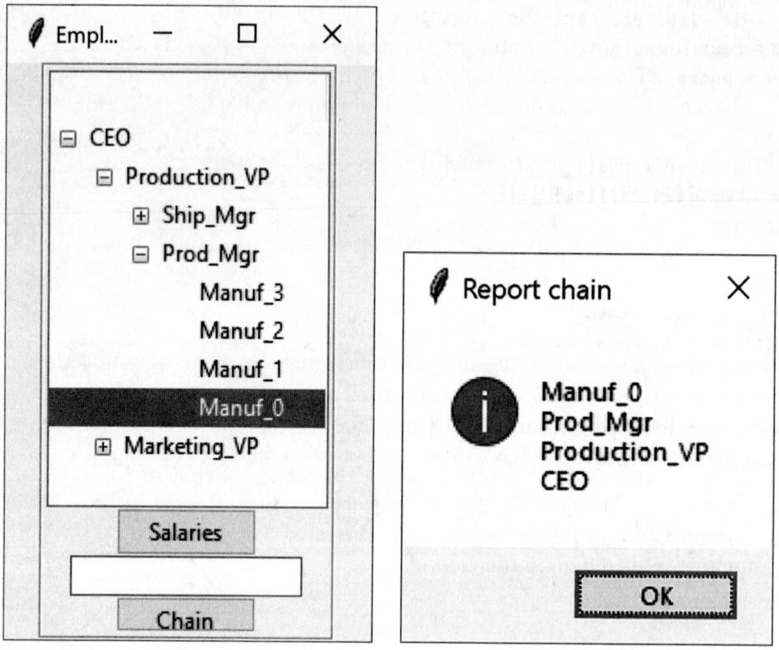

Figure 14-3 Chain of command display

Consequences of the Composite Pattern

The Composite pattern allows you to define a class hierarchy of simple objects and more complex composite objects so that they appear to be the same to the client program. Because of this simplicity, the client can be that much simpler because nodes and leaves are handled in the same way.

The Composite pattern also makes it easy for you to add new kinds of components to your collection, as long as they support a similar programming interface. On the other hand, this has the disadvantage of making your system overly general. You might find it harder to restrict certain classes, where this would normally be desirable.

A Simple Composite

The intent of the Composite pattern is to allow you to construct a tree of various related classes, even though some have different properties than others and some are leaves that do not have children. However, for very simple cases, you can sometimes use just a single class that exhibits both parent and leaf behavior. In the `SimpleComposite` example, we create an `Employee` class that always contains the List *employees*. This List of employees will either be empty or populated, which determines the nature of the values that you return from the `getChild` and `remove` methods. In this simple case, you do not throw exceptions, and you always allow leaf nodes to be promoted to have child nodes. In other words, you always allow execution of the add method.

While you may not regard this automatic promotion as a disadvantage, in systems where there are a very large number of leaves, it is wasteful to keep a List initialized and unused in each leaf node. In cases where there are relatively few leaf nodes, this is not a serious problem.

Other Implementation Issues

Other implementation issues include recursive calls, ordering components, and caching results.

Dealing with Recursive Calls

Both the `Boss` and `Employee` classes search the employee subordinate list recursively, meaning that the `getSalaries` method inside the `Boss` class calls itself to walk down the employee tree. This means that each new call is a new instance of the `Boss` class, so there would be new instance variables. Therefore, a reference to the Treeview cannot be kept inside the `Boss` class.

We solved this by creating a static `Tree` class that contains the reference to the Treeview that can be referred to as `Tree.tree`. This is initialized when the UI is created. We also searched down the Employee tree using the selected item in the Treeview display and then put that search in the `Tree` class as well:

```
class Tree():
    tree = None  # static variable
    index=0
    column=0

    # searches for the node that matches the
    # selected Treeview item.
    def findMatch(self,boss):
        curitem = Tree.tree.focus()  # get selected
        dict = Tree.tree.item(curitem)
        name = dict["text"]  # get name

        # search for match
        if name == boss.name:
            print(name, boss.name)
            newEmp = boss
        else:
            newEmp = self.boss.getChild(name)
        return newEmp
```

Ordering Components

In some programs, the order of the components may be important. If that order is somehow different from the order in which they were added to the parent, then the parent must do additional work to return them in the correct order. For example, you might sort the original List alphabetically and return the iterator to a new sorted list.

Caching Results

If you frequently ask for data that must be computed from a series of child components, as we did here with salaries, it may be advantageous to cache these computed results in the parent. However, unless the computation is relatively intensive and you are quite certain that the underlying data have not changed, this may not be worth the effort.

Programs on GitHub

- EmployeesConsole.py
- Employees.py
- DoublyLinked.py

15

The Decorator Pattern

The Decorator pattern provides us with a way to modify the behavior of individual objects without having to create a new derived class. Suppose that we have a program that uses eight objects, but three of them need an additional feature. You could create a derived class for each of these objects, and in many cases, this would be a perfectly acceptable solution. However, if each of these three objects requires *different* features, this would mean creating three derived classes. Further, if one of the classes has features of *both* the other classes, you would begin to create complexity that is both confusing and unnecessary.

Decorators can be used on visual objects such as buttons, but Python has a rich suite of nonvisual decorators that we will cover as well.

Now suppose that we wanted to draw a special border around some of the buttons in a toolbar. If we created a new derived button class, this means that all the buttons in this new class would always have this same new border, when this might not be our intent.

Instead, we create a `Decorator` class that *decorates* the buttons. Then we derive any number of specific Decorators from the main `Decorator` class, each of which performs a specific kind of decoration. To decorate a button, the `Decorator` has to be an object derived from the visual environment, so that it can receive paint method calls and forward calls to other useful graphic methods to the object that it is decorating. This is another case in which object containment is favored over object inheritance. The decorator is a graphical object, but it contains the object it is decorating. It may intercept some graphical method calls, perform some additional computation, and may pass them on to the underlying object it is decorating.

Decorating a Button

Applications running under Windows versions up through Windows 10 have a row of flat, unbordered buttons that highlight themselves with outline borders when you move your mouse over them. Some Windows programmers called this toolbar a CoolBar and call the buttons CoolButtons.

Let's consider how to create this Decorator. *Design Patterns* suggests that Decorators should be derived from some general Visual Component class and then every message for the actual button should be forwarded from the decorator.

Python does not make this easy to accomplish, so the Decorator in use here is derived from Button. All it does is intercept mouse movements. *Design Patterns* suggests that classes such as `Decorator` should be abstract classes and that you should derive all of your actual working (or concrete) decorators from the abstract class. Again, this is not easy in Python because all the base classes that inherit widget behavior are concrete.

Our decorator simply changes the button style when the mouse enters the button and restores it to flat upon exit.

```
# Derived Button intercepts mouse entry and changes
# the decoration of the button from flat to raised
class Decorator(Button):
    def __init__(self, master, **kwargs):
        super().__init__(master, **kwargs)

        self.configure(relief=FLAT)
        self.bind("<Enter>", self.on_enter)
        self.bind("<Leave>", self.on_leave)

    def on_enter(self, evt):
        self.configure(relief=RAISED)

    def on_leave(self, evt):
       self.configure(relief=FLAT)
```

Using a Decorator

Now that we've written a `Decorator` class, how do we use it? We simply create an instance of the Decorator as a button it is meant to decorate. We can do all of this right in the constructor. Let's consider a simple program with two CoolButtons and one ordinary Button. We create the layout as follows:

```
# creates the user interface
class Builder():
    def build(self):
        root = Tk()
        root.geometry("200x100")
        root.title("Tk buttons")
        #create two decorated buttons and one normal
        cbut = CButton(root)
        dbut = DButton(root)
        qbut = Button(root, text="Quit",
            command=quit)
        cbut.pack( pady=3)
        dbut.pack( pady=3)
        qbut.pack()
```

Figure 15-1 shows this program, with the mouse hovering over one of the buttons.

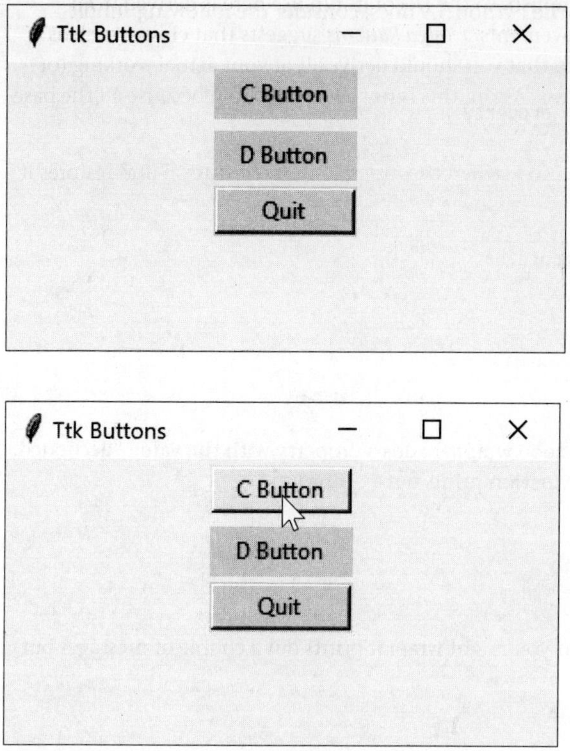

Figure 15-1 Mouse hovering over the C button

And it is then perfectly possible to have the two buttons with different decorators. A similar approach is possible using the tkinter ttk toolkit; an example is provided on our GitHub repository.

Using Nonvisual Decorators

Decorators are not limited to objects that enhance visual classes. You can add or modify the methods of any object in a similar way. In fact, nonvisual objects can be easier to decorate because there may be fewer methods to intercept and forward.

We have already seen the `@property` decorator and the `@staticmethod` decorator in previous chapters. At first, these appear to be compiler instructions or some sort of macro, but decorators are actually the names of functions that you call. For example, there is a `staticmethod()` function in Python, which you wrap around a method. This simple property marker is easier to read and less prone to error.

For a really simple example suggested by the Python 3.9 docs, consider the following simple wrapper and an empty function it wraps:

```
def deco(func):
    # adds a value to a new function property
    func.label = "decorated"
    return func

# Complete empty function,
# that is decorated by the "deco" decorator
@deco
def f():
    pass

print(f.label)
```

The function `f()` does nothing, but the `deco` wrapper adds a property with the value "decorated." When you run the program, the `print` function prints out `f.label` as

```
Decorated
```

Decorated Code

Now, let's consider another function that you might wrap. It prints out a couple of messages but doesn't do much.

```
# decorator that wraps a function
def mathFunc(func):
    def wrapper(x):
        print("b4 func")
        func(x)
        print("after func")
    return wrapper
```

We'll also create a simple two-line function to be wrapped.

```
# print out a name or phrase
def sayMath(x):
    print("math")
```

Now suppose we want to create a new version of `mathfunc` that wraps `sayMath`. We can do this directly, like this:

```
# create wrapped function
sayMath = mathFunc(sayMath)
```

Now, the `sayMath` function is replaced by the function wrapped by `mathFunc`. If we call

```
sayMath(12)
```

the program will print:

```
call after making decorator
b4 func
math
after func
```

In other words, the word math is wrapped by the wrapper info from `mathFunc`.

Now let's rewrite this wrapper code using a decorator:

```
# Decorator wraps sayMath
@mathFunc
def sayMath(x):
    print("math")
```

So, you can see that the `@mathFunc` decorator simply wraps the `sayMath` function just as if we had written this:

```
sayMath = mathFunc(sayMath)
print("call after making decorator")
```

And that is really all there is to Python decorators. These are one-line statements that replace a little more complex way of wrapping (or decorating) code. The only reason they are hard to explain is that there are so few simple examples that make them seem useful.

You can put all the decorators you create in a single file and import them as part of your code. But frankly, you probably won't think of too many times to do so.

The dataclass Decorator

One of the most useful decorators we have come across is the `dataclass` decorator.

Whenever you create a new class, you have to go through the boilerplate of setting up the `__init__` method and copying some values into the instance variables. For example, in this simple `Employee` class, you generally would write this:

```
class Employee:
    def __init__(self, frname:str, lname:str,
                        idnum:int):
        self.frname = frname
        self.lname = lname
        self.idnum = idnum
```

where you declare the arguments to the `init` method and then copy them into variables for that instance. Well, if this happens pretty much every time you create a class, why not automate it?

This is what the `dataclass` decorator does for you. If you use this decorator, your code is reduced to

```
@dataclass
class Employee:
    frname: str
    lname: str
    idnum: int
```

and the `init` method and the copying is filled in for you.

You also need to import the library that contains this function, but only once per module:

```
from dataclasses import dataclass
```

So, when you go to create an instance of `Employee`, you proceed as usual:

```
emp = Employee('Sarah', 'Smythe', 123)
print(emp.nameString())
```

The arguments are in the same order as in the variable list. In fact, IDEs such as PyCharm recognize this decorator (which is just a function call under the covers) and pop up the variable list shown in Figure 15-2.

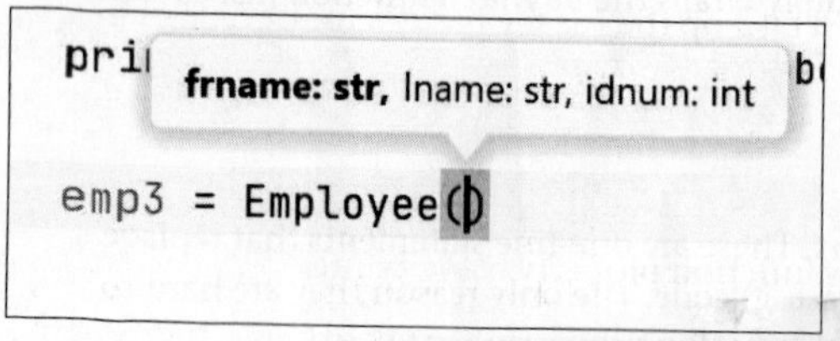

Figure 15-2 Info the PyCharm IDE displays regarding the Employee constructor

Using dataclass with Default Values

The `dataclass` decorator handles default values in the same way:

```
class Employee2:
    frname: str
    lname: str
    idnum: int
    town: str = "Stamford"
    state: str = 'CT'
    zip: str = '06820'
```

The class then works just fine. Doesn't that make class creation a lot easier?

Decorators, Adapters, and Composites

As noted in *Design Patterns*, there is an essential similarity among these classes that you may have recognized. Adapters also seem to "decorate" an existing class. However, their function is to change the interface of one or more classes to one that is more convenient for a particular program. Decorators add methods to functions but not to classes. You can also imagine that a composite consisting of a single item is essentially a decorator. Once again, however, the intent is different.

Consequences of the Decorator Pattern

The Decorator pattern provides a more flexible way to add responsibilities to a function in a class than by using inheritance. It also enables you to customize a class without creating subclasses high in the inheritance hierarchy. *Design Patterns* points out two disadvantages of the Decorator pattern, however. One is that a Decorator and its enclosed component are not identical. Thus, tests for object type will fail. The second is that Decorators can lead to a system with "lots of little objects" that all look alike to the programmer trying to maintain the code. This can be a maintenance headache.

Decorator and Façade evoke similar images in building architecture. In design pattern terminology, however, the Façade is a way of hiding a complex system inside a simpler interface, whereas Decorator adds function by wrapping a class. We'll take up the Façade pattern in the next chapter.

Programs on GitHub

- SimpleDecoratorTk.py: Adds value to a new function property using tkinter
- SimpleDecoratorTtk.py: Adds value to a new function property using the tkinter ttk toolkit
- DecoCode.py: Decorates a math function
- Decofunc.py: Interior function used as decorator
- Dclass.py: Employee class with dataclass
- Dclasse.py: Employee class without dataclass

16

The Façade Pattern

As your programs evolve and develop, they frequently grow in complexity. In fact, for all the excitement about using design patterns, these patterns sometimes generate so many classes that it is difficult to understand the program's flow. Furthermore, there may be a number of complicated subsystems, each of which has its own complex interface.

The Façade pattern enables you to simplify this complexity by providing a simplified interface to these subsystems. This simplification may in some cases reduce the flexibility of the underlying classes, but it usually still provides all the function needed for all but the most sophisticated users. These users can still, of course, access the underlying classes and methods.

Fortunately, we don't have to write a complex system to provide an example of where a Façade can be useful. Python provides a set of classes that connect to databases using an interface called Open Database Connectivity (ODBC). You can connect to any database for which the manufacturer has provided an ODBC connection class: almost every database on the market.

A database is essentially a set of tables in which columns in one table are related to some data in another table, such as stores, foods, and prices. You create queries that produce results computed from those tables. The queries are written in Structured Query Language (SQL) and the results are usually a new table that contains rows computed from the other tables.

The Python interface is more procedural than object oriented and can be simplified using a few objects based on the four data objects in Figure 16-1.

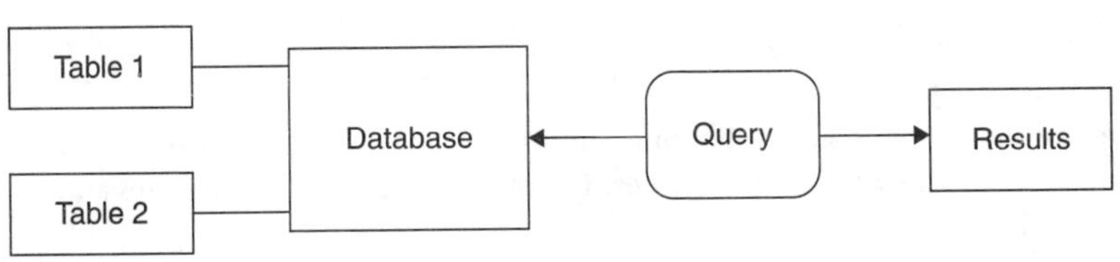

Figure 16-1 Database objects using Façade

We started down this path using the popular MySQL database, a full-fledged industrial-strength database that you can download and use for free. You can install it and run it on your laptop or on a server where a number of people can access the data. However, for simpler cases, where you don't need to share the data, a colleague suggested we also should look at the SQLite database.

In both cases, these databases run on nearly all computing platforms and Python provides drivers to connect to them. Each SQLite database is a separate file on your computer. It is not embedded in some complex management system, and you can easily send that file to another user when that is useful.

However, by designing a Façade consisting of a `Database` class and a `Results` class, we can build a much more usable system for any database you decide to use.

For our examples, we have created a groceries database with just three tables—Foods, Stores, and Prices. Figure 16-2 shows the Foods table. And we were able to create this simple database using the free MySQL Workbench application. There is a similar tool for SQLite called SQLite Studio.

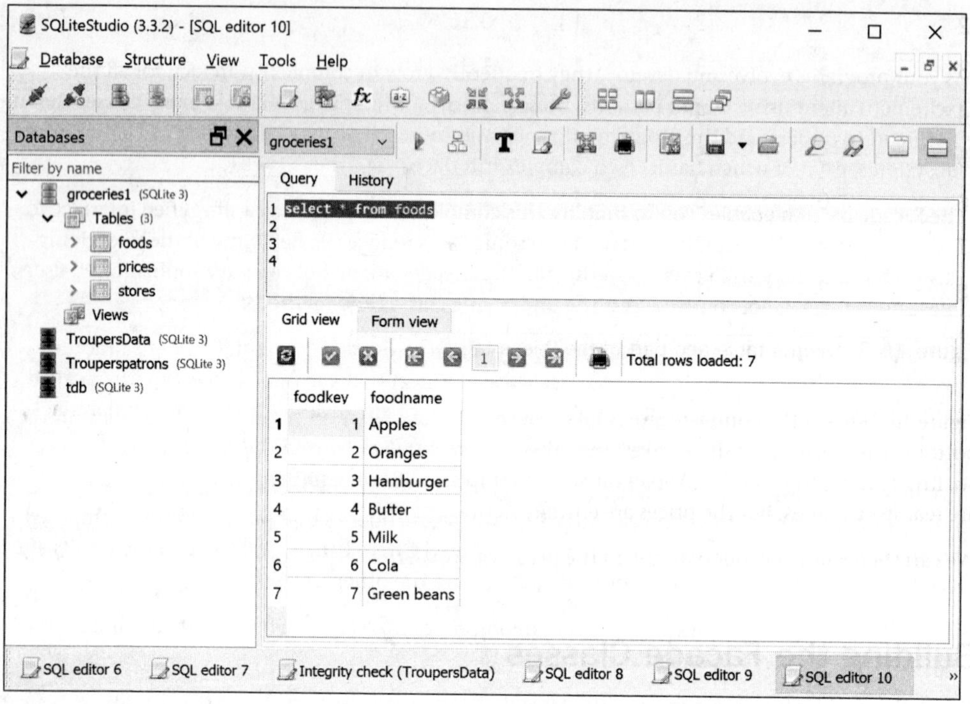

Figure 16-2 MySQL Workbench

Tables may have as many columns as you like, but one column must be the primary key (usually an integer). This table has only the key and food names. The other two tables are the stores and the prices (see Figure 16-3).

	storekey	storename
1	1	Stop and Shop
2	2	Village Market
3	3	Shoprite

	pricekey	foodkey	storekey	price
1	1	1	1	0.27
2	2	2	1	0.36
3	3	3	1	1.98
4	4	4	1	2.39
5	5	5	1	1.98
6	6	6	1	2.65
7	7	7	1	2.29
8	8	1	2	0.29

Figure 16-3 Stores table and part of the Prices table

Figure 16-3 shows the complete Stores table on the top and a section of the Prices table on the bottom. The Prices table shows a key from the Food table, a key from the Stores table, and a price. So, line 1 shows that Food 1 (Apples) at Store 1 (Stop and Shop) has a price of $0.27 each. (These are real store names, but the prices are entirely fictitious.)

We can then use a SQL query to get all the prices of apples, for example.

Building the Façade Classes

Now let's consider how to connect to the MySQL database. We first must load the database driver:

```
import pymysql
```

Then we use the `connect` function to connect to a database. Note that these arguments require keyword names.

```
db = pymysql.connect(host=self.host,
      user=self.userid, password=self.pwd)
```

These arguments are the server, the username, the password, and the database name.

If we want to list the names of the tables in the database, we need to query the database for the names:

```
db.cursor.execute("show tables")
rows = cursor.fetchall()
for r in rows:
    print(r)
```

This gives you the following, which are essentially single element tuples:

```
('foods',)
('prices',)
('stores',)
```

If you want to execute a query, to get the prices of apples, for example, you do it like this:

```
# execute SQL query using execute() method.
cursor.execute(
"""select foods.foodname, stores.storename, prices.price from prices
    join foods on (foods.foodkey=prices.foodkey)
    join stores on (stores.storekey = prices.storekey )
    where foods.foodname='Apples' order by price"""

row = cursor.fetchone()
while row is not None:
    print(row)
    row = cursor.fetchone()
```

The result is three tuples:

```
('Apples', 'Stop and Shop', 0.27)
('Apples', 'Village Market', 0.29)
('Apples', 'ShopRite', 0.33)
```

This is a little clunky to manage and is entirely procedural, with no classes.

One simplifying assumption we can make is that the exceptions that all these database class methods throw do not need complex handling. For the most part, the methods will work without error unless the network connection to the database fails. Thus, we can wrap all of these methods in classes in which we simply print the infrequent errors and take no further action.

This makes it possible to make four enclosing classes, as shown in Figure 16-1: the `Database` class, the `Table` class, the `Query` class, and the `Results` class. These constitute the Façade pattern we have been leading up to.

The `Database` class here not only connects to the server and opens a database, but it also creates an array of `Table` objects.

```
class MysqlDatabase(Database):
    def __init__(self, host, username, password,dbname):
        self._db = pymysql.connect(host=host, user=username,
                                   password=password, database=dbname)
        self._dbname = dbname
        self._cursor = self._db.cursor()
```

```
    @property
    def cursor(self):
        return self._cursor

    def getTables(self):
        self._cursor.execute("show tables")

        # create array of table objects
        self.tables = []
        rows = self._cursor.fetchall()
        for r in rows:
           self.tables.append(
                Table(self._cursor, r))
        return self.tables
```

The Table object gets the column names and stores them:

```
class Table():
    def __init__(self, cursor, name):
        self.cursor = cursor
        self.tname = name[0]    # first of tuple
        # get column names
        self.cursor.execute("show columns from " + self.tname)
        self.columns = self.cursor.fetchall()

    @property
    def name(self):     # gets table name
        return self.tname


# returns a list of columns
    def getColumns(self):
        return self.columns
```

The Query class executes the query and returns the results:

```
class Query():
    def __init__(self, cursor, qstring):
        self.qstringMaster = qstring  #master copy
        self.qstring = self.qstringMaster
        self.cursor = cursor

     # executes the query and returns all results
    def execute(self):
        print (self.qstring)
        self.cursor.execute(self.qstring)
        rows = self.cursor.fetchall()
        return Results(rows)
```

We store the query string in `qstringMaster` so that it can be copied and modified if you want to use the same query for different foods.

Finally, the simple `Results` class just keeps the rows.

```
class Results():
    def __init__(self, rows):
        self.rows = rows

    def getRows(self):
        return self.rows
```

You could enhance the class by adding an iterator to get the rows one by one and then formatting them if you wanted.

These simple classes allow us to write a program for opening a database; displaying its table names, column names, and contents; and running a simple SQL query on the database.

The DBObjects program accesses a simple database that contains food prices at three local markets (see Figure 16-4).

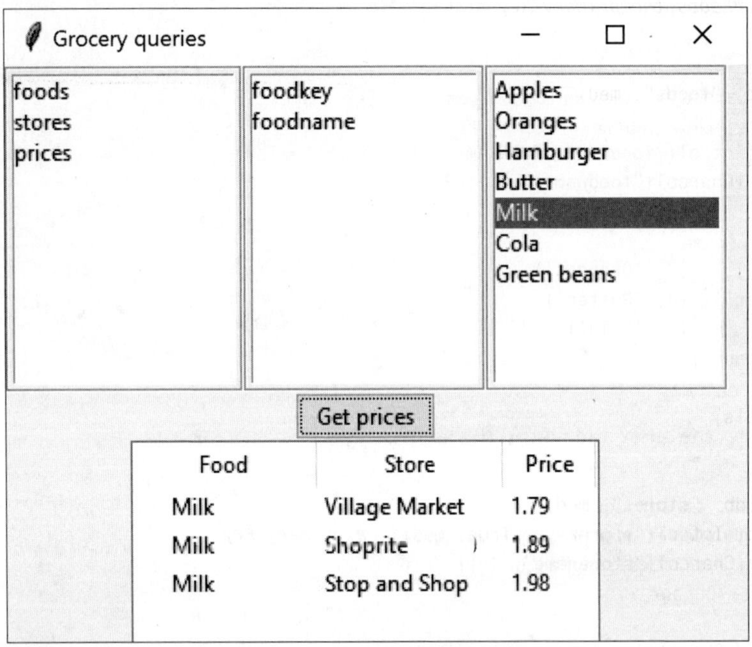

Figure 16-4 Grocery store pricing with DBObjects

Clicking a table name shows you the column names; clicking a column name shows you the contents of that column. If you click the Get Prices button, you display the food prices sorted by store for any food you pick from the list box on the right.

This program starts by connecting to the database and getting a list of the table names:

```
db = MysqlDatabase('localhost', 'newuser',
                   'new_user','groceries')
```

Then the program runs a simple query for table names. Each table runs a query for column names once when created. The list of column contents is generated by a query when you click the column name in the middle list box.

Creating Databases and Tables

With slight modifications to the `Database`, `Table`, and `Query` classes, you can create a database and create and populate tables. These classes then generate the needed SQL. You can find the complete code in our GitHub repository.

Here is how we create the database and tables for our groceries example.

```
db = Database("localhost", "newuser", "new_user")
db.create("groceries")
med = Mediator(db)  #keeps the primary key string

# Create food table
foodtable = Table(db, "foods", med)
# primary key
foodtable.addColumn(Intcol("foodkey", True, med))
foodtable.addColumn (Charcol("foodname", 45))
foodtable.create()

vals = [(1, 'Apples'),   (2, 'Oranges'),
        (3, 'Hamburger'), (4, 'Butter'),
        (5, 'Milk'),      (6, 'Cola'),
        (7, 'Green beans')
        ]
foodtable.addRows(vals)

# create store table
storetable  = Table(db, "stores", med)
storetable.addColumn( Intcol("storekey", True, med))  # primary key
storetable.addColumn(Charcol("storename", 45))
storetable.create()

vals = [(1, 'Stop and Shop'),
         (2, 'Village Market'),
         (3, 'Shoprite')]
storetable.addRows(vals)
```

Although the data for the Prices table is longer, the approach is exactly the same:

```
pricetable = Table(db, "prices", med)
pricetable.addColumn(Intcol("pricekey", True, med))  # primary key
```

```
pricetable.addColumn(Intcol("foodkey", False, med))
pricetable.addColumn(Intcol("storekey", False, med))
pricetable.addColumn(Floatcol("price"))
pricetable.create()

vals = [( 1, 1, 1, 0.27),
        (2, 2, 1, 0.36), (3, 3, 1, 1.98),
        (4, 4, 1, 2.39), (5, 5, 1, 1.98),
# and so forth
]
pricetable.addRows(vals)
```

Using the SQLite Version

There are only very small differences in the Database and Table code for Sqlite. And to illustrate the great power of classes, we can create a derived class from Database with some slight changes to the methods. For example, connecting to a SQLite database just means specifying a filename. And SQLite does not have a "show tables" SQL command, but you can still get the table names from a master table within the database file:

```
class SqltDatabase(Database):
    def __init__(self, *args):
        self._db = sqlite3.connect(args[0])
        self._dbname = args[0]
        self._cursor = self._db.cursor()

    def commit(self):
        self._db.commit()

    def create(self, dbname):
        pass

    def getTables(self):
        tbQuery = Query(self.cursor,
           """select name from
           sqlite_master where type='table'""")

        # create array of table objects
        rows = tbQuery.execute().getRows()
        for r in rows:
             self.tables.append(
                 SqltTable(self._db, r))
        return self.tables
```

Changes to the derived `SqltTable` class are likewise pretty simple, and the Groceries app using SQLite runs and looks exactly the same as the one for the MySQL version.

Consequences of the Façade

The Façade pattern shields clients from complex subsystem components and provides a simpler programming interface for the general user. However, it does not prevent advanced users from going to deeper, more complex classes when necessary.

In addition, the Façade pattern allows you to make changes in the underlying subsystems without requiring changes in the client code, and it reduces compilation dependencies.

Programs on GitHub

- Dbtest.py: test query without Façade
- SimpledbObjects.py: Queries without UI
- DBObjects.py: Complete set of DB classes
- MysqlDatabase.py: Connects to MySQL
- SqltDatabase.py: Connects to SqLite
- Makedatabase.py: Creates the groceries MySQL database
- Makesqlite.py: Creates a SQLite database
- Grocerydisplay.py: Displays groceries using MySQL
- GroceryDispLite: Displays groceries using SQLite

Notes on MySQL

MySQL was always an open source project, but it has a complicated history: It was sold to Sun Microsystems, which was then taken over by Oracle, who now supports MySQL for free, although it offers a paid version as well. The original MySQL developers left the project at that time, taking the MySQL code with them and forming MariaDB (which is also freely available).

You can download and install MySQL directly from the Oracle website (mysql.com) for most platforms. For Windows, use the .msi installer, which is supposed to install everything you need for Python to work with MySQL.

You will also need to install the pymysql library using `pip`:

```
pip install pymysql
```

For PyCharm, this can be done directly from the command line. For VSCODE, you need to open a command line within VSCODE to install this library in the right place.

When you install MySQL, you also need to create a user other than root. Make sure that Authentication Type is set to standard and that Administrative Roles is set to DBA.

Using SQLite

You can download the Windows ZIP file (as well as many others) from sqlite.com. Unzip it into any convenient directory and add that directory to your path. Sqlite Studio is available at sqlitestudio.pl.

References

https://dev.mysql.com/doc/refman/8.0/en/windows-installation.html

17

The Flyweight Pattern

Sometimes in programming, it seems that you need to generate a very large number of small class instances to represent data. You can greatly reduce the number of different classes that you need to instantiate if you can recognize that the instances are fundamentally the same except for a few parameters. If you can move those variables outside the class instance and pass them in as part of a method call, the number of separate instances can be greatly reduced by sharing them.

The Flyweight design pattern provides an approach for handling such classes. It refers to the instance's *intrinsic* data, which makes the instance unique, and the *extrinsic* data, which is passed in as arguments. The Flyweight pattern is appropriate for small, fine-grained classes such as individual characters or icons on the screen. For example, you might be drawing a series of icons on the screen in a window, where each represents a person or data file as a folder (see Figure 17-1).

In this case, it does not make sense to have an individual class instance for each folder that remembers the person's name and the icon's screen position. Typically, these icons are one of a few similar images, and the position where they are drawn is calculated dynamically based on the window's size.

In another example in *Design Patterns*, each character in a document is represented as a single instance of a character class, but the positions where the characters are drawn on the screen are kept as external data so that there needs to be only one instance of each character, rather than one for each appearance of that character.

What Are Flyweights?

Flyweights are sharable instances of a class. At first, it might seem that each class is a Singleton, but in fact there might be a small number of instances, such as one for every character or one for every icon type. The number of instances that are allocated must be decided as the class instances are needed. This is usually accomplished with a `FlyweightFactory` class. This factory class usually *is* a Singleton because it needs to keep track of whether a particular instance has been generated. The class then returns either a new instance or a reference to one it has already generated.

To decide whether some part of your program is a candidate for using Flyweights, consider whether it is possible to remove some data from the class and make it extrinsic. If this makes it possible to reduce greatly the number of different class instances your program needs to maintain, this might be a case where Flyweights will help.

Example Code

Suppose we want to draw a small folder icon with a name under it for each person in an organization. If this is a large organization, there could be a large number of such icons, but the icons are actually all the same graphical image with different text labels. Even if we have two icons, one for "is selected" and one for "not selected," the number of different icons is small. In such a system, having an icon object for each person, with its own coordinates, name, and selected state, is a waste of resources. Figure 17-1 shows two such icons.

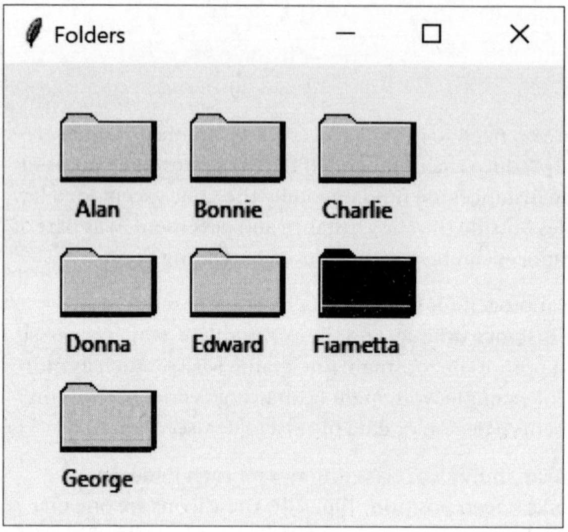

Figure 17-1 Folders as Flyweights

Instead, we'll create a `FolderFactory` that returns either the selected or the unselected folder drawing class but does not create additional instances after one of each has been created. Because this is such a simple case, we just create them both at the outset and then return one or the other:

```
# returns a selected or unselected folder
class FolderFactory():

    def __init__(self, canvas):
        brown = "#5f5f1c"
        self.selected = Folder(brown, canvas)
        self.unselected = Folder("yellow", canvas)

    def getFolder(self, isSelected):
        if isSelected:
            return self.selected
        else:
            return self.unselected
```

For cases where more instances could exist, the factory could keep a table of the ones it has already created and then create new ones only if they aren't already in the table.

The unique thing about using Flyweights, however, is that we pass the coordinates and the name to be drawn into the folder when we draw it. These coordinates are the extrinsic data that allow us to share the folder objects and, in this case, create only two instances. The complete folder class shown next simply creates a folder instance with one background color or the other and has a public `Draw` method that draws the folder at the point you specify.

```
# draws a folder
class Folder():
    W =50
    H=30

    def __init__(self, color, canvas:Canvas):
        self._color = color
        self.canvas = canvas
# draw the folder
    def draw (self, tx, ty, name):
        self.canvas.create_rectangle(tx, ty,
            tx+Folder.W, ty+Folder.H, fill="black")
        self.canvas.create_text(tx+20, ty+Folder.H+15, text=name)
        self.canvas.create_rectangle(
            tx+1, ty+1, tx + Folder.W-1,
            ty + Folder.H-1,
            fill=self._color)
        #----And so forth ----
```

To use a Flyweight class like this, your main program must calculate the position of each folder as part of its paint routine and then pass the coordinates to the folder instance. This is actually rather common because you need a different layout depending on the window's dimensions, and you do not want to have to keep telling each instance where its new location is going to be. Instead, we compute it dynamically during the paint routine.

Note that we could have generated an array of folders at the outset and simply scanned through the array to draw each folder. Such an array is not as wasteful as a series of different instances because it is actually an array of references to one of only two folder instances. However, because we want to display one folder as selected and we want to be able to change which folder is selected dynamically, we just use the `FolderFactory` itself to give us the correct instance each time:

```
def repaint(self):
    j = 0
    row = BuildUI.TOP
    x= BuildUI.LEFT

    # look for whether any is selected and
    # use the factory to create it
    for nm in self.namelist:
```

```
        f = self.factory.getFolder(
            nm == self.selectedName)
        f.draw( x, row, nm)
        x += BuildUI.HSPACE
        j += 1
        if j > BuildUI.ROWMAX:
            j = 0
            row += BuildUI.VSPACE
            x = BuildUI.LEFT
```

The `FlyCanvas` class is the main UI class where the folders are arranged and drawn. It contains one instance of the `FolderFactory` and one instance of the `Folder` class. The `FolderFactory` class contains two instances of `Folder`: selected and unselected. The `FolderFactory` returns one or the other of these to the `FlyCanvas`.

Selecting a Folder

Since we have two folder instances that we termed selected and unselected, we'd like to be able to select folders by moving the mouse over them. In the paint routine shown earlier, we simply remember the name of the folder that was selected and ask the factory to return a selected folder for it. The folders are not individual instances, so we can't listen for mouse motion within each folder instance. In fact, even if we did listen within a folder, we'd need to have a way to tell the other instances to deselect themselves.

Instead, we check for a mouse click at the canvas level. If the mouse is found to be within a folder rectangle, we make that corresponding name the selected name. This allows us to just check each name when we redraw and create a selected folder instance where it is needed:

```
# search to see if click is inside a folder
# changes the selected name so repaint draws
# a new selected folder
def mouseClick(self, evt):
    self.selectedName= ""
    found = False
    j = 0
    row =FlyCanvas.TOP
    x = FlyCanvas.LEFT
    self.selectedName = ""  #blank if not in folder
    for nm in self.namelist:
        if x < evt.x and evt.x < (x+ Folder.W):
            if row < evt.y and \
                  evt.y < (row+Folder.H):
                self.selectedName = nm
                found = True
        j += 1
        x += FlyCanvas.HSPACE
```

```
        if j > FlyCanvas.ROWMAX:
            j=0
            row += FlyCanvas.VSPACE
            x = FlyCanvas.LEFT
    self.repaint()
```

Copy-on-Write Objects

The Flyweight pattern uses just a few object instances to represent many different objects in a program. All of them normally have the same base properties as intrinsic data and a few properties representing extrinsic data that vary with each manifestation of the class instance. However, some of these instances might eventually take on new intrinsic properties (such as shape or folder tab position) and require a new specific instance of the class to represent them. Instead of creating these in advance as special subclasses, you can copy the class instance and change its intrinsic properties when the program flow indicates that a new separate instance is required. The class thus copies itself when the change becomes inevitable, changing those intrinsic properties in the new class. We call this process copy-on-write and can build this process into Flyweights as well as a number of other classes, such as the `Proxy` pattern discussed in the next chapter.

Program on GitHub

- FlyFolders.py

18

The Proxy Pattern

The Proxy pattern is used when you need to represent an object that is complex or time consuming to create by a simpler one. If creating an object is expensive in time or computer resources, a proxy enables you to postpone this creation until you need the actual object. A proxy usually has the same methods as the object it represents; when the object is loaded, it passes on the method calls from the proxy to the actual object.

There are several cases where a Proxy can be useful:

1. If an object, such as a large image, takes a long time to load.
2. If the object is on a remote machine and loading it over the network might be slow, especially during peak network load periods.
3. If the object has limited access rights. The proxy then can validate the access permissions for that user.

Proxies can also be used to distinguish between requesting an instance of an object and the actual need to access it. For example, program initialization may set up a number of objects that may not all be used right away. In this case, the proxy can load the real object only when it is needed.

Suppose that a program needs to load and display a large image. When the program starts, there must be some indication that an image is to be displayed so that the screen lays out correctly, but the actual image display can be postponed until the image loads completely. This is particularly important in programs such as word processors and web browsers that lay out text around the images even before the images are available.

Using the Pillow Image Library

The standard Python library supports only .png files and .ppm files. To display the more common .jpg files, you need an enhancement to Python called the Python Image Library (PIL), or Pillow. You can find the install file for your platform and Python version at https://pypi.org/project/Pillow/#files and then install it using pip.

First, go to your Python directory, `c:\users\`*`yourname`*`\Appdata\Local`.

Then go on down to `Programs\Python\Python38-32`.

Download the .whl file from the pypi site into this folder and then use pip to install it:

```
pip install Pillow-7 … etc.
```

Then restart your Python development environment to see Pillow now available.

Displaying an Image Using PIL

In the following examples, we'll start with a 24MB JPG file (5168 × 4009) and reduce it to 516 × 400 for faster loading and display.

You need the following imports to use PIL:

```
import tkinter as tk
from tkinter import Canvas, NW
from PIL import ImageTk, Image
```

Then in a few lines, you can read in the large .jpg file and scale it down to about 10% of its original size, creating a PhotoImage using PIL instead of the native Python image classes.

```
root = tk.Tk()
root.title("Edward")
w = 516
h = 400
root.configure(background='grey')
path = "Edward.jpg"

# Creates a Tkinter-compatible photo image,
# using PIL to read the JPG file
img = Image.open(path)
img = img.resize((w, h), Image.ANTIALIAS)
self.photoImg = ImageTk.PhotoImage(img)
```

Then you create a Canvas and display the image on it as using the `create_image` method of the Canvas class:

```
self.canv = Canvas(root, width = w+40, height = h+40)
self.canv.pack(side="bottom", fill="both", expand="yes")
self.canv.create_rectangle(20,20,w+20,h+20, width=3)
self.canv.create_image(20,20, anchor=NW, image=self.photoImg)
```

Using Threads to Handle Image Loading

Now, if this were a very large image or one that for some reason takes a long time to load, an image Proxy would be a good idea. We launch the main program, have it draw a frame where the image will be loaded, and then spin off a separate thread to go fetch and scale the image.

We start by creating the canvas and drawing the place-holding rectangle:

```
self.canv = Canvas(root, width = self.w+40, height = self.h+40)
self.canv.pack(side="bottom", fill="both", expand="yes")
self.canv.create_rectangle(20,20, self.w+20,self.h+20, width=3)
```

You then need to import the threading and time libraries: threading simply to run threads and time because we are going to introduce an artificial delay to represent a longer process:

```
import threading
import time
```

To spin off a thread, you need to create a function that the thread system calls. It can be a simple function in the current class or a much longer one.

The function must have at least one argument, which is the thread ID. It can be any string you want. The arguments are in an `*args` array, and you can fetch them by position: `args[0]` is the thread ID and the rest are arguments to the thread itself. Our single argument here is the filename for the image we are loading:

```
def thread_image(self,*args):
    name = args[0]        #thread identifier
    time.sleep(2)         # here is the delay
    # open the image, and scale it
    img = Image.open(args[1])    #image location
    img = img.resize((self.w, self.h),
                     Image.ANTIALIAS)
    self.photoImg = ImageTk.PhotoImage(img)
    self.canv.create_image(20, 20, anchor=NW,
                           image=self.photoImg)
```

To launch the thread from your main program, you create a `Thread` and call `start` on it:

```
# set up the imaging thread
x = threading.Thread(target=self.thread_image,
                     args=(1,path))
x.start()       # start tho thread here
```

Note that the `thread_image` function sleeps for 2 seconds. This represents the long delay that the thread is supposed to be using. The result of this program is first an empty frame and then, 2 seconds later, an image (see Figure 18-1).

Figure 18-1 Image displayed after 2 seconds

Logging from Threads

If you are writing simple single-threaded programs, you can follow their progress by adding `print` statements or by using a debugger. However, this gets trickier when you have more than one thread running because the other threads do not print to the console. To use logging, you must, of course, include the `import` statement:

```
import logging
```

There are five levels of logging: debug, info, warning, error, and critical. You can issue log messages using the methods `logging.debug`, `logging.info`, `logging.warning`, `logging.error`, and `logging.critical`. These messages are written to the console or to a file you select, and you can set the level of logging messages you see with the following method:

```
logging.basicConfig
```

For example:

```
format = "%(asctime)s: %(message)s"
logging.basicConfig(format=format,
             level=logging.INFO,
             datefmt="%H:%M:%S")
```

Then you can issue logging messages from anywhere in any thread:

```
logging.info("Thread %s: starting", name)
```

To write the messages to a file, include the filename in the config statement:

```
logging.basicConfig(format=format,
             level=logging.INFO,
             file= "logfile.log",
             datefmt="%H:%M:%S")
```

Logging is particularly useful when you need to debug multithreaded programs because you can't see the console output of those other threads.

Copy-on-Write

You can also use proxies to keep copies of large objects that may or may not change. If you create a second instance of an expensive object, a Proxy can decide there is no reason to make a copy yet. It then simply uses the original object. If the program makes a change in the new copy, the Proxy can copy the original object and make the change in the new instance. This can be a great time and space saver when objects do not always change after they are instantiated.

Comparing Related Patterns

Both the Adapter and the Proxy constitute a thin layer around an object. However, the Adapter provides a different interface for an object, whereas the Proxy provides the same interface for the object but interposes itself where it can postpone processing or data transmission effort.

A Decorator also has the same interface as the object it surrounds, but its purpose is to add additional (sometimes visual) function to the original object. A proxy, by contrast, controls access to the contained class.

Programs on GitHub

- Canvasversion.py: Displays an image using the PIL library
- ThreadCanvas.py: Displays a frame and then the image
- ThreadLogging.py: Logs the program using logging
- Edward.jpg: Picture for proxy loading

19

Summary of Structural Patterns

The chapters in Part II have covered the following patterns:

- The Adapter pattern, used to change the interface of one class to that of another one
- The Bridge pattern, designed to separate a class's interface from its implementation so that you can vary or replace the implementation without changing the client code
- The Composite pattern, a collection of objects, any one of which can be either a Composite or just a leaf object
- The Decorator pattern, a class that surrounds a given class, adds new capabilities to it, and passes all the unchanged methods to the underlying class
- The Façade pattern, which groups a complex set of objects and provides a new, simpler interface to access those data
- The Flyweight pattern, which provides a way to limit the proliferation of small, similar instances by moving some of the class data outside the class and passing it in during various execution methods
- The Proxy pattern, which provides a simple placeholder object for a more complex object that is in some way time-consuming or expensive to instantiate

The chapters in the next part of this book will cover Behavioral patterns.

PART IV

Behavioral Patterns

Behavioral patterns are those patterns that are most specifically concerned with communication between objects.

- The Chain of Responsibility allows a decoupling between objects by passing a request from one object to the next in a chain until the request is recognized.
- The Command pattern utilizes simple objects to represent execution of software commands, and allows you to support logging and undoable operations.
- The Interpreter provides a definition of how to include language elements in a program.
- The Iterator pattern formalizes the way we move through a list of data within a class.
- The Mediator defines how communication between objects can be simplified by using a separate object to keep all objects from having to know about each other.
- The Observer pattern defines the way a number of objects can be notified of a change.
- The State pattern allows an object to modify its behavior when its internal state changes.
- The Strategy pattern encapsulates an algorithm inside a class.
- The Template Method pattern provides an abstract definition of an algorithm.
- The Visitor pattern adds polymorphic functions to a class noninvasively.

These patterns are some of the most powerful and most commonly used of the basic 23 Design Patterns, so be sure to study them carefully.

20 Chain of Responsibility Pattern

[illegible]

The Chain of Responsibility pattern allows a number of classes to attempt to handle a request without any of them knowing about the capabilities of the other classes. It provides a loose coupling between these classes; the only common link is the request that is passed between them. The request is passed along until one of the classes can handle it.

One example of such a chain pattern is a Help system, where every screen region of an application invites you to seek help (see Figure 20.1). There are also window background areas where more generic help is the only suitable result.

Figure 20.1: Help demonstration [illegible]

When you select an area for help, that visual control forwards its ID or name to the chain. Suppose you click the New button. If the first module can handle the New button, it displays the help message. If not, it forwards the request to the next module. Eventually, the message is forwarded to an "All buttons" class that can display a general message about how buttons work. If no general button help is available, the message is forwarded to the general help module that tells you how the system works in general. If that doesn't exist, the message is lost and no information is displayed. This is illustrated in Figure 20.2.

20

Chain of Responsibility Pattern

The Chain of Responsibility pattern allows a number of classes to attempt to handle a request without any of them knowing about the capabilities of the other classes. It provides a loose coupling between these classes; the only common link is the request that is passed between them. The request is passed along until one of the classes can handle it.

One example of such a chain pattern is a Help system, where every screen region of an application invites you to seek help (see Figure 20-1). There are also window background areas where more generic help is the only suitable result.

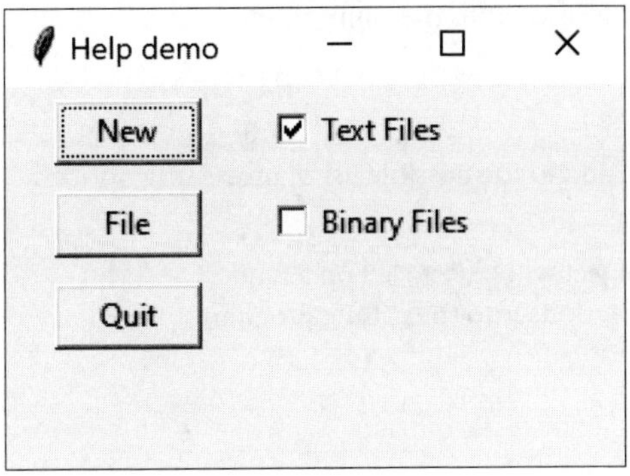

Figure 20-1 Help demonstration

When you select an area for help, that visual control forwards its ID or name to the chain. Suppose you click the New button. If the first module can handle the New button, it displays the help message. If not, it forwards the request to the next module. Eventually, the message is forwarded to an "All buttons" class that can display a general message about how buttons work. If no general button help is available, the message is forwarded to the general help module that tells you how the system works in general. If that doesn't exist, the message is lost, and no information is displayed. This is illustrated in Figure 20-2.

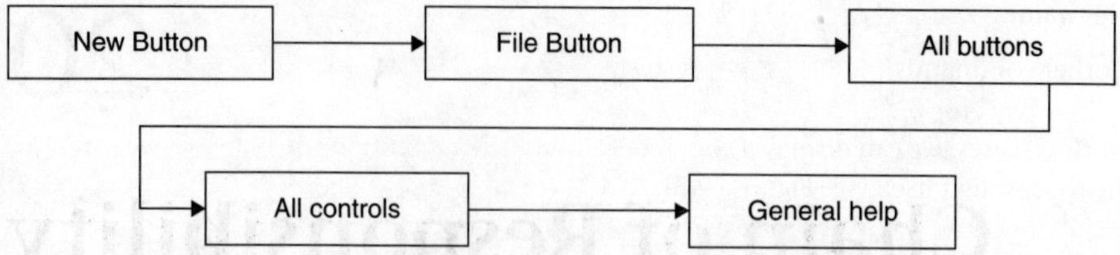

Figure 20-2 Help demo flowchart

There are two significant points we can observe from this example. First, the chain is organized from most specific to most general. Second, there is no guarantee that the request will produce a response in all cases. The Observer pattern defines the way a number of classes can be notified of a change.

When to Use the Chain

The Chain of Responsibility pattern is a good example of a pattern that helps keep knowledge separate from what each object in a program can do. In other words, it reduces the coupling between objects so that they can act independently. This also applies to the object that constitutes the main program and contains instances of the other objects. You will find this pattern helpful in certain cases:

- Several objects have similar methods that could be appropriate for the action the program is requesting. However, it is more appropriate for the objects to decide which one is to carry out the action than it is for you to build this decision into the calling code.
- One of the objects may be most suitable, but you don't want to build in a series of if-else statements to select a particular object.
- There might be new objects that you want to add to the possible list of processing options while the program is executing.
- There might be cases when more than one object will have to act on a request and you don't want to build knowledge of these interactions into the calling program.

Sample Code

The help system we just described is a little involved for a first example. Instead, let's start with a simple visual command interpreter program that illustrates how the chain works. This program displays the results of typed-in commands. This first case is constrained to keep the example code tractable, but we'll see that this Chain of Responsibility pattern is commonly used for parsers and even compilers.

In this example, the commands can be

- Image filenames
- General filenames

- Color names
- All other commands

In the first three cases, we can display a concrete result of the request. In the last case, we can only display the request text itself (see Figure 20-3).

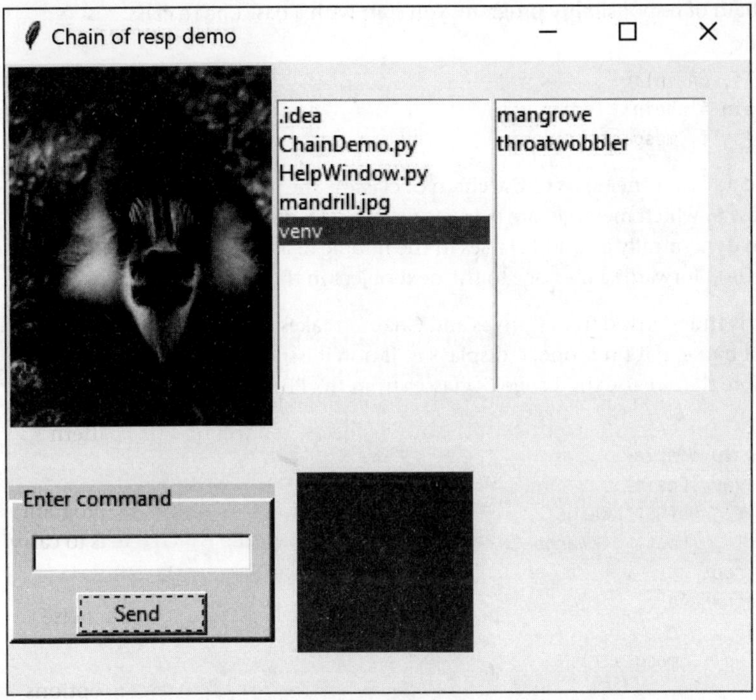

Figure 20-3 Chain of responsibility demo (Credit: Mandrill image, Jasni/Shutterstock)

Figure 20-3 illustrates these steps:

1. Type “Mandrill” to see a display of the image mandrill.jpg.
2. Type “venv” and that filename is highlighted in the center listbox.
3. Type “blue” and that color is displayed in the lower center panel.

Finally, if we type anything that is neither a filename nor a color, that text is displayed in the final listbox at the right (see Figure 20-4).

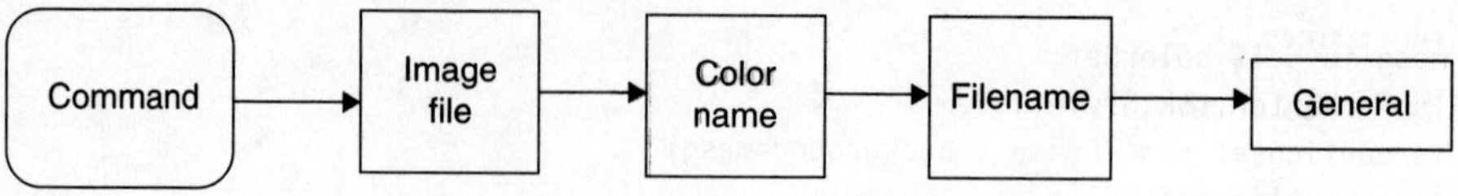

Figure 20-4 Flowchart for Chain of Responsibility demo

To write this simple chain of responsibility program, you start with a base `Chain` class:

```
class Chain():
    def addChain(self, chain):
        self.nextChain = chain
    def sendToChain(self, mesg:str): pass
```

The `addChain` method adds another class to the chain of classes. The `nextChain` property returns the current class to which messages are being forwarded. These two methods allow us to modify the chain dynamically and add classes in the middle of an existing chain. The `sendToChain` method forwards a message to the next object in the chain.

The `ImageChain` class is thus derived from Canvas and Chain. It takes the message and looks for .jpg files with that root name. If it finds one, it displays it. If not, it issues an exception and goes on down the chain. Note that we use the `ImageTk` classes from the PIL library to read the JPEG files.

```
# looks for jpg file to display
class ImageChain(Canvas, Chain):
    def __init__(self, root, **kwargs):
        super().__init__(root, **kwargs)
        self.root = root
        self.nextchain=None

    def sendToChain(self, mesg:str):
        try:
            img = Image.open(mesg + ".jpg")
            self.photoImg = ImageTk.PhotoImage(img)
            self.create_image(0, 0, anchor=NW,
                              image=self.photoImg)
        except:
            self.nextChain.sendToChain(mesg)
```

In a similar fashion, the `ColorFrame` class simply interprets the message as a color name and displays it if it can. The tkinter library supports eight named colors; we can put them in a set and check to see if the entered message is a member of that set.

```
self.colorSet = { "white", "black", "red", "green",
                  "blue", "cyan",
                  "yellow","magenta"}

def sendToChain(self, mesg:str):
    # if message is one of these colors
    # display it
```

```
    if mesg in self.colorSet:
        s = tkinter.ttk.Style()
        s.configure('new.TFrame', background=mesg)
        self.configure(style='new.TFrame')
    else:
        self.nextChain.sendToChain(mesg)
```

The Listboxes

Both the file list and the list of unrecognized commands are ordinary listboxes. The `ErrorList` class is the end of the chain, and any command that reaches it is simply displayed in the list. However, to allow for convenient extension, we could forward the message to other classes as well.

```
class ErrorList(Listbox, Chain):
    def __init__(self, root):
        super().__init__(root)

    def sendToChain(self, mesg: str):
        self.insert(END, mesg)
```

The `FileList` class is quite similar. The only differences are that it loads a list of the files in the current directory into the list when using the call to `os.dir` to get the file list.

```
class FileList(Listbox, Chain):
    def __init__(self, root):
        super().__init__(root)
        self.files = os.listdir('.')
        for f in self.files:
            self.insert(END, f)
```

Then the `sendToChain` method looks for a match in this list and highlights that filename if it finds it.

```
def sendToChain(self, mesg:str):
    index = 0
    found = False
    for f in self.files:
        if mesg == f.lower():
            self.selection_set(index)
            found = True
        index += 1
    if not found:
        self.nextChain.sendToChain(mesg)
```

Finally, we link these classes together in the constructor to form the Chain:

```
# construct the chain
    self.entrychain.addChain(self.imgchain)
    self.imgchain.addChain(self.flistbox)
    self.flistbox.addChain(self.cframe)
    self.cframe.addChain(self.errList)
```

The `EntryChain` class is the initial class that implements the Chain interface. It receives the button clicks and obtains the text from the text field. It passes the command on to the `ImageChain` class, the `FileList` class, the `ColorImage` class, and finally the `ErrorList` class.

Programming a Help System

As we noted at the beginning of this discussion, help systems provide good examples of how to use the Chain of Responsibility pattern. Now that we've outlined a way to write such chains, we'll consider a help system for a window with several controls. The program pops up a help dialog message when the user presses the F1 (help) key. The message depends on which control is selected when the F1 key is pressed.

If no control is selected, a general message pops up (see Figure 20-5).

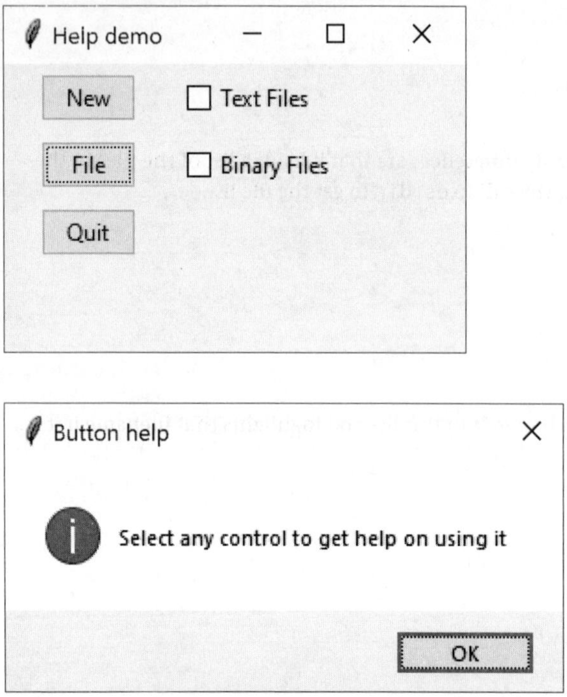

Figure 20-5 General help if no control is selected

To write this help system, we create the five widgets shown earlier, each as its own class. Here we derive `NewButton`, `Filebutton`, and `Quitbutton` from the same `DButton` class we have been using all along; you derive `TextCheck` and `BinCheck` from the `Checkbox` class we created in

Chapter 2, "Visual Programming in Python." All these classes also inherit from the Chain class, which is much the same as in the earlier example, except that we pass the actual event into the classes:

```
# Chain base class
class Chain():
    def addChain(self, chain):
        self._nextChain = chain

    def sendToChain(self, evt):pass
```

Therefore, we write the previous five classes and combine them into a chain, as follows:

```
# construct the Chain of Responsibility
self.newButton.addChain(self.fileButton)
self.fileButton.addChain(self.quitButton)
self.quitButton.addChain(self.textCheck)
self.textCheck.addChain(self.binCheck)
```

Receiving the Help Command

Now you need to assign keyboard listeners to look for the F1 keypress. At first, you might think we need six such listeners, for the three buttons, the two checkboxes, and the background window. However, we really only need one listener, for the Frame window itself. We simply check to see which component has the focus.

We add the <Key> listener in this way:

```
# connect the keystroke event monitor
self.frame.bind("<Key>", self.keyPress)
```

Note that we obtain the component that has the current focus using `self.focus_get()` and send that component along the chain to obtain the most specific help message the system provides. In each help object, there is a test for whether the object is the one described by that help message; either the message is displayed, or the object is forwarded to the next chain element. For the File button, the class looks like the following:

```
# the File button and help message
class FileButton(DButton, Chain):

    def __init__(self, root, **kwargs):
        super().__init__(root, text="File",
                         **kwargs)

    def sendToChain(self, evt):
        sel = self.focus_get()._name
        nm = self._name
```

```
        if sel.find(nm) >= 0:
            messagebox.showinfo("File button", "Opens an existing file")
        else:
            self.nextChain.sendToChain(evt)
```

The First Case

One important lesson of programming is learning to check for end cases. One of our end cases is the final element of the chain, the `BinCheck` class. However, the focus name is always matched and the `sendToChain` is never called beyond that.

But, the first case is problematic. Suppose that when the program starts, *none* of the objects have the focus. Then the following method fails:

```
sel = self.focus_get()._name
```

This is because the object that has the focus is the Frame, and it has no `_name` method. You can correct this problem in two ways: Either catch an exception for the unknown method or test the results of

```
sel = self.focus_get()
```

This returns the name of the Frame, which is just a single period. So, for the first element of the chain, we must test for this and then produce the general help message shown earlier.

```
s1 = str(self.focus_get()) #check name of focus
if len(s1)>1:              #if it is "." its the frame
    sel = self.focus_get()._name #get the real focus
    nm = self._name      #and the name of this class

    if sel.find(nm) >=0:  #sel will start with a "!"
        messagebox.showinfo("New button",
                            "Creates a new file")
    else:
        self.nextChain.sendToChain(evt)
else:
    # if no object has focus display general message
    messagebox.showinfo("Button help",
            "Select any control using the Tab key\n"
             + "to get help on using it" )
```

A Chain or a Tree?

Of course, a Chain of Responsibility pattern does not have to be linear. The *Smalltalk Companion* suggests that it is more generally a tree structure with a number of specific entry points, all pointing upward to the most general node (see Figure 20-6).

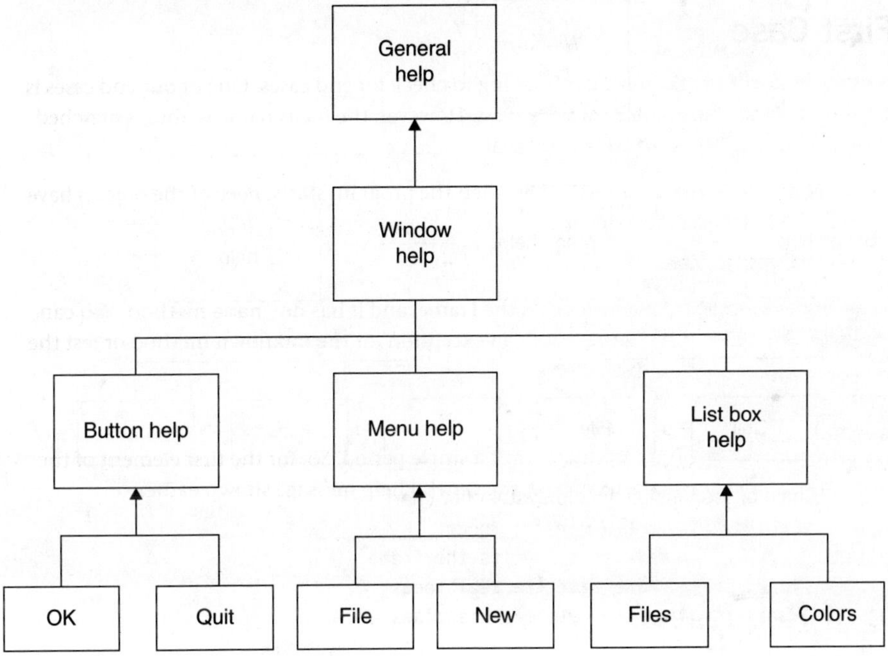

Figure 20-6 A tree-structured help system

However, this sort of structure seems to imply that each button, or its handler, knows where to enter the chain. This can complicate the design in some cases and may preclude the need for the chain at all.

Another way to handle a treelike structure is to have a single entry point that branches to the specific button, menu, or other widget types and then "unbranches" to more general help cases. There is little reason for that complexity: you could align the classes into a single chain, starting at the bottom and then going left to right and up a row at a time until the entire system is traversed (see Figure 20-7).

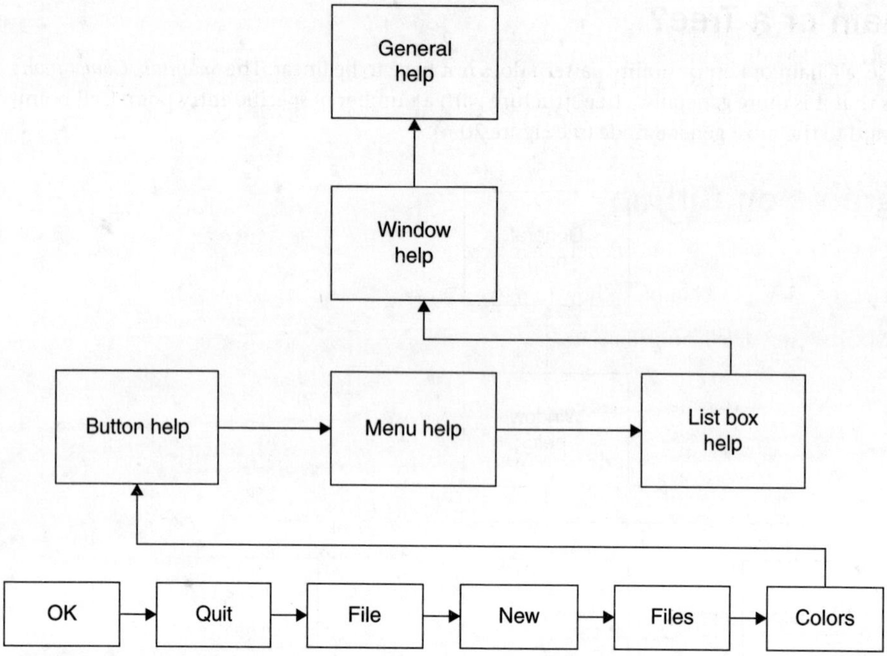

Figure 20-7 Chain of responsibility help system flowchart

Kinds of Requests

The request or message passed along the Chain of Responsibility may well be a great deal more complicated than just the string or event that we conveniently used on these examples. For instance, the information might include various data types or a complete object with a number of methods. Because various classes along the chain may use different properties of such a request object, you might end up designing an abstract `Request` type and any number of derived classes with additional methods.

Consequences of the Chain of Responsibility

Consequences of the Chain of Responsibility pattern include the following:

1. As with several other patterns, the main purpose of this pattern is to reduce coupling between objects. An object only needs to know how to forward the request to other objects.
2. Each object in the chain is self-contained. It knows nothing of the others and only needs to decide whether it can satisfy the request. This makes writing each one very easy, and constructing the chain very easy.

3. You can decide whether the final object in the chain handles all requests it receives in some default fashion or just discards them. However, you do need to know which object is last in the chain for this to be effective.

Programs on GitHub

- ChainDemo.py: Example of chain using colors and a mandrill
- HelpWindow.py: Example of how to make a help window
- Mandrill.jpg: The mandrill itself

21

The Command Pattern

The Chain of Responsibility pattern forwards requests along a chain of classes, but the Command pattern forwards a request only to a specific object. It encloses a request for a specific action inside an object and gives it a known public interface. It lets you give the client the ability to make requests without knowing anything about the actual action that will be performed, and it allows you to change that action without affecting the client program in any way.

We have, of course, seen this command interface already, as we have been using our DButton class, which includes a comd method that is called when you click the button.

When to Use the Command Pattern

When you build a Python user interface, you provide menu items, buttons, checkboxes, and so forth to allow the user to tell the program what to do. When a user selects one of these controls, the program calls a specified function. Suppose that you build a very simple program that allows you to select the menu items File | Open and File | Exit, and click a button marked Red that turns the background of the window red. Figure 21-1 illustrates this program.

Figure 21-1: Command button turns the background red

21

The Command Pattern

The Chain of Responsibility pattern forwards requests along a chain of classes, but the Command pattern forwards a request only to a specific object. It encloses a request for a specific action inside an object and gives it a known public interface. It lets you give the client the ability to make requests without knowing anything about the actual action that will be performed. It also allows you to change that action without affecting the client program in any way.

We have, of course, seen this command interface already, as we have been using in our `DButton` class, which includes a `comd` method that is called when you click the button.

When to Use the Command Pattern

When you build a Python user interface, you provide menu items, buttons, checkboxes, and so forth to allow the user to tell the program what to do. When a user selects one of these controls, the program calls a specified function. Suppose that you build a very simple program that enables you to select the menu items File | Open and File | Exit, and then click a button marked Red that turns the background of the window red. Figure 21-1 illustrates this program.

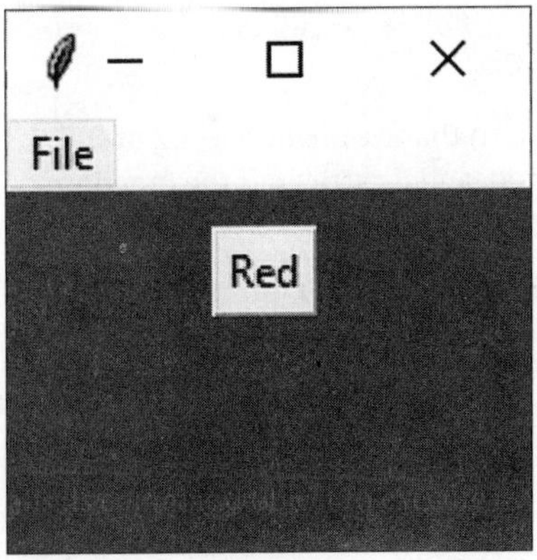

Figure 21-1 Command button turns the background red

Command Objects

One way to ensure that every object receives its own commands directly is to use the Command pattern and create individual `Command` objects. A `Command` object always has a `comd()` method (or an `execute()` method) that is called when an action occurs on that object. Most simply, a `Command` object implements at least the following interface:

```
# Command interface
class Command():
    def comd(self):pass
```

The objective of using this interface is to simplify access to the actions the button calls when clicked. In this book, we have used the `comd` method for this, but others have suggested calling it an `execute` method. We'll use both, as you will see shortly.

If we can call an `execute` or `comd` method for each object that carries out a desired action, we keep the knowledge of what to do inside the object where it belongs instead of having another part of the program make these decisions.

One important purpose of the Command pattern is to keep the program and user interface objects completely separate from the actions they initiate. In other words, these program objects should be separate from each other and should not have to know how other objects work. The user interface receives a command and tells a `Command` object to carry out whatever duties it has been instructed to do.

The UI does not—and should not—need to know what tasks will be executed. This decouples the UI class from the execution of specific commands, making it possible to modify or completely change the action code without changing the classes containing the user interface.

The `Command` object can also be used when you need to tell the program to execute the command when the resources are available rather than executing immediately. In such cases, you are *queuing* commands to be executed later. Finally, you can use `Command` objects to remember operations so that you can support `Undo` requests.

A Keyboard Example

In the previous example, we have a menu item and a push button that we might select. But the user interface is the same for all cases: You call the `comd` method, and it carries out the function you want, such as changing a color or opening a file.

Although this is common in programs with GUIs such as tkinter, it really isn't limited to graphical objects. For example, you could start up a console-based program, select an object by pressing a key, and have it call a `comd` method in the same way.

One example in which this might be helpful is if you want to launch a command using a single character. You are probably familiar with the Python `input` method to get characters from the console; you can also use the keyboard library to receive and act on single characters in much the same way. You can easily install this library with `pip`:

```
pip install keyboard
```

Then you can use the library as described in its documentation. The keyboard library is pretty extensive, but we're only going to use a few of its features.

You start, of course, by importing the library:

```
import keyboard
```

The main program for this keyboard command system is:

```
# program starts here
kmod = KeyModerator()    # set up command classes

# wait for key presses
keyboard.on_press(callback=kmod.getKey, suppress=True)

#Wait for keys but relinquish time when not used
print("Enter commands: r, b, c or q")
while True:
    time.sleep(1000)
```

The `KeyModerator` class received all the key events in its `getkey` method. Because this program is monitoring the keyboard continuously, we have to give up time to other processes that need the keyboard. Thus, we create the `time.sleep(n)` method, where *n* is some number of seconds. If you don't do this, other windows will access the keyboard sporadically and slowly.

As you can see from the prompt text, the four commands are `r`, `b`, `c`, and `q`. All they simply do is

- Turn the text red
- Turn the text blue
- Compute the elapsed time since you started
- Exit the program

The first two `Command` objects here are the red text and the elapsed time computation. Note that the operations all take place in their `comd` methods.

```
# A series of Command objects
class Ckey(Command):
    def __init__(self):
        self.start =time.time() # start timer
    def comd(self):
        self.end = time.time()
        elapsed = self.end - self.start #compute elapsed time
        print('elapsed: ',elapsed)
        self.start = self.end # new starting time

# prints green on red message
class Rkey(Command)    :
    def comd(self):
        cprint('Hello, World!', 'green', 'on_red')
```

The code for printing text in color is contained in the termcolor library, which you also can install with `pip`. That's where the earlier `cprint` method comes from. We introduced this library just to keep the overall example simple.

The other two classes are shown here:

```
# print blue on yellow message
class Bkey(Command):
    def comd(self):
        cprint('Feeling blue', 'blue','on_yellow')

# exits from the program
class Qkey(Command):
    def comd(self):
        print('exiting')
        os._exit(0)
```

If you are using the keyboard module, you *must* use the `os._exit` command to end the program.

Calling the Command Objects

The important point is that all these little classes are `Command` objects and all are called using the same `comd` method. So we can set up the `KeyModerator` class to create those instances and make a dictionary of which one to call:

```
class KeyModerator():
    def __init__(self):
        # create instances of each command class
        self.rkey = Rkey()
        self.bkey = Bkey()
        self.qkey = Qkey()
        self.ckey = Ckey()
        self.funcs = {'r': self.rkey,
                      'b': self.bkey,
                      'q': self.qkey,
                      'c': self.ckey }
```

And the actual `getkey` method does all the work, using that dictionary:

```
def getKey(self, keyval):

    # call any command object using the dictionary
    # to fetch the right function
    func = self.funcs.get(keyval.name)
    func.comd()
```

The method looks up the class in the dictionary and calls its command object to execute it. The final program output looks like Figure 21-2.

Figure 21-2 Screen shot of keyboard output

As you can see, the Command pattern is useful even without a GUI. You can use it whenever there are several classes to choose from that have analogous functions in them.

Building Command Objects

There are several ways to go about building Command objects for a program like the one in Figure 21-1, and each has some advantages. We'll start with the simplest one: deriving new classes from the `MenuItem` and `Button` classes and implementing the Command interface in each. Here are examples of extensions to the `Button` and `Menu` classes for our simple program:

```
# Button creates a red background
class RedButton(DButton):
    def __init__(self, root):
        super().__init__(root, text="Red")
        self.root = root
    def comd(self):
        self.root.configure(bg='red')

   //-----------------------------------------
# exit menu
class Exititem(Command):
    def __init__(self, fmenu):
        fmenu.add_command(label="Exit",
                          command=self.comd)
    def comd(self):
        sys.exit()
```

This certainly lets us simplify the calls made in the `comd` method, but it requires that we create and instantiate a new class for each action we want to execute.

```
# create menu bar
menubar = Menu(root)
root.config(menu=menubar)

# create top File menu
filemenu = Menu(menubar, tearoff=0)
menubar.add_cascade(label="File", menu=filemenu)
```

```
# add three menu items
fileitem = Openitem(filemenu)
svmn = SaveMenu(filemenu)
exititem = Exititem(filemenu)

rbutton = RedButton(root)          # red button
```

Note that the menu and button command classes can then be external to the main class and can even be stored in separate files, if you prefer.

The Command Pattern

Now, while it is advantageous to encapsulate the action in a `Command` object, binding that object into the element that causes the action (such as the menu item or button) is not exactly what the Command pattern is about.

Instead, the `Command` object should be separate from the invoking client so you can vary the invoking program and the details of the command action separately. Rather than having the command be part of the menu or button, we make the menu and button classes *containers* for a `Command` object that exists separately.

This simple interface simply says that there is a way to put a `Command` object into the invoking object and a way to obtain that object to call its `Execute` method.

Consequences of the Command Pattern

The main disadvantage of the Command pattern is a proliferation of little classes that clutter up either the main class (if they are inner classes) or the program namespace (if they are outer classes).

Even if we put all of our `comd` events in a single basket, we usually call little internal methods to carry out the actual function. It turns out that these internal methods are just about as long as our little inner classes, so there is frequently little difference in complexity between inner and outer class approaches.

Providing the Undo Function

The most powerful reason for using Command design patterns is that they provide a convenient way to store and execute an `Undo` function. Each command object can remember what it just did and restore that state when requested to do so if the computational and memory requirements are not too overwhelming. At the top level, we simply redefine the Command interface to have two methods:

```
# Command object interface
class Command():
    def execute(self):pass
    def undo(self):pass
```

Then we have to design each command object to keep a record of what it last did so that it can undo it. This can be a little more complicated than it first appears because having a number of interleaved Commands being executed and then undone can lead to some hysteresis. In addition, each command needs to store enough information about each execution of the command that it can know what specifically has to be undone.

The problem of undoing commands is actually a multipart problem. First, you must keep a list of the commands that have been executed. Second, each command has to keep a list of its executions. To illustrate how we use the Command pattern to carry out undo operations, let's consider a program that draws successive red or blue lines on the screen using two buttons to draw a new instance of each line (see Figure 21-3). You can undo the last line you drew with the Undo button.

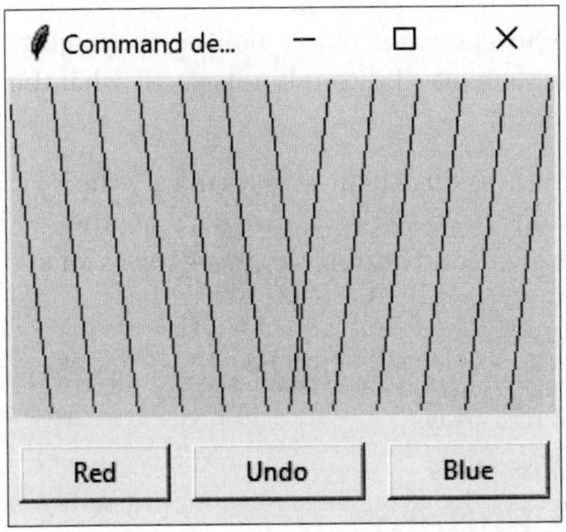

Figure 21-3 Red and blue lines displayed

If you click Undo several times, you expect the last several lines to disappear, no matter what order the buttons were clicked in (see Figure 21-4).

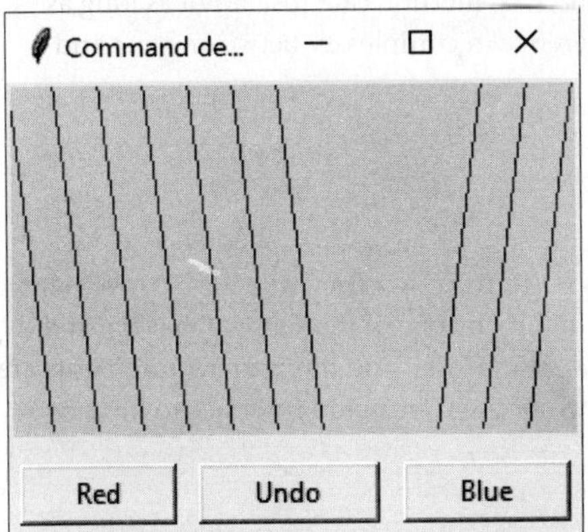

Figure 21-4 Undoing some of the later lines

In our design, we keep a List of the Commands executed as a stack, where you append to the end and remove from the end with the pop method. The `execute` method of each Command draws that single line on the screen.

Here is the simple Command object:

```
# Button command,
class ButtonCommand(Command):
    def __init__(self, button, x1, y1,
                 x2, y2, color):
        self.canvas = button.getCanvas()
        self.button = button
        self.x1, self.x2 = x1, x2
        self.y1, self.y2 = y1, y2
        self.color = color

    def execute(self):
        self.canvas.create_line(self.x1,
                self.y1, self.x2, self.y2,
                        fill=self.color)
    def undo(self):
        self.button.undo()
```

The `CommandStack` is just an array of these commands. Each time you click on Red or Blue, an instance of `ButtonCommand` is created and appended to this array.

```
# stack of commands generated by the Red and Blue buttons
class CommandStack():
    def __init__(self, canvas):
        self.commands = []  # stack of commands
        self.canvas = canvas
    # add line and draw it
    def addDraw(self, command):
        self.commands.append(command)
        command.execute()   # draw the line

    # redraw all the lines
    def redraw(self):
        # remove lines
        self.canvas.delete('all')

        for comd in self.commands:
            # redraw remaining
            comd.execute()


    # pops last command off the stack
    # and returns command to call its Undo
    def undo(self):
        comd=None
```

```
        if len(self.commands) > 0:
            comd = self.commands.pop()
            self.redraw()
        return comd
```

Creating the Red and Blue Buttons

Clicking either button creates a `ButtonCommand` object and pushes it onto the command stack. The Red button then advances *x* by 20 pixels. The corresponding Blue button moves *x* to the left by 20 pixels.

```
# draws red diagonal line and advances x coord
class RedButton(DButton):
    def __init__(self, root,
                 canvas:Canvas,stack:CommandStack):
        super().__init__(root, text="Red")
        self.root = root
        self.canvas=canvas
        self.stack = stack
        self.x = self.y = 0

# create a button command on the stack and draw it
    def execute(self):
        bcomd = ButtonCommand(self,
                    self.x,self.y,
                    self.x+20,self.y+150,'red')
        self.x += 20                # move red to right
        self.stack.addDraw(bcomd) # push it and draw

    # returns canvas
    def getCanvas(self):
        return self.canvas

    # resets x coord back one line
    def undo(self):
        self.x -= 20
```

Undoing the Lines

The Undo button simply removes the last command from the list and then redraws the remaining lines. It also calls the Button's undo method to move *x* back 20 pixels so that the line coordinate is ready for the next drawing command.

```
# Undo button pops one command off the stack
# and calls its Undo
class UndoButton(DButton):
    def __init__(self, root, stack:CommandStack):
        super().__init__(root, text="Undo")
        self.root = root
        self.stack = stack
```

```
    def execute(self):
        comd = self.stack.undo() # remove last comd
        if comd != None:
            comd.undo()      # undo x coordinate
```

Summary

We have seen the Command interface and used it in the DButton derived class and in the derived Menu class in Chapter 2, "Visual Programming in Python." This makes all of these objects conform to the Command interface.

However, the Command pattern we introduced here introduces Command objects that actually do the work for the buttons and menus and, with the help of the CommandStack, provide a simple way to undo commands.

References

1. https://github.com/boppreh/keyboard#keyboard
2. https://pypi.org/project/termcolor/

Programs on GitHub

- keyboardCommand.py: Commands using the keyboard
- RedCommand.py: Menu and Red button
- UndoDemo.py: Draws and undoes red and blue lines

22

The Interpreter Pattern

Some programs benefit from having a language to describe operations they can perform. The Interpreter pattern generally describes defining a grammar for that language and using that grammar to interpret statements in that language.

When to Use an Interpreter

When a program presents a number of different but somewhat similar cases that it can deal with, it can be advantageous to use a simple language to describe these cases and then have the program interpret that language. Such cases can be as simple as the sort of Macro language recording facilities a number of office suite programs provide or as complex as VBA in Microsoft Office.

One of the problems we must deal with is how to recognize when a language can be helpful. The Macro language recorder simply records menu and keystroke operations for later playback and just barely qualifies as a language; it may not actually have a written form or grammar. Languages such as VBA, on the other hand, are quite complex and are frequently beyond the capabilities of the individual application developer. Furthermore, embedding commercial languages such as VBA may require substantial licensing fees, which make them less attractive to all but the largest developers.

Where the Pattern Can Be Helpful

Recognizing cases where an interpreter can be helpful is much of the problem, and programmers without formal language/compiler training frequently overlook this approach. There are not large numbers of such cases, but there are three general places where languages are applicable:

1. When you need a command interpreter to parse user commands. The user can type queries of various kinds and obtain a variety of answers.
2. When the program must parse an algebraic string. This case is fairly obvious. The program is asked to carry out its operations based on a computation where the user enters an equation of some sort. This frequently occurs in mathematical-graphics programs, where

the program renders a curve or surface based on any equation it can evaluate. Programs such as Mathematica and graph-drawing packages embedded in Python work that way.

3. When the program must produce varying kinds of output. This case is a little less obvious but far more useful. Consider a program that can display columns of data in any order and sort them in various ways. These programs are frequently referred to as Report Generators. Although the underlying data might be stored in a relational database, the user interface to the report program is usually much simpler than the SQL language you saw in Chapter 16, "The Façade Pattern." In fact, in some cases, the simple report language may be interpreted by the report program and translated into SQL.

A Simple Report Example

Let's consider a simplified report generator that can operate on five columns of data in a table and return various reports on these data. Suppose you have the following sort of results from the familiar swimming competition data:

```
Amanda McCarthy        12  WCA     29.28
Jamie Falco            12  HNHS    29.80
Meaghan O'Donnell      12  EDST    30.00
Greer Gibbs            12  CDEV    30.04
Rhiannon Jeffrey       11  WYW     30.04
Sophie Connolly        12  WAC     30.05
Dana Helyer            12  ARAC    30.18
```

where the five columns are `frname`, `lname`, `age`, `club`, and `time`. If we consider the complete race results of 51 swimmers, we realize that it might be convenient to sort these results by club, last name, or age. Since there are a number of useful reports we could produce from these data in which the order of the columns changes as well as the sorting; using a language is one useful way to handle these reports.

Here we define a very simple nonrecursive grammar of the sort:

```
Print lname frname club time Sortby time Thenby club
```

For the purposes of this example, we define the three verbs shown earlier here:

```
Print
Sortby
Thenby
```

These are the five column names listed earlier:

```
Frname
Lname
Age
Club
Time
```

For convenience, we'll assume that the language is not case sensitive. Also note that the simple grammar of this language is punctuation free and amounts in brief to

Print var[var] [sortby var [thenby var]]

Finally, there is only one main verb used, and although each statement is a declaration, there is no assignment statement or computational ability in this grammar.

Interpreting the Language

Interpreting the language takes place in three steps:

1. Parsing the language symbols into tokens
2. Reducing the tokens into actions
3. Executing the actions

We parse this simple language by separating the string into tokens using the string's `split` method, then creating `Variable` and `Verb` objects containing them, and placing them onto a stack.

After parsing, your stack might look like this:

Type	**Token**	
Var	Club	<-top of stack
Verb	Thenby	
Var	Time	
Verb	Sortby	
Var	Time	
Var	Club	
Var	Frname	
verb	Lname	

However, we quickly realize that the verb `Thenby` has no real meaning other than clarification, and it is more likely that we'd parse the tokens and skip the `Thenby` word altogether. The initial stack, then, looks like this:

```
Club
Time
Sortby
Time
Club
Frname
Lname
Print
```

We can then reduce the stack by copying variable names into an array in the next variable. It goes down a step at a time like this:

Time [Club] Sortby Time Club Frname Lname Print	Sortby [Time, Club] Time Club Frname Lname Print

Then the SortBy verb is executed on the two arguments, Time and Club, and removed from the stack. The four variables are reduced and copied in a similar way.

Time Club Frname Lname Print	Club [Time] Frname Lname Print	Frname[Club, Time] Lname Print	Lname[Frname, Club, Time] Print

Finally, the verb Print contains all the arguments:

```
Print [Lname, Frname, Club, Time]
```

When it is executed, it generates the string for each field and adds them into a List that is passed to the Interp command to display in the Listbox.

How Parsing Works

Parsing consists of separating the string to be interpreted into single-word tokens and then creating Variable and Verb objects from them. We can use the Python set representation to see whether a token is a member of the legal variables or verbs.

```
class Parser():
    verbs= {"print", "sortby"}
    variables = {"lname", "frname", "club",
                 "time", "age"}
```

Then you split the command line into tokens:

```
tokens = commands.split()
```

Then we create Verb or Variable objects using the set in operator to decide which category each token belongs to. Then we add (push) each object onto the stack.

```
for tok in tokens:
    if tok.lower() in Parser.verbs:     # it's a Verb
        self.stack.append(Verb(tok,
                          self.swmrs, bldr))
```

```
    # or a Variable
     if tok.lower() in Parser.variables:
         self.stack.append(Variable(tok))
```

The Variable and Verb classes are quite similar. Each contains a List of the tokens that accumulate as the objects are combined.

```
class Variable():
    def __init__(self,varname):
        self.varlist = []
        self.varlist.append(varname)

# appends all the variables from previous token
    def append(self,var:Variable):
        vlist = var.getList()
        for v in vlist:
            self.varlist.append(v)

    def getList(self):
        return self.varlist
```

The Verb class is quite similar, except that it also contains a comd method, making a Command object as well. This command is executed when all the tokens are added to that verb and it then acts on them, performing either a Sort or a Print command. This is quite straightforward because there are only two possible verbs:

```
def comd(self):
    # Sort by one field
    if self.getName().lower() == "sortby":
        sorter = Sorter(self.swmrs)
        self.varlist.pop(0)    #remove "sortby"
        for v in self.varlist: # multiple sorts here
            sorter.sortby(v)

    # generate a List of lines to display
    if self.varname.lower() == "print":
        self.varlist.pop(0)  # remove "print"
        pres = Printres( self.varlist, self.bldr)
        plist = pres.create(self.swmrs)
```

Sorting Using attrgetter()

The problem here is that the keyword variables are field names within the Swimmer class: frname, age, time, and so forth. But how do we get the value of these fields for each swimmer?

Python provides the attrgetter operator for that purpose. Suppose we want to know the value of a field, but we don't know at coding time which one it will be. We can use this operator to a create a function to fetch the contents of any field, assuming that it isn't made semiprivate with a leading underscore.

```
def sortby(self, vname):
    # bubble sort on one field
    f = attrgetter(vname) #function to access field
```

Then the function `f` returns the contents of the field that has that name. So if we write

```
f = attrgetter("frname")
```

then the following statement returns the contents of `sw.frname`:

```
name = f(sw)
```

We use that in the bubble sort here:

```
f = attrgetter(vname) #function to access field
for i in range(0, len(self.swmrs)):
    for j in range(i, len(self.swmrs)):
        if f(self.swmrs[i]) > f(self.swmrs[j]):
            temp=self.swmrs[i]
            self.swmrs[i] =self.swmrs[j]
            self.swmrs[j] = temp
```

The Print Verb

We also use the `attrgetter` operator in executing the `Print` verb. Here we have to generate an array of these functions: one for each variable to be printed.

```
# create list of functions to fetch from Swimmer
for v in varlist:
    self.functions.append(attrgetter(v))
```

and then we use that array to create the results string for each Swimmer.

```
for sw in swmrs:
    sline=""
    for f in self.functions:  # go through functions
        sline += str(f(sw)) +"   " # and swimmers
    self.printList.append(sline)   # save in List
```

The Console Interface

You can run this whole program from the command line because you have to type in the string for it to interpret. The calling code is simply the `Builder` class.

```
# creates the needed classes and reads in the file
class Builder():
    def __init__(self):
        self.plist = []
```

```
def setPlist(self, pl):
    self.plist = pl
def getPlist(self):
    return self.plist
def build(self):
    swmrs = Swimmers("100free.txt")

    commands = ""
    while commands != 'q':
        commands = input('Enter command: \n')
        interp = Interp(self)
        interp.comd(commands)
        # result is returned in self.plist
                # print it out
        for p in self.plist:
            print(p)
```

You can see a little of the output here:

```
Enter command:
Print lname frname club time Sortby time Thenby club
Slater   Emily   BRS   57.26
Amendola   Alesha   BRS   57.34
McLellan   Ashley   CDEV   56.85
Fiore   Stephanie   CDEV   58.14
Schwartz   Robyn   CDEV   59.02
Gibbs   Greer   CDEV   59.04
```

The User Interface

Alternatively, you can make a little entry field and listbox-based user interface. It does the same thing, except that it fills the listbox instead of printing the results.

You can alter the command string and view the results right away by again pressing the Interp button (see Figure 22-1).

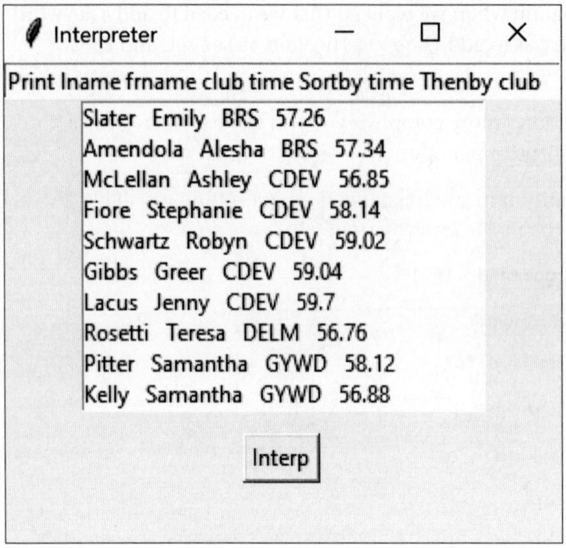

Figure 22-1 Interpreter demo

Consequences of the Interpreter Pattern

Whenever you introduce an interpreter into a program, you need to provide a simple way for the program user to enter commands in that language. It can be as simple as the Macro record button, or it can be an editable text field such as the one in the previous program.

However, introducing a language and its accompanying grammar also requires fairly extensive error checking for misspelled terms or misplaced grammatical elements. This can easily consume a great deal of programming effort unless some template code is available for implementing this checking. Furthermore, effective methods for notifying the users of these errors are not easy to design and implement.

In the Interpreter example, the only error handling is that keywords that are not recognized are not converted to Variables and pushed onto the stack. Thus, nothing happens because the resulting stack sequence probably cannot be parsed successfully—or, if it can, the item represented by the misspelled keyword will not be included.

You can also consider generating a language automatically from a user interface of radio and command buttons and list boxes. While it may seem that having such an interface reduces the necessity for a language at all, the same requirements of sequence and computation still apply. When you need a way to specify the order of sequential operations, a language is a good way to do so, even if the language is generated from the user interface.

The Interpreter pattern offers the advantage of extending or revising the grammar fairly easily after you have built the general parsing and reduction tools. You can also add new verbs or variables quite easily once the foundation is constructed.

In fact we had completely tested this program when we realized that we needed to add a keyword for Age. The only change we had to make was to add "age" to the Variables set, and the program worked perfectly.

Finally, as the syntax of the grammar becomes more complex, you run the risk of creating a hard-to-maintain program. That is more or less the upper bound of using Interpreters.

Although interpreters are not all that common in solving general programming problems, the Iterator pattern we look at next is one of the most common ones you'll be using.

Programs on GitHub

In all these samples, be sure to include the data file (100free.txt) in the same folder as the Python file. Also make sure the files are part of the project in Vscode or PyCharm.

- InterpretConsole.py: The console version
- Interpreter.py: The complete program
- 100free.txt: The data set of swimmers

The Iterator Pattern

The Iterator pattern is one of the simplest and most frequently used of the design patterns. It enables you to move through a list or collection of data using a standard interface without having to know the details of the internal representation of that data. You can also define special iterators that perform some special procedure and return only specified elements of the data collection.

Why We Use Iterators

The Iterator provides a defined way to move through a set of data elements without exposing what is taking place inside the class. Because the Iterator is an interface, you can implement it in any way that is convenient for the data you are returning. Design Patterns suggests that a suitable interface for an Iterator might look like this:

```
class Iterator:
    def first(): pass
    def next(): pass
    def isDone(): pass
    def currentItem(): pass
```

You can move to the top of the list, move through the list, find out if there are more elements, and find the current list item. This interface is easy to implement and has certain advantages, but the Iterator of choice in Python is the simple two-method iterator:

```
def iter(): pass
def next(): pass
```

Not having a method to move to the top of a list might seem restrictive at first, but this not a very serious problem in Python because it is customary to obtain a new instance of the Iterator each time you want to move through a list.

Iterators in Python

We have already seen iterators in Python throughout this book. The for loop is always an iterator under the covers, used here to go through a List

23

The Iterator Pattern

The Iterator pattern is one of the simplest and most frequently used of the design patterns. It enables you to move through a list or collection of data using a standard interface without having to know the details of the internal representations of that data. In addition, you can define special iterators that perform some special processing and return only specified elements of the data collection.

Why We Use Iterators

The Iterator provides a defined way to move through a set of data elements without exposing what is taking place inside the class. Because the Iterator is an interface, you can implement it in any way that is convenient for the data you are returning. *Design Patterns* suggests that a suitable interface for an Iterator might look like this:

```
class Iterator
    def first(): pass
    def next(): pass
    def isDone(): pass
    def currentItem(): pass
```

You can move to the top of the list, move through the list, find out if there are more elements, and find the current list item. This interface is easy to implement and has certain advantages, but the Iterator of choice in Python is the simple two-method iterator:

```
def iter(): pass
def next(): pass
```

Not having a method to move to the top of a list might seem restrictive at first, but it is not a serious problem in Python because it is customary to obtain a new instance of the iterator each time you want to move through a list.

Iterators in Python

We have already seen iterators in Python throughout this book. The `for` loop is always an iterator under the covers, used here to go through a List.

```
# Iterate through an array
people = ["Fred", "Mary", "Sam"]
for p in people:
    print (p)
```

Of course, this produces the following result:

```
Fred
Mary
Sam
```

You can also iterate through sets, tuples, dictionaries, and even files. All of these are called *iterable containers* and you can get an iterator from them, as the `for` keyword does above.

A Fibonacci Iterator

Suppose that you want to create a class you can iterate through that isn't one of these built-in iterable types. To make an iterable class, it must have the methods:

```
__init__()
__iter__()
__next__()
```

Because these methods are surrounded by double underscores, they are sometimes referred to as *dunder methods*.

The `__init__()` is optional, but the `__iter__()` *must* return an iterator, which is almost always `self`. You terminate the iterator by raising the `StopIteration` exception. In this case, this happens when the return value exceeds 1000. This is, of course, adjustable in the `__init__` method if you like.

```
class FiboIter():
    def __init__(self):
        self.current = 0     # initialize variables
        self.prev = 1
        self.secondLast = 0

    def __iter__(self):
        return self              # must return iterator

    # each iteration computes a new value
    def __next__(self):
        if self.current < 1000:   # stops at 1000
            # copy n-1st
            self.secondLast = self.prev
            self.prev = self.current # copy nth to p

            # compute next x as sum of previous 2
            self.current = self.prev
                     + self.secondLast
            return self.current
        else:
            raise StopIteration
```

To create and call the iterator, you create an instance and call it until it reaches past 1000.

```
fbi = FiboIter()    # create iterator

# print out values until 1000 is exceeded
for val in fbi:
    print(val, end=" ")
print("\n")
```

Getting the Iterator

You can get the actual iterator itself using the `iter()` function and then use `next()` to get each successive value. This is useful if you can't use `for` to run the iteration for you.

```
val = 0
fbi = FiboIter()
fbit = iter(fbi)

while val<1000:
    val = next(fbit)
    print(val, end=" ")
```

In both cases, the program prints the following:

```
1 1 2 3 5 8 13 21 34 55 89 144 233 377 610 987 1597
```

You can also use the iterator to pull out elements of an array to store elsewhere:

```
# iterate to get elements and store them
person = ["Fred", "Smith", "80901210"]
pIter = iter(person)

frname = next(pIter)
lname = next(pIter)
serial = next(pIter)
print(frname, lname, serial)
```

Filtered Iterators

A *filtered* iterator returns only values that meet some particular criteria. For example, you could return the data ordered in some particular way or return only those objects that match a particular criterion.

Suppose, for example, that we want to enumerate only those swimmers who belonged to a certain club. This is very simple: We just check for club membership before returning each name. We create an iterator whose `__init__` method takes in the List of swimmers and the club name to filter for.

```
# Filtered iterator returns only members of one club
class SwmrIter():
    def __init__(self, club, swmrs):
        self.club = club
        self.swmrs = swmrs
```

```
    def __iter__(self):
        self.index = 0
        return self

    # Next operation returns next swimmer in list
    # that is a club member
    # Terminated with StopIteration when the index
    # pass the end of the list
    def __next__(self):
        found = False
        while not found and \
                self.index < len(self.swmrs):
            swm = self.swmrs[self.index]
            if swm.club == self.club:
                found = True
                self.index += 1
                return swm.getName()
            else:
                self.index += 1
                found = False
        raise StopIteration
```

All the work is done in the `next()` method, which iterates through the collection for another swimmer who belongs to the club specified in the constructor and either saves that swimmer in the swm variable or sets it to `null`. Then `next()` returns either `true` or `false`. When the code runs out of swimmers in the list, it falls through to raise the `StopIteration` exception.

Figure 23-1 shows a simple program that displays all the swimmers on the left side. It fills a combo box with a list of the clubs and then allows the user to select a club; the program fills the list box on the right with the swimmers who belong to a single club.

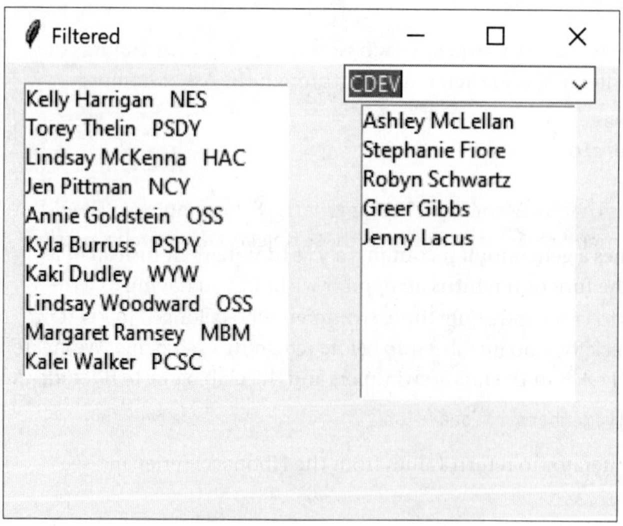

Figure 23-1 Filtered iterator display

It is interesting that we don't need a list of all the clubs; We can just create one by adding the club names to an empty set. This set can then be copied to a list and sorted.

```
# creates a set of club names
# using the set to eliminate duplicates
self.clubs = set()
for sw in self.swimmers:
    self.clubs.add(sw.club)
```

The Iterator Generator

These approaches work perfectly well, but you also can use a Python generator to create the iterator for you. Although *generator* describes the approach, the important new concept is the `yield` keyword. Generators are functions that return iterators you can use to go through a sequence of values.

One of the motivations for Python adding generators is to provide a way to iterate through very large data sets that may not fit in available memory. The PEP-255 document describes this in detail.

The main difference in creating a generator function is that, instead of returning data with a `return` statement, it returns the data using `yield`. When you use `yield`, the function and all its internal variables remain alive, and the function resumes after returning that value using `yield`.

Let's consider a really simple example that makes this clear. Suppose we need to write a function to square a series of sequential numbers.

```
def sqrit(max=0):
    n = 0
    while n < max:
        yield n*n          # return each result
        n += 1             # code resumes here
```

This function starts at zero and returns successive squares each time it is called. The calling code calls this function once and gets the iterator, and then it iterates through the list of numbers:

```
# call sqrit and iterate up to max
sq = sqrit(10)  # returns an iterator
for s in sq:
    print(s)
```

The ordinary function `sqrit` becomes a generator if it contains a `yield` statement instead of a `return` statement. As you can see, the function returns an iterator without you having to write any annoying dunder method code.

A Fibonacci Iterator

Let's write a slightly more advanced iterator to return values from the Fibonacci series and see how much simpler this one is.

Here is our generator function:

```
def fibo(max=0):
    current, prev = 0, 1      # initialize variables

    while current < max:      # but stops at max
        secondLast, prev = prev, current

        # compute next x as sum of previous 2
        current = prev + secondLast
        yield current         # returns next value in series
```

And the calling routine is pretty much the same:

```
fb = fibo(100)
for f in fb:
    print(f, end=', ')
```

The result is as you expect:

```
1, 1, 2, 3, 5, 8, 13, 21, 34, 55, 89, 144,
```

Generators in Classes

Of course, there is no reason why you can't create a class that contains a generator. This approach gets around the awkwardness of stray functions that don't seem to belong to anyone. A method inside a class becomes an iterator generator if that method contains a `yield` statement.

You can also create rather complex iterators using the Python itertools package. Although all these iterators can be written directly in Python, the itertools library gives you significantly faster execution.

Consequences of the Iterator Pattern

The consequences of the iterator pattern include the following:

1. *Data modification.* The most significant question iterators may raise is the question of iterating through data while it is being changed. If your code is wide ranging and only occasionally moves to the next element, it is possible that an element might be added or deleted from the underlying collection while you are moving through it. It is also possible that another thread could change the collection. There are no simple answers to this problem. You can make an enumeration thread-safe by declaring the loop to be synchronized, but if you want to move through a loop using an iterator and delete certain items, you must be careful of the consequences. Deleting or adding an element might mean that a particular element is skipped or accessed twice, depending on the storage mechanism you are using.
2. *Privileged access.* Iterator classes may need some sort of privileged access to the underlying data structures of the original container class so they can move through the data. If the

data are stored in a List, this is pretty easy to accomplish, but if the data are stored in some other collection structure contained in a class, you probably need to make that structure available through a get operation. Alternatively, you could make the Iterator a derived class of the containment class and access the data directly.

3. *External versus internal iterators.* The *Design Patterns* book describes two types of iterators: external and internal. Thus far, we have only described external iterators. Internal iterators are methods that move through the entire collection, performing some operation on each element directly without any specific requests from the user. These are less common in Python, but you can imagine methods that normalize a collection of data values to lie between 0 and 1 or that convert all the strings to a particular case. In general, external iterators give you more control because the calling program accesses each element directly and can decide whether to perform an operation.

Composites and Iterators

Iterators are also an excellent way to move through Composite structures. In the Composite of an employee hierarchy that we developed in the previous chapter, each Employee contains a List whose iterator allows you to continue to enumerate down that chain. If that Employee has no subordinates, there is nothing to iterate.

Programs on GitHub

- Simple iter examples.py: Simple examples
- Fiboiter.py: Iterator that gets the next member of a Fibonacci series
- FilteredIter.py: Iterates through a list of swimmers, returning only those in the selected club
- Fibogen.py: Generator version of an iterator
- Fiboclass.py: Generator in a class
- 100free.txt: Data file used by FilteredIter

24

The Mediator Pattern

When a program is made up of a number of classes, the logic and computation are divided among these classes. However, as more of these isolated classes are developed in a program, the problem of communication between these classes becomes more complex. The more each class needs to know about the methods of another class, the more tangled the class structure can become. This makes the program harder to read and harder to maintain. Furthermore, it can become difficult to change the program, since any change may affect code in several other classes.

The Mediator pattern addresses this problem by promoting looser coupling between classes. Mediators accomplish this by being the only class that has detailed knowledge of the methods of a number of other classes. Classes send information to the Mediator when changes occur, and the Mediator passes them on to any other classes that need to be informed.

We find that along with Command and Factory, the Mediator is the pattern we use the most, especially in visual programming. You probably will, too!

An Example System

Let's consider a program that has several buttons, two listboxes, and a text entry field (see Figure 24-1).

When the program starts, the Copy and Clear buttons are disabled.

1. When you select one of the names in the list box on the left, it is copied into the text field for editing and the Copy button is enabled.
2. When you click Copy, that text is added to the list box on the right, and the Clear button is enabled (see Figure 24-1).

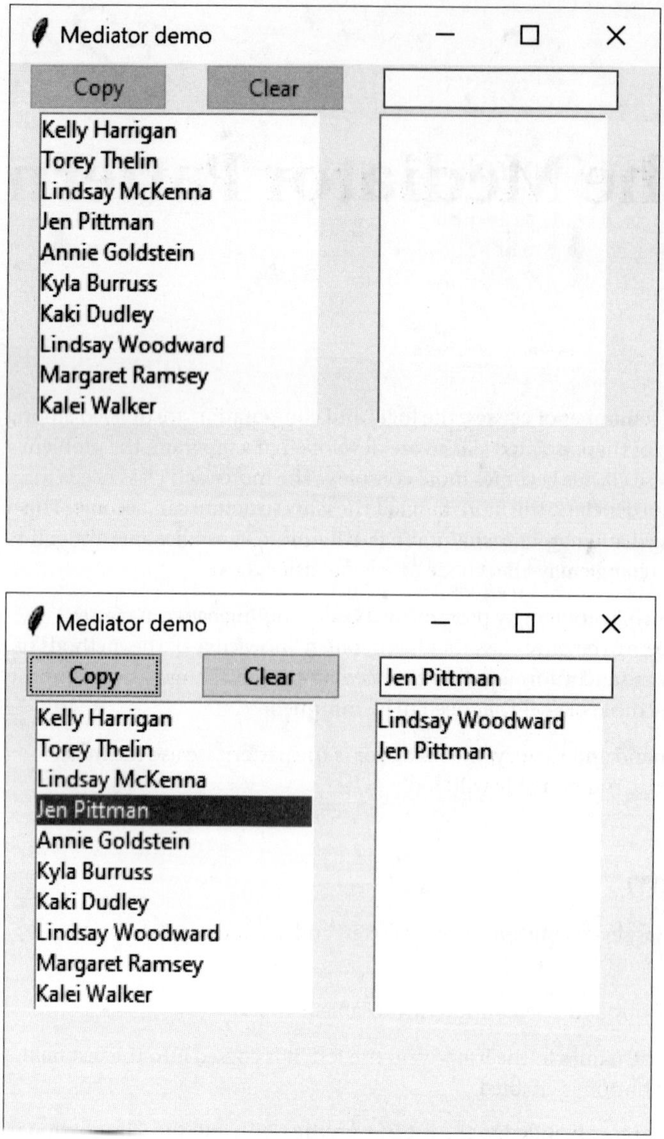

Figure 24-1 UI to demonstrate the Mediator pattern

If you click the Clear button, the rightmost list box and the text field are cleared, the list box is deselected, and the two buttons are again disabled.

User interfaces such as this one are commonly used to select lists of people or products from longer lists. They are usually even more complicated than this one, involving insert, delete, and undo operations as well.

Interactions Between Controls

The interactions between the visual controls are pretty complex, even in this simple example. Each visual object needs to know about two or more others, leading to a tangled relationship diagram (see Figure 24-2).

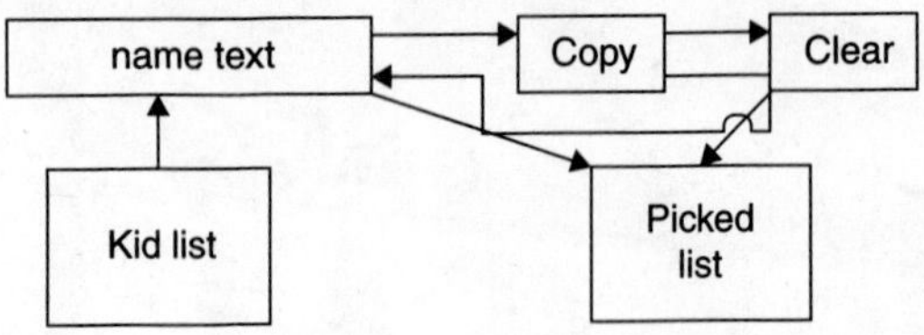

Figure 24-2 Tangled interactions between controls without a Mediator

The Mediator pattern simplifies this system by being the only class that is aware of the state of other classes in the system. Each control that the Mediator communicates with is called a colleague. Each colleague informs the Mediator when it has received a user event, and the Mediator decides which other classes should be informed of this event. Figure 24-3 illustrates this simpler interaction scheme.

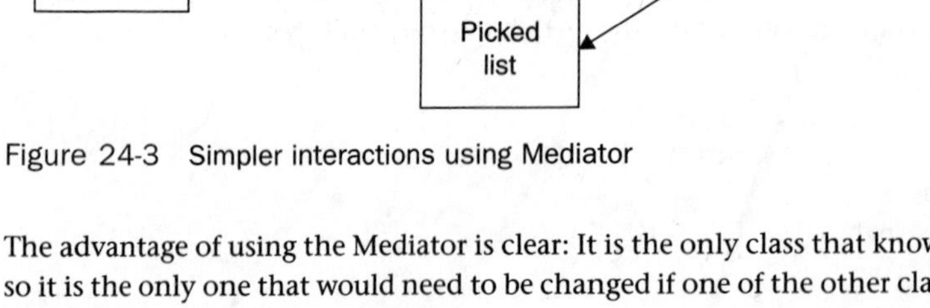

Figure 24-3 Simpler interactions using Mediator

The advantage of using the Mediator is clear: It is the only class that knows of the other classes, so it is the only one that would need to be changed if one of the other classes changes or if other interface control classes are added.

Sample Code

Let's consider this program in detail and decide how each control is constructed. The main difference in writing a program using a Mediator class is that each class needs to be aware of the existence of the Mediator. You start by creating an instance of the Mediator and then pass the instance of the Mediator to each class in its constructor.

```
self.swlist = Listbox(root, width=25) # swimmer list
slist = self.swmrs.getSwimmers()
med = Mediator(slist)      # create the Mediator
med.setSwlist(self.swlist) # pass in list box

# right list box filled by Copy button
self.sublist = Listbox(root)
med.setSublist(self.sublist)

# buttons and entry go in frame
frame =Frame(root)
frame.grid(row=0, columnspan=2)

# Copy button
copyb = CopyButton(frame, med)
copyb.pack(side=LEFT, padx=10)
med.setCopyButton(copyb)

#Clear button
clearb = ClearButton(frame, med)
clearb.pack(side=LEFT, padx=10)
med.setClearButton(clearb)

# Entry field
entryf=Entry(frame)
med.setEntryfield(entryf)
entryf.pack(side=LEFT, padx=10)
```

The two buttons use the Command interface and register themselves with the Mediator during their initialization. Their command events tell the mediator to carry out their job:

```
class CopyButton(DButton):
    def __init__(self, root, med:Mediator):
        super().__init__(root, text="Copy")
        self.med = med
        self.med.setCopyButton(self)

    def comd(self):
        self.med.copyClick()
```

(The Clear button works similarly.)

The Swimmer name list is based on the one used in the last two examples but has been expanded so that the data loading of the list takes place within the Mediator. The builder program registers the list click to call the Mediator when it happens.

```
# connect click event to Mediator
self.swlist.bind('<<ListboxSelect>>', med.listClicked)
```

The text field is even simpler: It simply registers itself with the mediator. The mediator then loads and clears the text field when the buttons are clicked.

When you click the listbox to select a name, the Mediator gets the name, copies it into the entry field, and enables the Copy button:

```
def listClicked(self,evt):
    self.copyb.enable()

# get the selected name from the list box
    nm =self.swlist.get(self.swlist.curselection())
    self.entryf.delete(0, END)  # clear entry field
    self.entryf.insert(END, nm) # insert new name
```

When you click the Copy button, the Mediator copies the text from the Entry field into the right list and enables the Clear button:

```
# copy button is clicked
def copyClick(self):
    nm = self.entryf.get()  # entry to right list
    self.sublist.insert(END, nm)
    self.clearb.enable()     #enable the clear button
```

When you click the Clear button, it empties the right list, clears the entry field, unselects any object in the left list box, and disables both buttons:

```
def clearClick(self):
    self.sublist.delete(0, END)
    self.entryf.delete(0, END)
    self.copyb.disable()
    self.clearb.disable()
    self.swlist.select_clear(0, END)
```

As you can see, the Mediator class simplifies the code by localizing all the interactions in a single class.

Mediators and Command Objects

The two buttons in this program are command objects. As we noted earlier, this makes processing the button click events simple. For example, the Copy button has a comd method that calls a method in the Mediator:

```
def comd(self):
    self.med.copyClick()
```

and the Clear button has the analogous `comd` method:

```
def comd(self):
    self.med.clearClick()
```

In either case, this represents the solution to one of the problems noted in Chapter 21, "The Command Pattern": In that chapter, each button needed knowledge of many of the other user interface classes in order to execute its command. Here we delegate that knowledge to the Mediator so that the Command buttons do not need any knowledge of the methods of the other visual objects.

Consequences of the Mediator Pattern

The consequences of the Mediator pattern include the following:

1. The Mediator pattern keeps classes from becoming entangled when actions in one class need to be reflected in the state of another class.
2. Using a Mediator makes it easy to change a program's behavior. For many kinds of changes, you can merely change or subclass the Mediator, leaving the rest of the program unchanged.
3. You can add new controls or other classes without changing anything except the Mediator.
4. The Mediator solves the problem of each `Command` object needing to know too much about the objects and methods in the rest of a user interface.
5. The Mediator can become a "god class," having too much knowledge of the rest of the program. This can make it hard to change and maintain. Sometimes you can improve this situation by putting more of the function into the individual classes and less into the Mediator. Each object should carry out its own tasks, and the Mediator should only manage the interaction between objects.
6. Each Mediator is a custom-written class that has methods for each colleague to call and knows what methods each colleague has available. This makes it difficult to reuse Mediator code in different projects. On the other hand, most Mediators are quite simple, and writing this code is far easier than managing the complex object interactions any other way.

Mediators are not limited to use in visual interface programs, but this is their most common application. You can use Mediators whenever you are faced with the problem of complex inter-communication between multiple objects.

Single Interface Mediators

The Mediator pattern we have described above acts as a kind of Observer pattern: It observes changes in each of the colleague elements, with each element having a custom interface to the Mediator. Another approach is to have a single method in your Mediator and pass that method various objects that tell the Mediator which operations to perform.

In this approach, we avoid registering the active components and create a single action method with different polymorphic arguments for each action element.

This approach is more difficult in Python because it is essentially a one-pass compiler, and references to objects that have not yet been created are difficult to control.

Programs on GitHub

- MedDemo.py: Visual demo of Mediator used in Figure 24-1
- 100free.txt: Data for MedDemo.py

The Memento Pattern

Suppose you would like to save the internal state of an object so that you can restore it later. For example, you might want to save the color, size, pattern, or shape of objects in a drawing or painting program. Ideally, it should be possible to save and restore this state without making each object take care of this task and without violating encapsulation. This is the purpose of the Memento pattern.

When to Use a Memento

Objects normally shouldn't expose much of their internal state using public methods. However, you would still like to be able to save the entire state of an object because you might need to restore it later. In some cases, you can obtain enough information from the public interfaces (such as the drawing position of graphical objects) to save and restore that data. In other cases, the color, shading, angle, and connection relationships to other graphical objects need to be saved, and this information may not be readily available. This sort of information saving and restoration is common in systems that need to support Undo commands.

If all the information describing an object is available in public variables, saving them in some external store is not difficult. However, making these data public makes the entire system vulnerable to change by external program code, when we usually expect data inside an object to be private and encapsulated from the outside world.

Python has no private or protected variables. However, you can follow the custom of naming variables with a leading underscore if you want to indicate that they should not be accessed directly.

The Memento pattern attempts to solve this problem by having privileged access to the state of the object you want to save. Other objects may have only more restricted access to the object, thus preserving their encapsulation. This pattern defines three roles for objects:

- The Originator is the object whose state you want to save.
- The Memento is another object that saves the state of the Originator.
- The Caretaker manages the timing of the saving of the state, saves the Memento, and, if needed, uses the Memento to restore the state of the Originator.

25

The Memento Pattern

Suppose you would like to save the internal state of an object so that you can restore it later. For example, you might want to save the color, size, pattern, or shape of objects in a drafting or painting program. Ideally, it should be possible to save and restore this state without making each object take care of this task and without violating encapsulation. This is the purpose of the Memento pattern.

When to Use a Memento

Objects normally shouldn't expose much of their internal state using public methods. However, you would still like to be able to save the entire state of an object because you might need to restore it later. In some cases, you can obtain enough information from the public interfaces (such as the drawing position of graphical objects) to save and restore that data. In other cases, the color, shading, angle, and connection relationships to other graphical objects need to be saved, and this information may not readily be available. This sort of information saving and restoration is common in systems that need to support Undo commands.

If all the information describing an object is available in public variables, saving them in some external store is not difficult. However, making these data public makes the entire system vulnerable to change by external program code, when we usually expect data inside an object to be private and encapsulated from the outside world.

Python has no private or protected variables. However, you can follow the custom of naming variables with a leading underscore if you want to indicate that they should not be accessed directly.

The Memento pattern attempts to solve this problem by having privileged access to the state of the object you want to save. Other objects may have only more restricted access to the object, thus preserving their encapsulation. This pattern defines three roles for objects:

- The Originator is the object whose state you want to save.
- The Memento is another object that saves the state of the Originator.
- The Caretaker manages the timing of the saving of the state, saves the Memento, and, if needed, uses the Memento to restore the state of the Originator.

Saving the state of an object without making all its variables publicly available is tricky and can be done with varying degrees of success in various languages. In Python, everything is potentially public, but you probably don't want everything to be used publicly.

Sample Code

Let's consider a simple prototype of a graphics drawing program that creates rectangles and enables you to select them and move them around by dragging them with the mouse. This program has a toolbar with three buttons: Rectangle, Undo, and Clear (see Figure 25-1).

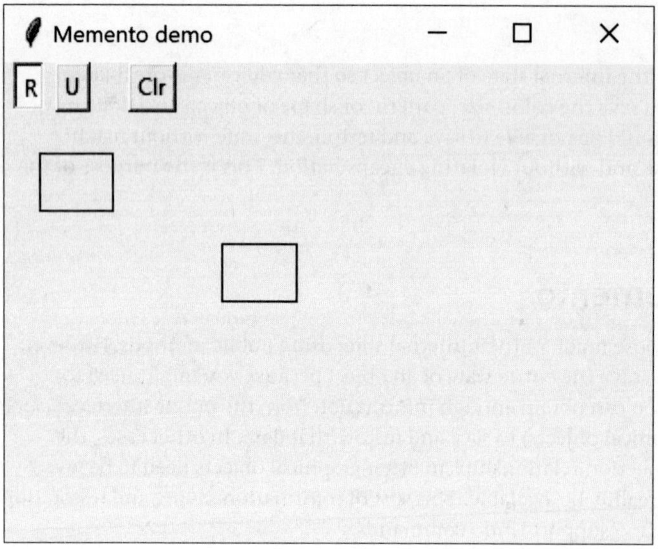

Figure 25-1 Graphics drawing program

The Rectangle checkbox (shown as a button by setting `indicatoron` to 0) stays selected until you uncheck that button. If you click anywhere in the main window when this button is selected, it draws a rectangle.

When you have drawn the rectangle, you can click in any rectangle to select it. If you click outside any rectangle, the current rectangle is deselected, as you see in Figure 25-2.

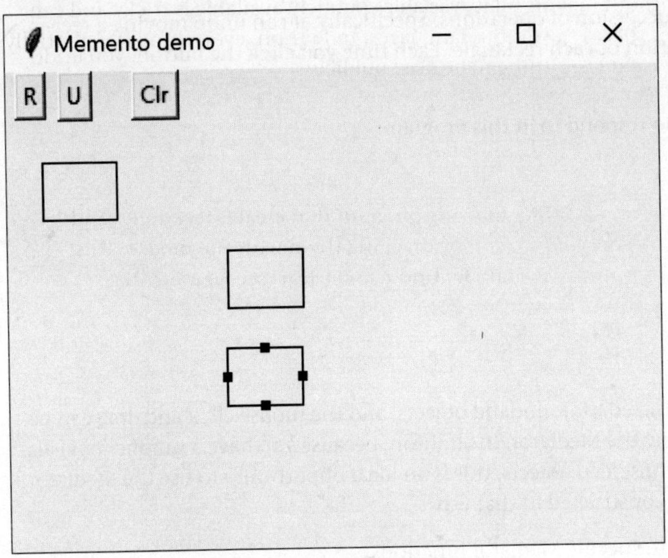

Figure 25-2 Showing the selected rectangle

After you select a rectangle, you can drag it to a new position using the mouse (see Figure 25-3).

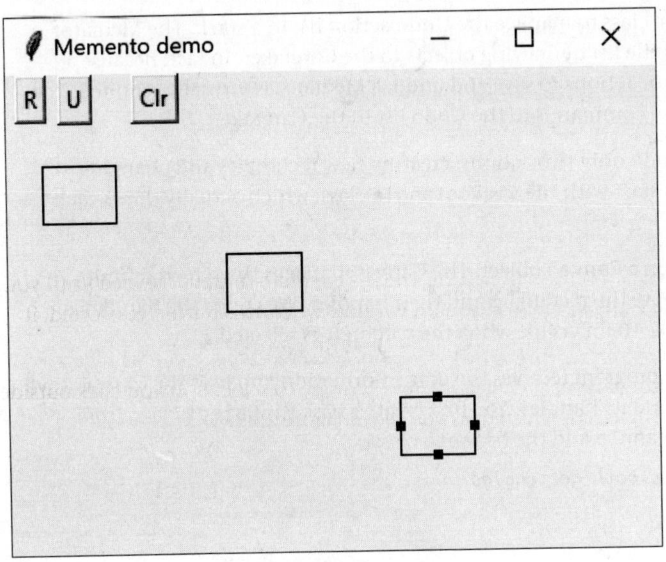

Figure 25-3 After dragging the rectangle

The Undo button can undo a succession of operations. Specifically, it can undo moving a rectangle, and it can undo the creation of each rectangle. Each time you click the button, you undo one more operation.

There are five actions we need to respond to in this program:

- Rectangle checkbox click
- Undo button click
- Clear button click
- Mouse click
- Mouse drag

The three buttons can be constructed as Command objects, and the mouse click and drag can be treated as events to be handled by the Mediator. In addition, because you have a number of visual objects that control the display of screen objects, this is an ideal opportunity to use the Mediator pattern. In fact, this program is constructed in that way.

Here we bind the mouse events to specific Mediator functions:

```
# binds the mouse events
canvas.bind("<Button-1>", med.buttonDown)
canvas.bind("<B1-Motion>", med.drag)
canvas.bind("<ButtonRelease-1>", med.buttonUp)
```

We will also create a `Caretaker` class to manage the Undo action list in a stack. The Mediator manages the actions and sends the list of drawing objects to the Caretaker. In fact, because a program can have any number of actions to save and undo, a Mediator is virtually required: You need a single place to send these commands to the Undo list in the Caretaker.

In this program, we save and undo only two actions: creating new rectangles and changing the position of rectangles. Let's start with the `visRectangle` class, which actually draws each instance of the rectangles.

In Python, we draw rectangles on a `Canvas` object. The Canvas manages the screen refresh/redraw, and we only need to create the rectangles and their handles. We create the handles at once, but hidden; then you make them visible when the rectangle is selected.

When you drag a rectangle, the program receives the drag information and uses the Canvas `move` method to move the rectangle and its handles. You first create a base `VisObject` class, from which you derive both the `Rectangle` and the `Memento` classes:

```
# abstract class representing both Rectangles
# and Mementos
class VisObject():
    def undo(self): pass
    def contains(self, x,y):
        return False
    def isSelected(self):
        return False
```

Then the Rectangle is based on this simple base class:

```
class Rectangle(VisObject):
    def __init__(self,x, y, canvas):
        self.x = x  # save coordinates
        self.y = y
        self.canvas = canvas
        self._selected = False
        self.corners = []   #create corners array
        fillcol='black'     # rect and handles

        #create main Rectangle
        self.crect = self.canvas.create_rectangle(
            x - 20, y - 15, x + 20, y + 15,
            outline=fillcol)

        # and create the four (hidden) handles
        c = self.canvas.create_rectangle(x - 22,
                y - 2, x - 18, y + 2, fill=fillcol,
                    state=HIDDEN)
        self.corners.append(c)
        c = self.canvas.create_rectangle(x + 18,
                    y - 2, x + 22, y + 2, fill=fillcol,
                      state=HIDDEN)
        self.corners.append(c)
        c = self.canvas.create_rectangle(x - 2,
                y - 17, x + 2, y - 13, fill=fillcol,
                    state=HIDDEN)
        self.corners.append(c)
        c = self.canvas.create_rectangle(x - 2,
                y + 17, x + 2, y + 13, fill=fillcol,
                      state=HIDDEN)
        self.corners.append(c)
```

Drawing the rectangle is pretty straightforward because the tkinter library keeps the screen refreshed after you create the rectangle. To show the hidden handles, you simply call the following:

```
if self._selected:
   for c in self.corners:
       self.canvas.itemconfigure(c, state=NORMAL)
```

To move the rectangle and handles when the Mediator receives a mouse drag event, you just calculate the `deltax` and `deltay` values and apply them to the rectangle and the handles:

```
def move(self, x, y):
    oldx = self.x
    oldy = self.y

    self.x = x
    self.y = y
```

```
        deltax= x - oldx      # calc deltas
        deltay = y - oldy

      # move rect
        self.canvas.move(self.crect, deltax, deltay)

        # move handles
        for c in self.handles:
            self.canvas.move(c, deltax, deltay)
```

Now, let's look at the simple `Memento` class.

```
# Memento stores last position of rectangle
# before dragging
# and restores it by clicking undo button

class Memento(VisObject):
    def __init__(self, x, y, rect:Rectangle):
        self.rect = rect
        self.oldx = x
        self.oldy = y
    def undo(self):
        self.rect.move(self.oldx, self.oldy )
```

When we create an instance of the `Memento` class, we pass it the `visRectangle` instance we want to save. It copies the size and position parameters and saves a copy of the instance of the `visRectangle` itself. Later, when you want to restore these parameters, the Memento knows which instance it has to restore them to and can do so directly, as you see in the undo method.

The undo method here simply decides whether to reduce the drawing list by one or to invoke the Memento. This is trivial because both the Memento and the Caretaker have the same undo method that is called from the Mediator when the Undo button is pressed.

In both cases, the Mediator calls the undo method in the Caretaker, which pops the last `visObject` off the stack and calls its undo method. If this is a rectangle, the rectangle gets deleted from the screen; if this is a Memento, it restores the rectangle's previous position.

Here is the `Caretaker` class:

```
# Manages the stack of Rectangles and Mementoes
class Caretaker():
    def __init__(self, med):
        self.med = med
        self.rectList= []
        med.setCare(self)
    #append latest visObj
    def append(self, visobj):
        self.rectList.append(visobj)
    #get the top of the stack and undo the visObj
    def undo(self):
        if len(self.rectList) > 0:
```

```
            visobj = self.rectList.pop()
            visobj.undo()
    # clear the canvas
    def clear(self):
        while len(self.rectList) > 0:
            visobj = self.rectList.pop()
            visobj.undo()
```

Consequences of the Memento Pattern

The Memento pattern provides a way to preserve the state of an object while preserving encapsulation, in languages where this is possible.

On the other hand, the amount of information that a Memento has to save might be quite large, thus taking up a fair amount of storage. This further affects the `Caretaker` class (here, the Mediator), which may have to design strategies to limit the number of objects for which it saves state. In our simple example, we impose no such limits. In cases where objects change in a predictable manner, each Memento may be able to get by with saving only incremental changes of an object's state.

Program on GitHub

- MementoRectHide.py: Memento demo shown in Fig 25-1

26

The Observer Pattern

In our sophisticated windowing world, we often would like to display data in more than one form at the same time and have all the displays reflect any changes in that data. For example, we might represent stock price changes as both a graph and a table or listbox. Each time the price changes, we'd expect both representations to change at once without any action on our part.

We expect this sort of behavior because there are any number of Windows applications, such as Excel, where we see that behavior. Now, there is nothing inherent in Windows to allow this activity and, as you may know, programming directly in Windows in C or C++ is complicated. In Python, however, we can easily make use of the Observer design pattern to cause our program to behave in this way.

The Observer pattern assumes that the object containing the data is separate from the objects that display the data and, furthermore, that these display objects *observe* changes in that data (see Figure 26-1).

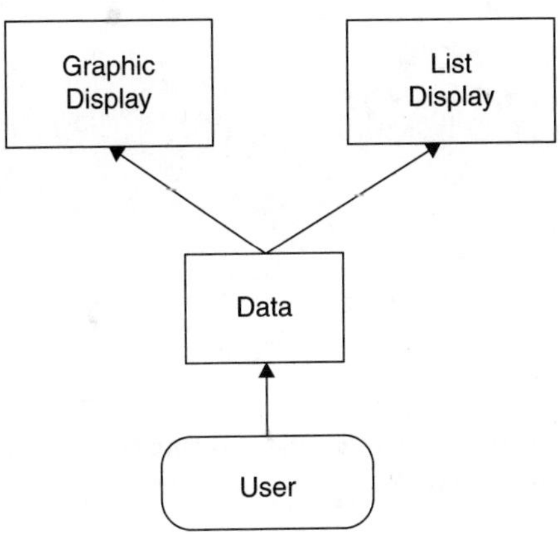

Figure 26-1 Observer pattern

When we implement the Observer pattern, we usually refer to the data as the Subject and each of the displays as Observers. Each of these Observers registers its interest in the data by calling a public method in the Subject. Then each observer has a known interface that the subject calls when the data change. We can define these interfaces as follows:

```
# interface all observers must have
class Observer:
    def sendNotify(self):
        pass
# interface the Subject must have
class Subject:
    def registerInterest(self, obs:Observer):
        pass
```

The advantage of defining these abstract interfaces is that you can write any sort of class objects you want, as long as they implement these interfaces. You can declare these objects to be of type Subject and Observer, no matter what else they do.

Example Program for Watching Colors Change

Let's write a simple program to illustrate how we can use this powerful concept. This program shows a display frame containing three radio buttons, named Red, Blue, and Green (see Figure 26-2).

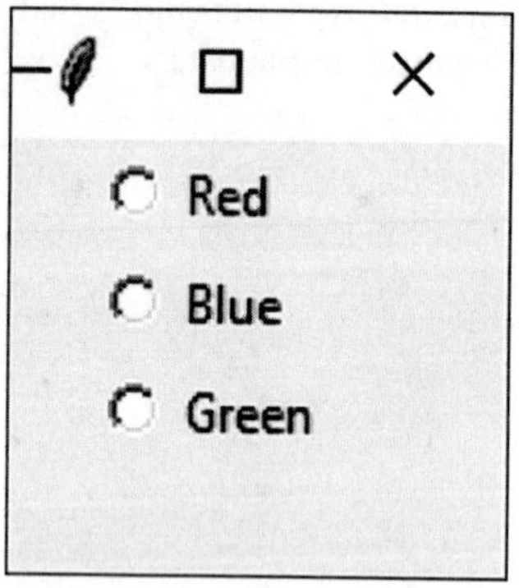

Figure 26-2 UI for simple Observer demo

This main window is the Subject or data repository object. We create this window using the `ChoiceButton` code we derived from the `RadioButton` in Chapter 2:

```
class ColorRadio(Subject):
    def __init__(self, root):
        root.geometry("100x100")
        root.title("Subj")
        self.subjects = []
        self.var = tk.IntVar()
```

```
    self.colors=["red", "blue", "green"]

    ChoiceButton(root, 'Red', 0, self.var, command=self.colrChange)
    ChoiceButton(root, 'Blue', 1, self.var, command=self.colrChange)
    ChoiceButton(root, 'Green', 2, self.var, command=self.colrChange)
    self.var.set(None)  # No buttons selected
```

Note that the main frame class is derived from `Subject`. Thus, it must provide a public method for registering interest in the data in this class. This method is the `registerInterest` method, which just adds Observer objects to a List:

```
# Observers tell the Subject they want to know of changes
def registerInterest(self, subj:Subject):
    self.subjects.append(subj)
```

Now we create the radio button frame and two observers, one that displays the color (and its name) and another that adds the current color to a list box.

```
root = tk.Tk()
colr = ColorRadio(root)       # create radio frame

cframe = ColorFrame(None)     # create color frame
colr.registerInterest(cframe) # and register it

clist = ColorList(None)       # create color list
colr.registerInterest(clist)  # and register it
```

The `registerInterest` method just adds the Observers to a list:

```
# Observers tell the Subject
# they want to know of changes
def registerInterest(self, subj:Subject):
    self.subjects.append(subj)
```

Then, when you click a `RadioButton`, it calls the command interface, which looks up the actual color and sends it to the observers.

```
def oolrChange(self):
    cindex = self.var.get()     # get index of the color
    color = self.colors[cindex] # look in color list

    #send notification to all the observers
    for subj in self.subjects:  # send color name
        subj.sendNotify(color)
```

When we create the `ColorFrame` and `ColorList` windows, we register our interest in the data in the main program, as shown earlier.

Meanwhile, in the main program, every time someone clicks one of the radio buttons, it calls the `sendNotify` method of each Observer that has registered interest in these changes by simply running through the objects in the observers List.

The ColorFrame is quite simple because the message is an actual color name it can use to change the background of the frame, so little code is involved:

```
# a Frame that is filled with the chosen color
class ColorFrame(Observer):
    def __init__(self, master=None):
        self.frame = Toplevel(master)
        self.frame.geometry("100x100")
        self.frame.title("Color")

    def sendNotify(self, color:str):
        self.frame.config(bg = color)
```

In the case of the Listbox observer, it just adds the text to the list and recapitalizes the leading character:

```
# list box that displays
# the text of the chosen color
class ColorList(Observer):
    def __init__(self, master=None):
        frame = Toplevel(master)
        frame.geometry("100x100")
        frame.title("Color list")
        self.list = Listbox(frame)
        self.list.pack()

    def sendNotify(self, color: str):
        self.list.insert(END, color.capitalize())
```

Figure 26-3 shows the final program running.

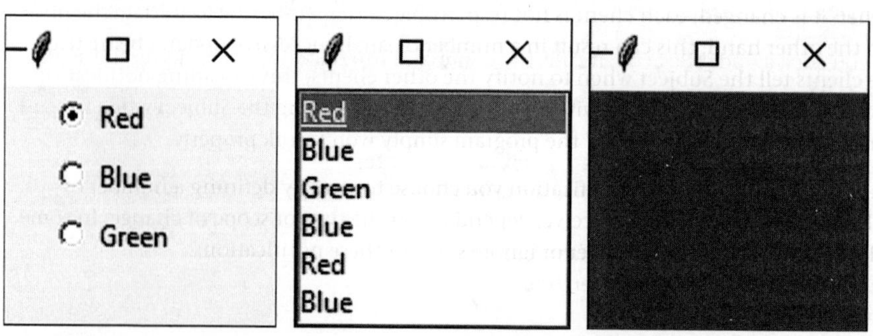

Figure 26-3 Radiobuttons with Listbox and Canvas observers

The Message to the Media

What kind of notification should a subject send to its observers? In this carefully circumscribed example, the notification message is the string representing the color itself. When we click one of the radio buttons, we can get the index for that button, look up the color, and send it to the observers. Of course, this assumes that all the observers can handle that string representation. In more realistic situations, this might not always be the case, especially if the observers can also be used to observe other data objects.

In more complicated systems, we might have observers that demand specific, but different, kinds of data. Instead of having each observer convert the message to the right data type, we could use an intermediate `Adapter` class to perform this conversion.

Another problem observers may have to deal with is the case where the data of the central subject class can change in several ways. For example, we could delete points from a list of data, edit their values, or change the scale of the data we are viewing. In these cases, we need to either send different change messages to the observers or send a single message and then have the observer ask which sort of change has occurred.

Consequences of the Observer Pattern

Observers promote abstract coupling to Subjects. A subject doesn't know the details of any of its observers. However, this has the potential disadvantage of successive or repeated updates to the Observers when there are a series of incremental changes to the data. If the cost of these updates is high, it may be necessary to introduce some sort of change management so that the Observers are not notified too soon or too frequently.

When one client makes a change in the underlying data, you need to decide which object will initiate the notification of that change to the other observers. If the Subject notifies all the observers when it is changed, each client is not responsible for remembering to initiate the notification. On the other hand, this can result in a number of small successive updates being triggered. If the clients tell the Subject when to notify the other clients, this cascading notification can be avoided, but the clients are left with the responsibility of telling the Subject when to send the notifications. If one client "forgets," the program simply won't work properly.

Finally, you can specify the kind of notification you choose to send by defining a number of update methods for the Observers to receive, depending on the type or scope of change. In some cases, the clients thus will be able to filter or ignore some of these notifications.

Programs on GitHub

- Observer.py: Code for radio button observers

27

The State Pattern

The State pattern is used when you want to have an object represent the state of your application and then switch application states by switching objects. For example, you could have an enclosing class switch between a number of related contained classes and then pass method calls on to the current contained class. *Design Patterns* suggests that the State pattern switch between internal classes in such a way that the enclosing object appears to change its class. In Python, at least, this is a bit of an exaggeration, but the actual purpose to which the classes are put can change significantly.

Many programmers have experienced creating a class that performs slightly different computations or displays different information based on the arguments passed into the class. This frequently leads to some sort of `if-else` statements inside the class that determine which behavior to carry out. The State pattern seeks to replace this inelegance.

Sample Code

Let's consider the case of a drawing program similar to the one we developed for the `Memento` class. This program has toolbar buttons for Select, Rectangle, Fill, Circle, and Clear (see Figure 27-1).

Each one of the tool buttons does something different when it is selected and you click or drag your mouse across the screen. Thus, the *state* of the graphical editor affects the behavior the program should exhibit; these states are Pick, Rectangle, Circle, and Fill, suggesting some sort of design using the State pattern.

Initially, we might design our program like Figure 27-2, with a Mediator managing the actions of five command buttons.

However, this initial design puts the entire burden of maintaining the state of the program on the Mediator. As you know, the main purpose of a Mediator is to coordinate activities among various controls, such as buttons. Keeping the state of the buttons and the desired mouse activity inside the Mediator can make it unduly complicated, as well as lead to a set of `if` tests that further make the program difficult to read and maintain.

In addition, this set of large, monolithic conditional statements might have to be repeated for each action the Mediator interprets, such as `mouseUp`, `mouseDrag`, `rightClick`, and so forth. This makes the program very hard to read and maintain.

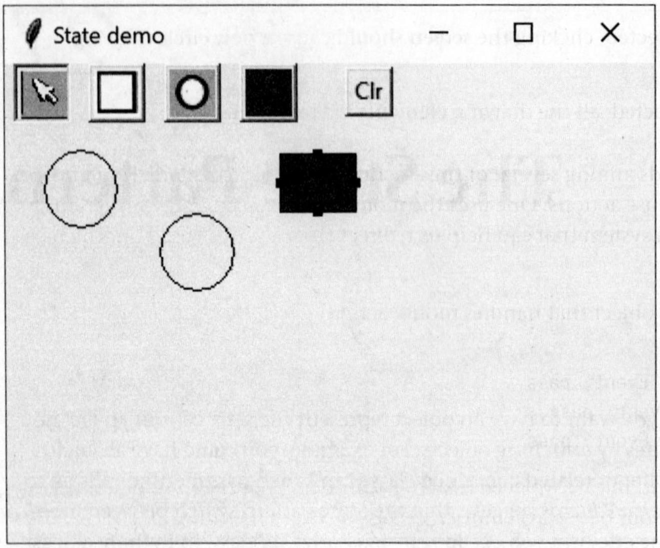

Figure 27-1 Drawing program for State pattern

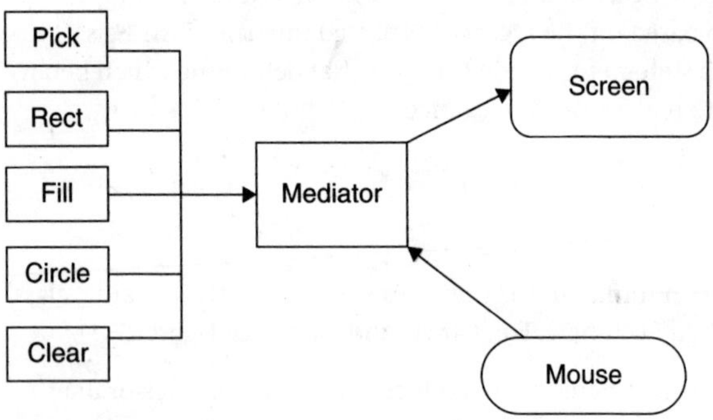

Figure 27-2 Tool button states and Mediator

Instead, let's analyze the expected behavior for each of the buttons:

1. If the Pick button is selected, clicking inside a drawing element should cause it to be highlighted or appear with "handles." If the mouse is dragged and a drawing element is already selected, the element should move on the screen.

2. If the Rect button is selected, clicking the screen should cause a new rectangle drawing element to be created.

3. If the Fill button is selected and a drawing element is already selected, that element should be filled with the current color. If no drawing is selected, clicking inside a drawing should fill it with the current color.

4. If the Circle button is selected, clicking the screen should cause a new circle drawing element to be created.

5. If the Clear button is selected, all the drawing elements are removed.

There are some common threads among several of these actions we should explore. Four of them use the mouse click event to cause actions. One uses the mouse drag event to cause an action. Thus, we really want to create a system that can help us redirect these events, based on which button is currently selected.

Let's consider creating a `State` object that handles mouse activities:

```
class State():
    def mouseDown(self, evt:Event):pass
    def mouseUp(self, evt:Event):pass
    def mouseDrag(self, evt:Event):pass
```

We'll include the `mouseUp` event, in case we need it later. Because none of the cases described need all these events, we'll give our base class empty methods instead of creating an abstract base class. Then we'll create four derived `State` classes for Pick, Rect, Circle, and Fill and put instances of all of them inside a `StateManager` class, which sets the current state and executes methods on that state object. In *Design Patterns*, this `StateManager` class is referred to as a *Context*. This object is illustrated in Figure 27-3.

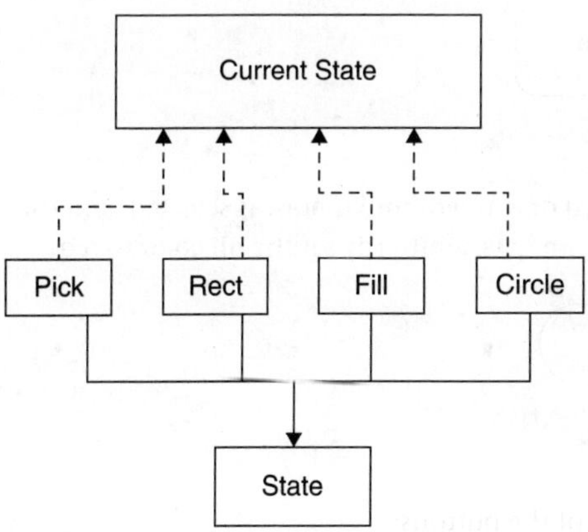

Figure 27-3 StateManager interacting with tool buttons

A typical `State` object simply overrides event methods that it must handle specially. For example, this is the complete `Rectangle` state object:

```
class RectState(State):
    def __init__(self, med):
        self.med = med
    def mouseDown(self, evt:Event):
        # create new rectangle if box checked
        newrect = Rectangle(evt.x, evt.y, self.med.canvas)
```

```
        rectList = self.med.getRectlist()
        rectList.append(newrect)  # save in stack
```

The RectState object simply tells the Mediator to add a rectangle drawing to the drawing list. Similarly, the Circle state object tells the Mediator to add a circle to the drawing list:

```
class CircState(State):
    def __init__(self, med):
        self.med = med
    def mouseDown(self, evt:Event):
        # create new circle
        newrect = Circle(evt.x, evt.y,
                         self.med.canvas)
        rectList = self.med.getRectlist()
        rectList.append(newrect)  # save in stack
```

The only tricky button is the Fill button because we have defined two actions for it.

1. If an object is already selected, fill it.
2. If the mouse is clicked inside an object, fill that one.

To carry out these tasks, we need to add the select method to your base State class. This method is called when each tool button is selected:

```
class State():
    def mouseDown(self, evt:Event):pass
    def mouseUp(self, evt:Event):pass
    def mouseDrag(self, evt:Event):pass
    def select(self):pass
```

The Drawing argument is either the currently selected drawing or null if none is selected, and the color is the current fill color. In this simple program, we have arbitrarily set the fill color to red. So, the Fill state class becomes this:

```
class FillState(State):
    def __init__(self, med):
        self.med = med

# if a figure is selected, fill it
    def select(self):
        rect = self.med.getSelected()
        if rect != None:
            rect.fillObject()

# otherwise fill the next figure you click on
    def mouseDown(self, evt:Event):
        rectList = self.med.getRectlist()
        for r in rectList:
            if r.contains(evt.x, evt.y):
                r.fillObject()
                self.selectRect = r
```

Switching Between States

Now that we have defined how each state behaves when mouse events are sent to it, we need to examine how the `StateManager` switches between states. We simply set the `currentState` variable to the state, as indicated by the button that is selected.

```
# switches between states depending
# on the button you click
class StateManager():
    def __init__(self, med):
        self.med = med
        # create instances of each state
        self.pickState = PickState(med)
        self.curState = self.pickState
        self.rectState = RectState(med)
        self.fillState =  FillState(med)
        self.circState = CircState(med)


    # switch states as you click on buttons
    def setRect(self):
        self.curState = self.rectState
    def setCirc(self):
        self.curState = self.circState
    def setFill(self):
        self.curState = self.fillState
    def setPick(self):
        self.curState = self.pickState
```

In this version of the `StateManager`, we create an instance of each state during the `__init__` method and copy the correct one into the state variable when the set methods are called. It would also be possible to use a Factory to create these states on demand; this might be advisable if there are a large number of states that each consume a fair number of resources.

The remainder of the `StateManager` code simply calls the methods of whichever state object is current. This is the critical piece: No conditional testing occurs. Instead, the correct state is already in place, and its methods are ready to be called.

```
# here are the three events we act on
def mouseDown(self, evt):
    self.curState.mouseDown(evt)
def mouseDrag(self, evt):
    self.curState.mouseDrag(evt)
def select(self):
    self.curState.select()
```

How the Mediator Interacts with the StateManager

Earlier, you learned that it is clearer to separate the state management from the Mediator's button and mouse event management. The Mediator is the critical class, however, because it tells the `StateManager` when the current program state changes.

Each button can be in a selected or unselected state, with these states represented by using the button borders to show the "up" or "down" for each button. These settings are part of the derived `DButton` class.

```
# derived button class with an abstract comd method
class DButton(Button, Command):
    def __init__(self, master,  **kwargs):
        super().__init__(master, command=self.comd,
                                 **kwargs)
    def select(self):
        self.config(relief=SUNKEN)
    def deselect(self):
        self.config(relief=RAISED)
```

When you click any button, that button receives that click event, turns off any buttons by calling the Mediator's `deselect` method, calls the `select` method on that button, and sends that state to the `StateManager`.

```
# When selected you can create rectangles
class RectButton(DButton):
    def __init__(self, rt,  med):
        super().__init__(rt)
        self.photo =  \
            PhotoImage(file="rectforbutton.png")
        self.config(image=self.photo)
        self.med = med
        med.addButton(self) # add to button list

    def comd(self):
        # deselect all buttons
        self.med.unselectButtons()
        self.select()   # select this one
        # set the statemanager to Rect state
        self.med.statemgr.setRect()
```

Note that each button click calls one of these methods and changes the state of the application. The remaining statements in each method simply turn off the other toggle buttons, so that only one button at a time can be depressed.

```
# Mediator manages the button and mouse events
class Mediator():
    def __init__(self, canvas):
        self.canvas = canvas
        self.selectRect=None    # not selected
```

```
        self.dragging = False   # not dragging
        self.memento = None     # variable goes here
        self.rectList=[]
        self.buttons = []
        # create the StateManager
        self.statemgr = StateManager(self)
    def getRectlist(self):
        return self.rectList


def addButton(self, but:DButton):
        self.buttons.append(but)

    #unselect all 4 buttons
    def unselectButtons(self):
        for but in self.buttons:
            but.deselect()
    # button 1 has been clicked
    def buttonDown(self, evt):
        self.statemgr.mouseDown(evt)

    # circle button sets Circle state
    def circleClicked(self):
        self.statemgr.setCirc()

    # selected rect or circle stored
    def setSelected(self, r):
        self.selectRect = r

    # gets the selected drawing object
    def getSelected(self):
        return self.selectRect

    # drag rectangle/circle to new position
    def drag(self, evt):
        self.statemgr.mouseDrag(evt)

    # clear all objects
    def clear(self):
        while len(self.rectList) > 0:
            visobj = self.rectList.pop()
            visobj.undo()
```

The rest of the code is essentially the same as in the Memento example, with the Undo methods eliminated for simplicity.

Consequences of the State Pattern

The consequence of the State pattern include the following:

1. The State pattern creates a subclass of a basic `State` object for each state that an application can have and switches between them as the application changes between states.
2. You don't need to have a long set of conditional `if` statements associated with the various states; each one is encapsulated in a class.
3. There is no variable anywhere that specifies which state a program is in; this approach reduces errors caused by programmers forgetting to test this state variable.
4. You can share state objects among several parts of an application, such as separate windows, as long as none of the state objects has specific instance variables. In this example, only the `FillState` class has an instance variable, and this could be easily rewritten to be an argument passed in each time.
5. This approach generates a number of small class objects but, in the process, simplifies and clarifies the program.

State Transitions

The transition between states can be specified internally or externally. In the example in this chapter, the Mediator tells the `StateManager` when to switch between states. However, it is also possible that each state can decide automatically what each successor state will be. For example, when a rectangle or circle drawing object is created, the program could automatically switch back to the `Arrow-object` State.

Program on GitHub

- StateMaster.py: Program showing how States are used, as in Figure 27-1

28

The Strategy Pattern

The Strategy pattern is much like the State pattern in outline but is a little different in intent. The Strategy pattern consists of related algorithms encapsulated in a driver class called the Context. Either your client program can select one of these differing algorithms, or, in some cases, the Context might select the best one for you. As with the State pattern, the intent is to switch easily between algorithms without any monolithic conditional statements. The difference between the State and Strategy patterns is that the user generally chooses which of several strategies to apply, and only one strategy at a time is likely to be instantiated and active within the Context class. By contrast, as we have seen, it is likely that all of the different States will be active at once, and switching may occur frequently between them. In addition, the Strategy pattern encapsulates several algorithms that do more or less the same thing, whereas the State pattern encapsulates related classes that perform somewhat different operations. Finally, the concept of transition between states is completely missing in the Strategy pattern.

Why We Use the Strategy Pattern

A program that requires a particular service or function and that has several ways of carrying out that function is a candidate for the Strategy pattern. Programs choose between these algorithms based on computational efficiency or user choice. Any number of strategies can be used, and more can be added. Additionally, any strategy can be changed at any time.

There are a number of cases in programs where we'd like to do the same thing in several different ways:

- Save files in different formats
- Compress files using different algorithms
- Capture video data using different compression schemes
- Use different line-breaking strategies to display text data
- Plot the same data in different formats (for example, line graph, bar chart, or pie chart)

In each case, we could imagine the client program telling a driver module (Context) which of these strategies to use and then asking it to carry out the operation.

The idea behind the Strategy pattern is to encapsulate the various strategies in a single module and provide a simple interface to allow choice between these strategies. Each of them should have the same programming interface, although they need not all be members of the same class hierarchy. However, they do have to implement the same programming interface.

Sample Code

Let's consider a simplified graphing program that can present data as a line graph or a bar chart. You start with an abstract `PlotStrategy` class and derive the two plotting classes from it (see Figure 28-1).

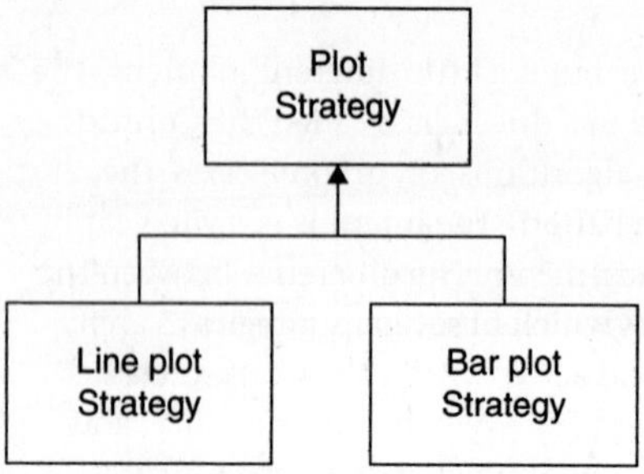

Figure 28-1 Two plot strategies

Because each plot appears in its own frame, the base `PlotStrategy` class reads in and scales the data. The child classes are derived from `TopLevel`, so they open independent windows.

```
class PlotStrategy():
    def __init__(self, title):
        self.width = 300
        self.height = 200
        self.title = title
        self.color = "black"
        frame = Toplevel(None, width=300, height=200)
        frame.title(self.title)
        self.canvas = Canvas(frame, width=300, height=200)
        self.canvas.pack()
        #read in the file and find its bounds
        self.readFile("data.txt")
        self.findBounds(self.xp, self.yp)

    # abstract plot method,
    # filled in by derived classes
    def plot(self, xp, yp):pass
```

```
    def setPencolor(self, c): self.color = c

    # finds the max and min of each array
    def findBounds(self, x, y):
        self.minx = min(x)
        self.miny = 0
        self.maxx  = max(x)
        self.maxy = max(y)

    # compute scaling factors
    def calcScale(self, h, w):
        self.xfactor = (0.9 * w) / (self.maxx - self.minx)
        self.yfactor = (0.9 * h) / (self.maxy - self.miny)

        self.xpmin = (int)(0.05 * w)
        self.ypmin = (int)(0.05 * h)
        self.xpmax = w - self.xpmin
        self.ypmax = h - self.ypmin
```

The important part is that all the derived classes must implement a method called `plot` that operates on two float arrays. Each of these classes can do any kind of plot that is appropriate.

The Context

The `Context` class is the traffic cop that decides which strategy is to be called. The decision is usually based on a request from the client program, and all that the `Context` needs to do is to set a variable to refer to one concrete strategy or another.

In this simple example, you just use the two buttons in Figure 28-2 to select which strategy to choose.

The Program Commands

This simple program is just a panel with two buttons that call the two plots (see Figure 28-2).

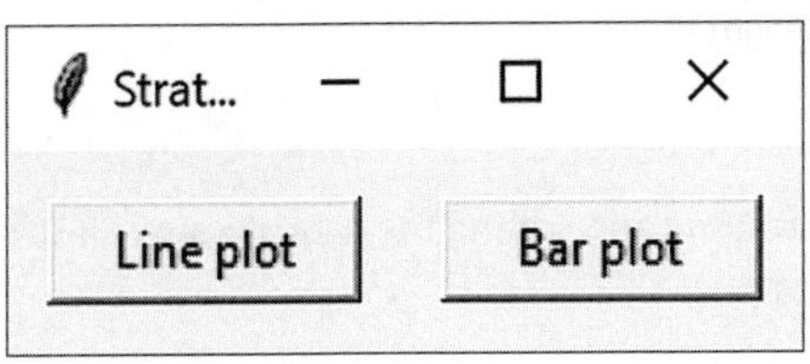

Figure 28-2 Command buttons to select strategies

Each button is a command object that sets the correct strategy and then calls its plot routine. For example, this is the complete Line graph button class:

```
# Button launches the line plot window
class LineButton(DButton):
    def __init__(self, root, **kwargs):
        super().__init__(root,
            text="Line plot", **kwargs)
    def comd(self):
        lst = LineStrategy()
        lst.plot()
```

The Line and Bar Graph Strategies

The two strategy classes are pretty much the same: They set up the window size for plotting and call a plot method specific for that display panel. Both are derived from the base `PlotStrategy` class, which reads in the data file and calculates the `min` and `max` values and scaling factors for the number of pixels (300 × 200).

Here is the Line graph strategy:

```
# strategy for line plot
class LineStrategy(PlotStrategy):
    def __init__(self, master=None):
        super().__init__("Line plot")

    def plot(self):
        w = self.width
        h = self.height
        self.calcScale(h, w)
    # Line plot of the two arrays
        coords = []         #array of x,y pairs
        for i in range(0, len(self.xp)):
            x = self.calcx(self.xp[i])
            y = self.calcy(self.yp[i], h)
            coords.append(x)
            coords.append(y)
        # plot x,y data
        self.canvas.create_line(coords,
                        fill=self.color)
```

The basic `PlotStrategy` class does the dirty work of reading and scaling the data. Because all the plots are on a canvas, it also initializes one.

```
class PlotStrategy():
    def __init__(self, title):
        self.width = 300
        self.height = 200
        self.title = title
```

```
        self.color = "black"  # default color
        frame = Toplevel(None)
        frame.title(self.title)

        self.canvas = Canvas(frame,
               width=self.width, height=self.height)
        self.canvas.pack()
        #read in the file and find its bounds
        self.readFile("data.txt")
        self.findBounds(self.xp, self.yp)

    # abstract plot method,
    # filled in by derived classes
    def plot(self, xp, yp):pass

    def setPencolor(self, c):
        self.color = c
```

Here are the scaling methods:

```
# finds the max and min of each array
def findBounds(self, x, y):
    self.minx = min(x)
    self.miny = 0
    self.maxx  = max(x)
    self.maxy = max(y)

# compute scaling factors
def calcScale(self, h, w):
    self.xfactor = (0.9 * w) / (self.maxx -
                               self.minx)
    self.yfactor = (0.9 * h) / (self.maxy -
                               self.miny)

    self.xpmin = (int)(0.05 * w)
    self.ypmin = (int)(0.05 * h)
    self.xpmax = w - self.xpmin
    self.ypmax = h - self.ypmin

# calculate x pixel position
def calcx(self,xp):
    x= (xp - self.minx) * self.xfactor + self.xpmin
    return x
# calculate y pixel position
def calcy(self, yp, h):
    y = h - (yp - self.miny)*self.yfactor
    return y
```

Figure 28-3 shows the final two plots.

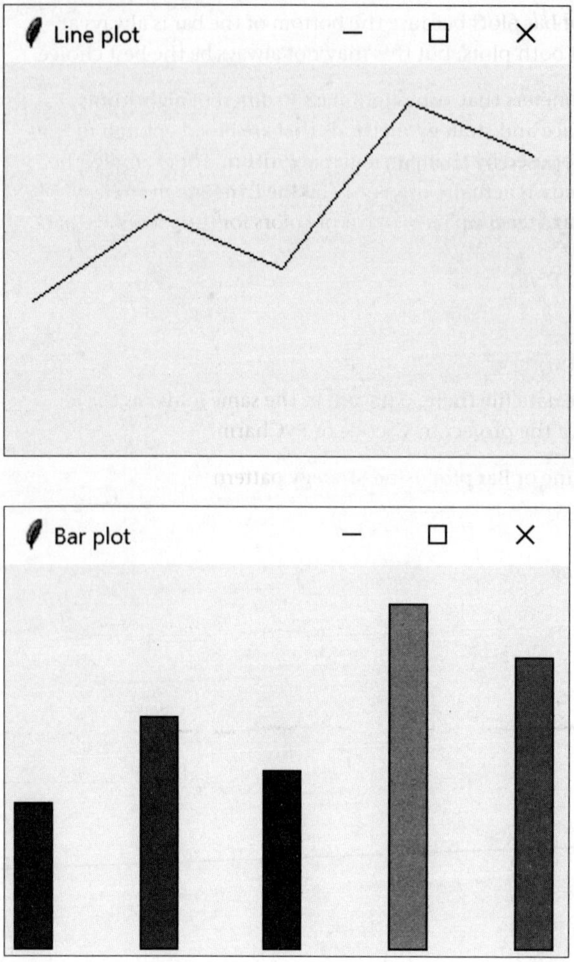

Figure 28-3 Line and Bar plot strategies

Consequences of the Strategy Pattern

The Strategy pattern enables you to select one of several algorithms dynamically. These algorithms can be related in an inheritance hierarchy, or they can be unrelated, as long as they implement a common interface. Because the Context switches between strategies at your request, you have more flexibility than if you simply called the desired derived class. This approach also avoids the sort of condition statements that can make code hard to read and maintain.

On the other hand, strategies don't hide everything. The client code must be aware that there are a number of alternative strategies and have some criteria for choosing among them. This shifts an algorithmic decision to the client programmer or the user.

For example, scaling might be different for bar plots because the bottom of the bar is always at `y = 0`. In this case, we force `ymin` to `0` for both plots, but this may not always be the best choice.

Since there are a number of different parameters that you might pass to different algorithms, you may have to develop a Context interface and strategy methods that are broad enough to allow for passing in parameters that are not used by that particular algorithm. For example, the `setPenColor` method in our `PlotStrategy` is actually used only by the `LineGraph` strategy. It is ignored by the `BarGraph` strategy, since it sets up its own list of colors for the successive bars it draws.

Programs on GitHub

In all these samples, be sure to include the data file (here, data.txt) in the same folder as the Python file. Also make sure they are part of the project in VScode or PyCharm.

- StrategyPlot.py: Program chooses Line or Bar plot using Strategy pattern
- Data.txt: Data for the StrategyPlot

Programs on GitHub

29

The Template Pattern

Whenever you write a parent class in which you leave one or more of the methods to be implemented by derived classes, you are in essence using the Template pattern. The Template pattern formalizes the idea of defining an algorithm in a class but leaving some of the details to be implemented in subclasses. In other words, if your base class is an abstract class, as often happens in these design patterns, you are using a simple form of the Template pattern.

Why We Use Template patterns

Templates are so fundamental; you have probably used them dozens of times without even thinking about it. The idea behind the Template pattern is that some parts of an algorithm are well defined and can be implemented in the base class, while other parts may have several implementations and are best left to derived classes. Another main theme is recognizing that there are some basic parts of a class that can be factored out and put in a base class so that they do not need to be repeated in several subclasses.

For example, in developing the plot classes we used in the Strategy pattern examples in this book, we discovered that in plotting both line graphs and bar charts, we needed similar code to scale the data and compute the *x* and *y* pixel positions.

```
# calculate x pixel position
def calcx(self,xp):
    x= (xp - self.minx) * self.xfactor + self.xpmin
    return x
# calculate y pixel position
def calcy(self, yp, h):
    y = h - (yp - self.miny) * self.yfactor
    return y
```

Thus, these methods all belonged in a base `PlotStrategy` class without any actual plotting capabilities. Note that the `plot` method sets up all the scaling constants. The actual `plot` method is deferred to the derived classes. The Template pattern is similar in this regard.

Kinds of Methods in a Template Class

A Template has four kinds of methods that you can use in derived classes:

1. Complete methods that carry out some basic function that all the subclasses want to use, such as `calcx` and `calcy` in the previous example. These are called *concrete methods.*
2. Methods that are not filled in at all and must be implemented in derived classes. In Python, you declare these as *empty* methods with a `pass` statement where the code would appear.
3. Methods that contain a default implementation of some operations but that can be overridden in derived classes. These are called *hook* methods. Of course, this naming is somewhat arbitrary because in Python, you can override any method in the derived class; still, Hook methods are intended to be overridden, whereas Concrete methods are not.
4. Finally, a `Template` class may contain methods that themselves call any combination of `abstract`, `hook`, and `concrete` methods. These methods are not intended to be overridden; they describe an algorithm without actually implementing its details. *Design Patterns* refers to these as `Template` methods.

Sample Code

Let's consider a simple program for drawing triangles on a screen. We'll start with an abstract `Triangle` class and then derive some special triangle types from it.

For simplicity, we use the `Point` class to represent the `x,y` pairs that define the vertices:

```
class Point():
    def __init__(self, x, y):
        self.x = x
        self.y = y
```

Note that you can access the *x* and *y* properties directly, without going through accessor functions.

The abstract `Triangle` class illustrates the Template pattern:

```
class Triangle():
    def __init__(self, canvas: Canvas, a: Point,
                 b: Point, c: Point):
        self.p1 = a
        self.p2 = b
        self.p3 = c
        self.canvas = canvas

    # draws a line between two points
    def drawLine(self, a, b):
        self.canvas.create_line(a.x, a.y, b.x, b.y)
```

```
    #draws the complete triangle
    def draw(self):
        self.drawLine(self.p1, self.p2)
        current = self.draw2ndLine(self.p2, self.p3)
        self.closeTriangle(current)

    # this is filled in by the derived classes
    def draw2ndLine(self, a: Point, b: Point):
        pass

    #closes the triangle from c back to p1
    def closeTriangle(self, c: Point):
        self.drawLine(c, self.p1)
```

This `Triangle` class saves the coordinates of three lines, but the *draw* routine draws only the first and the last lines. The all-important `draw2ndLine` method that draws a line to the third point is left as an abstract method. That way, the derived class can move the third point to create the kind of triangle you want to draw.

This is a general example of a class using the Template pattern. The `draw` method calls two concrete base class methods and one abstract method that must be overridden in any concrete class derived from `Triangle`.

Another very similar way to implement the base `Triangle` class is to include default code for the `draw2ndLine` method.

```
def draw2ndLine(self, a: Point, b: Point):
    self.drawLine(a, b)
    return b
```

In this case, the `draw2ndLine` method becomes a Hook method that can be overridden for other classes.

Drawing a Standard Triangle

To draw a general triangle with no restrictions on its shape, we simply implement the `draw2ndLine` method in a derived `stdTriangle` class:

```
# A simple standard triangle
class StdTriangle(Triangle):
    def __init__(self, canvas, a, b, c):
        super().__init__(canvas, a, b, c)

    def draw2ndLine(self, a: Point, b: Point):
        self.drawLine(a, b)
        return b
```

Drawing an Isosceles Triangle

This class computes a new third data point that makes the two sides equal in length and saves that new point inside the class.

```
class IsoscelesTriangle(Triangle):

    def __init__(self, canvas, a, b, c):
        super().__init__(canvas, a, b, c)
        dx1 = b.x - a.x
        dy1 = b.y - a.y
        dx2 = c.x - b.x
        dy2 = c.y - b.y

        side1 = self.calcSide(dx1, dy1)
        side2 = self.calcSide(dx2, dy2)

        if (side2 < side1):
            incr = -1
        else:
            incr = 1

        slope = dy2 / dx2
        intercept = c.y - slope * c.x

      # move point c
      # so that this is an isosceles triangle
        self.newcx = c.x
        self.newcy = c.y
        while math.fabs(side1 - side2) > 1:
            self.newcx += incr  # iterate a pixel
            self.newcy = (int)(slope * self.newcx
                                + intercept)
            dx2 = self.newcx - b.x
            dy2 = self.newcy - b.y
            side2 = self.calcSide(dx2, dy2)

        self.newc = Point(self.newcx, self.newcy)

    # calculate length of side
    def calcSide(self, dx, dy):
        return math.sqrt(dx * dx + dy * dy)
```

When the Triangle class calls the draw method, it calls this new version of draw2ndLine and draws a line to the new third point. Further, it returns that new point to the draw method so that it draws the closing side of the triangle correctly.

```
# draws 2nd line using saved new point
def draw2ndLine(self, b, c):
    self.drawLine(b, self.newc)
    return self.newc
```

The Triangle Drawing Program

The main program simply creates instances of the triangles you want to draw.

```
# coordinates of standard triangle
    p1 = Point(100, 40)
    p2 = Point(75, 100)
    p3 = Point(175, 150)

    stdTriangle = StdTriangle(canvas, p1, p2, p3)
    stdTriangle.draw()

# starting coordinates for isosceles triangle
    p4 = Point(150, 200)
    p5 = Point(240, 140)
    p6 = Point(175, 250)

    isoTriangle = \
        IsoscelesTriangle(canvas, p4, p5, p6)
    isoTriangle.draw()
    mainloop()
```

Figure 29-1 shows an example of the standard triangle and the same code using an isosceles triangle.

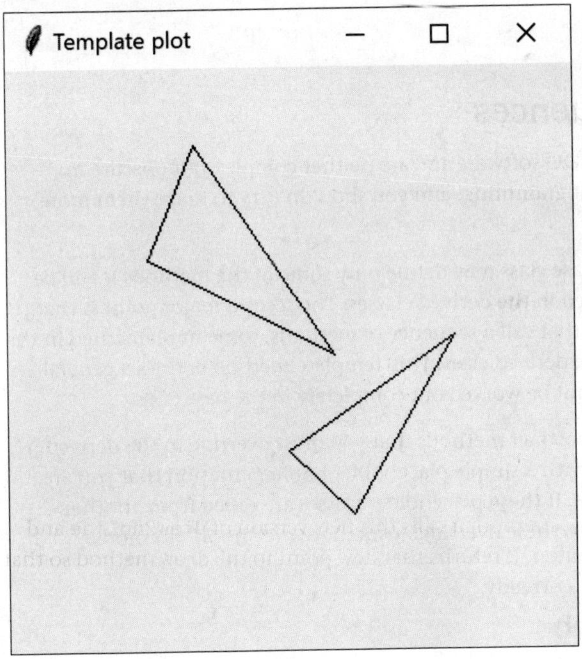

Figure 29-1 Standard and isosceles triangles

Templates and Callbacks

Design Patterns points out that Templates can exemplify the Hollywood Principle: "Don't call us, we'll call you." The idea here is that methods in the base class seem to call methods in the derived classes. The operative word here is *seem*. If we consider the `draw` method in our base `Triangle` class, we can see that there are three method calls:

```
def draw(self):
    self.drawLine(self.p1, self.p2)
    current = self.draw2ndLine(self.p2, self.p3)
    self.closeTriangle(current)
```

Now `drawLine` and `closeTriangle` are implemented in the base class. However, as we have seen, the `draw2ndLine` method is not implemented at all in the base class, and various derived classes can implement it differently. Because the actual methods that are being called are in the derived classes, it appears as though they are being called from the base class.

If this idea makes you uncomfortable, you will probably take solace in recognizing that *all* the method calls originate from the derived class and that these calls move up the inheritance chain until they find the first class that implements them. If this class is the base class, fine. If not, it could be any other class in between. Now, when you call the `draw` method, the derived class moves up the inheritance tree until it finds an implementation of `draw`. Likewise, for each method called from within `draw`, the derived class starts at the currently executing class and moves up the tree to find each method. When it gets to the `draw2ndLine` method, it finds it immediately in the current class. Thus, it isn't really called from the base class, but it does sort of seem that way.

Summary and Consequences

Template patterns occur all the time in OO software and are neither complex nor obscure in intent. They are a normal part of OO programming, and you shouldn't try to make them more abstract than they actually are.

The first significant point is that your base class may define only some of the methods it will be using, leaving the rest to be implemented in the derived classes. The second major point is that there may be methods in the base class that call a sequence of methods, some implemented in the base class and some implemented in the derived class. This Template method defines a general algorithm, although the details might not be worked out completely in the base class.

Template classes frequently have some abstract methods that you must override in the derived classes and may also have some classes with a simple placeholder implementation that you are free to override where this is appropriate. If these placeholder classes are called from another method in the base class, then we refer to these overridable methods are "hook" methods.

Example Code on GitHub

- TemplateTriangles.py: Displays the two triangles as in Figure 29-1 using a Template pattern.

30

The Visitor Pattern

The Visitor pattern turns the tables on the object-oriented model and creates an external class to act on data in other classes. This is useful if there are a fair number of instances of a small number of classes and you want to perform some operation that involves all or most of them.

When to Use the Visitor Pattern

While at first it may seem “unclean” to put operations that should be inside one class into another class instead, there are good reasons for doing it. Suppose each of multiple drawing object classes has similar code for drawing itself. The drawing methods may be different, but they probably all use underlying utility functions that we might have to duplicate in each class. Furthermore, a set of closely related functions is scattered throughout a number of different classes as shown in Figure 30-1.

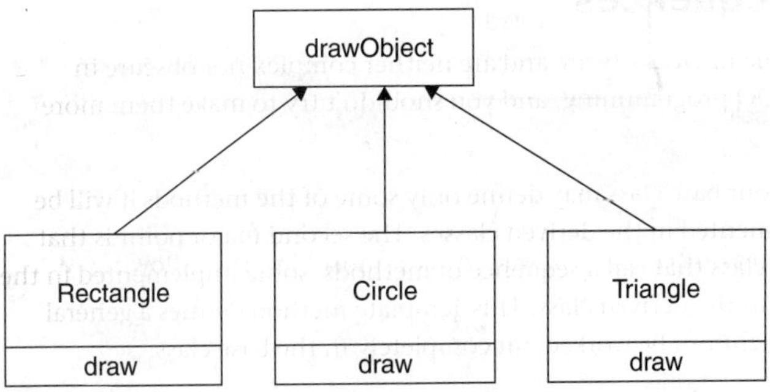

Figure 30-1 Functions scattered among classes

Instead, we write a `Visitor` class that contains all the related `draw` methods and have it visit each of the objects in succession (see Figure 30-2).

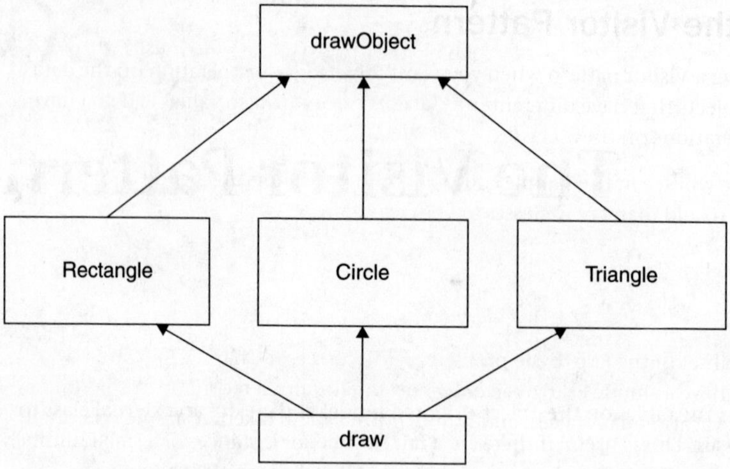

Figure 30-2 Draw visits each class

The question that most people who first encounter this pattern ask is, "What does visiting mean?" There is only one way that an outside class can gain access to another class, and that is by calling its public methods. In the `Visitor` case, visiting each class means that you are calling a method already installed for this purpose, called `accept`. The `accept` method has one argument: the instance of the visitor. In return, it calls the `visit` method of the `Visitor`, passing itself as an argument (see Figure 30-3).

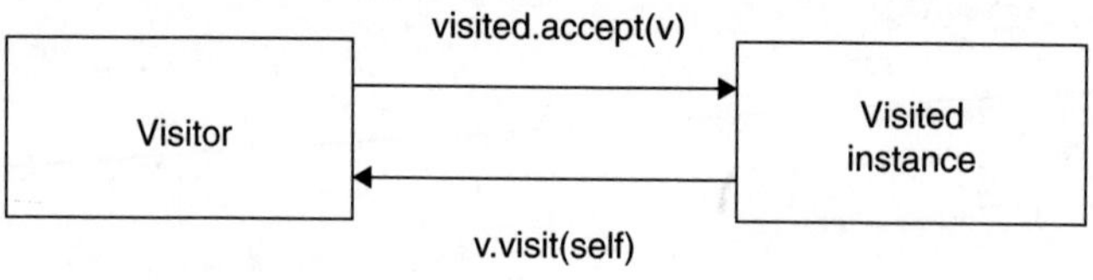

Figure 30-3 Visitor diagram

Putting it in simple code terms, every object that you want to visit must have the following method:

```
def accept(self, v:Visitor):
    v.visit(self)
```

In this way, the `Visitor` object receives a reference to each of the instances, one by one, and can then call its public methods to obtain data, perform calculations, generate reports, or just draw the object on the screen.

Working with the Visitor Pattern

You should consider using a Visitor pattern when you want to perform an operation on the data contained in multiple objects that have different interfaces. Visitors are also valuable if you have to perform unrelated operations on these classes.

On the other hand, as we will see in the sample code that follows, Visitors are a good choice only when you do not expect to add many new classes to your program.

Sample Code

Let's consider a simple subset of the `Employee` problem we discussed in Chapter 14, "The Composite Pattern." We have a simple `Employee` object that maintains a record of an employee's name, salary, number of vacation days taken, and number of sick days taken. A simple version of this class follows:

```
class Employee():
    def __init__(self, name, salary,
                    vacdays, sickdays):
        self.vacDays = vacdays  # save the days
        self.sickdays = sickdays
        self.salary = salary    #salary
        self.name = name        #and name

    # return the name
    def getName(self):  return self.name
    # and vacation days
    def getVacDays(self): return self.vacDays
    def getSalary(self): return self.salary

    # accept the Visitor and call it
    def accept(self, v: Visitor):
        v.visit(self)
```

Note that we have included the `accept` method in this class. Now suppose that we want to prepare a report on the number of vacation days that all employees have taken so far this year. We could just write some code in the client to sum the results of calls to each Employee's `getVacDays` function, or we could put this function into a Visitor.

In this first simple example, we only have Employees, so the basic abstract `Visitor` class is just

```
# abstract base class
class Visitor():
    def visit(self, emp):
        pass
```

Notice that there is no indication what the Visitor does with each class in either the client classes or the abstract `Visitor` class. We can, in fact, write a whole lot of visitors that do different things to the classes in this program. The Visitor we are going to write here first just sums the vacation data for all employees:

```
class VacationVisitor(Visitor):
    def __init__(self):
        self.totaldays = 0

    # sum the vacation days
    def visit(self, emp: Employee):
        self.totaldays += emp.getVacDays()

    def getTotalDays(self):
        return self.totaldays
```

Visiting Each Class

Now all we have to do to compute the total vacation days taken is go through a list of the employees, visit each of them, and then ask the Visitor for the total.

```
vac = VacationVisitor()  # create the 2 visitors
# do the visitation
for emp in self.employees:
    emp.accept(vac)

# print out sum
print(vac.getTotalDays()))
```

Let's reiterate what happens for each visit:

1. We move through a loop of all the Employees.
2. The Visitor calls each Employee's `accept` method.
3. That instance of the Employee calls the Visitor's `visit` method.
4. The Visitor fetches the vacation days and adds them into the total.
5. The main program prints the total when the loop is complete.

Visiting Several Classes

The Visitor becomes more useful when there are a number of different classes with different interfaces and we want to encapsulate how we get data from these classes. Let's extend our vacation days model by introducing a new Employee type called Boss. Let's further suppose that, at this company, Bosses are rewarded with bonus vacation days (instead of money). So the `Boss` class has a couple extra methods to set and obtain the bonus vacation day information:

```
class Boss(Employee):
    def __init__(self, name, salary, vacdays,
                 sickdays):
```

```
        super().__init__(name, salary, vacdays,
                         sickdays)
        self.bonusdays = 0

    def setBonusdays(self, bd):
        self.bonusdays = bd

    def getBonusdays(self):
        return self.bonusdays

    # accept the Visitor and call it
    def accept(self, v: Visitor):
        v.visit(self)
```

For any concrete Visitor classes we write, we must provide polymorphic `visit` methods for both the Employee and the Boss class. With the vacation day counter, you need to ask the Bosses for both regular and bonus days taken, so the visits are now different. Here you write a new `BVacationVisitor` class that accounts for this difference:

```
class BVacationVisitor(VacationVisitor):
    def __init__(self):
        self.totaldays = 0

    def visit(self, emp: Employee):
        self.totaldays += emp.getVacDays()

    # adds in total days including bonus days
    def visit(self, emp: Boss):
        self.totaldays += emp.getVacDays()
        if isinstance(emp, Boss):
            self.totaldays += emp.getBonusdays()
```

Note that while in this case `Boss` is derived from `Employee`, it need not be related at all, as long as the `Boss` class has an `accept` method for the `Visitor` class. It is quite important, however, that you implement a `visit` method in the Visitor for *every class* you will be visiting; do not count on inheriting this behavior because the `visit` method from the parent class is an Employee instead of a Boss visit method. Likewise, each of your derived classes (`Boss`, `Employee`, and so on) must have its own `accept` method instead of calling one in its parent class.

This level of polymorphism is not supported by Python (because of duck typing), and we need to check the type of employee before calling the `getBonusDays` method.

Bosses Are Employees, Too

The following simple application carries out both Employee visits and Boss visits on the collection of Employees and Bosses. The original `VacationVisitor` treats Bosses as Employees and gets only their ordinary vacation data. The `BVacationVisitor` gets both.

```
vac = VacationVisitor()  # create the 2 visitors
bvac = BVacationVisitor()
```

```
self.clearFields()
# do the visitations
for emp in self.employees:
    emp.accept(vac)
    emp.accept(bvac)
# put the totals in the two fields
self.total.insert(0, str(vac.getTotalDays()))
self.btotal.insert(0, str(bvac.getTotalDays()))
```

The two lines of displayed data represent the two sums that are computed when the user clicks the Visit button (see Figure 30-4).

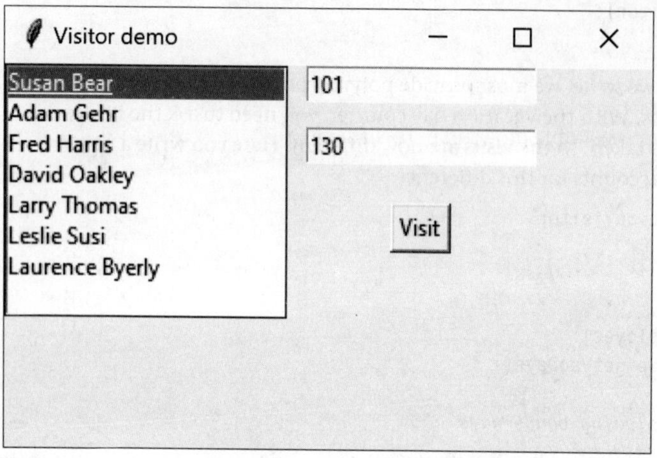

Figure 30-4 Visitor demo for total vacation days

The program also lets you click any employee and see their vacation days (see Figure 30-5).

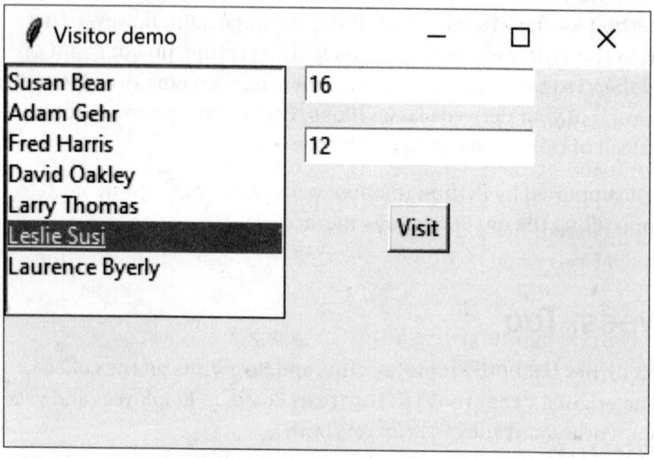

Figure 30-5 Visitor demo for one employee's vacation days

Double Dispatching

No article on the Visitor pattern is complete without mentioning that you are really dispatching a method twice for the Visitor to work. The Visitor calls the polymorphic `accept` method of a given object, and the `accept` method calls the polymorphic *visit* method of the Visitor. This bidirectional calling enables you to add more operations on any class that has an `accept` method because each new `Visitor` class we write can carry out whatever operations we might think of using for the data available in these classes.

Traversing a Series of Classes

The calling program that passes the class instances to the Visitor must know about all the existing instances of classes to be visited and must keep them in a simple structure such as a List. Another possibility would be to pass the List to the Visitor. Finally, the Visitor itself could keep the list of objects that it is to visit. The simple example program in this chapter uses a List of objects, but any of the other methods would work equally well.

Consequences of the Visitor Pattern

The Visitor pattern is useful when you want to encapsulate fetching data from a number of instances of several classes. *Design Patterns* suggests that the Visitor provides additional functionality to a class without changing it. We prefer to say that a Visitor can add functionality to a collection of classes and encapsulate the methods it uses.

The Visitor is not magic, however, and should not obtain private data from classes; it should be limited to the data available from public methods. This might force you to provide public methods that you would otherwise not provide. However, the Visitor can obtain data from a disparate collection of unrelated classes and use it to present the results of a global calculation to the user program.

It is easy to add new operations to a program using Visitors because the Visitor contains the code instead of each of the individual classes. Furthermore, Visitors can gather related operations into a single class instead of forcing you to change or derive classes to add these operations. This can make the program simpler to write and maintain.

Visitors are less helpful during a program's growth stage because each time you add new classes that must be visited, you have to add an abstract `visit` operation to the abstract `Visitor` class; additionally, you must add an implementation for that class to each concrete Visitor you have written. Visitors can be powerful additions when the program reaches the point where many new classes are unlikely.

Visitors can be used very effectively in Composite systems. The boss–employee system we just illustrated could well be a Composite like the one we used in Chapter 14.

Example Code on GitHub

- EmployeeVisits.py: Example of Visitor for Boss and Employees

PART V

A Brief Introduction to Python

If you haven't worked in Python before, these chapters summarize the Python language. These chapters start at the beginning, giving you the grammar and syntax and then take you through the basics of working with Python.

31

Variables and Syntax in Python

Python has all the features of any powerful modern language. If you are familiar with C, C++, or Java, you will find most of its syntax very familiar.

You use *variables* in Python to represent numbers and strings that might change during the program. Usually variable names are written all in lower case.

In Python, case is significant, and if we write

```
y = m * x + b            # all lower case
```

or

```
Y = m * x + b            # Y differs from y
```

we mean two different variables: Y and y. This might seem awkward at first, but having the ability to make such distinctions is sometimes very useful. For example, programmers often capitalize symbols that refer to constants:

```
PI = 3.1416              # implies a constant
```

Programmers also sometimes define data types using mixed case and variables of that data type in lower case. Here we create a class called `Temperature` and a variable of that type in lower case.

```
class Temperature            # begin definition

temp = Temperature(37.2)     # an instance
```

To see much more about how to use classes, refer to Chapter 1, "Introduction to Objects."

Data Types

The major data types in Python mirror those in C and Java.

Boolean	True or False
int	Integers can be long
float	Floating point, always double precision
string	Characters
complex	A two-part number with .real and .imag parts

Boolean variables can only take on the values represented by the reserved words True and False. Boolean variables often result from comparisons and other logical operations:

```
gtnum = k >6            # true if k is greater than 6
```

Unlike in C, you cannot assign numeric values to a Boolean variable, and you cannot convert between Boolean and any other type. Python Boolean True evaluates to 1 and False evaluates to 0.

However, you can also reassign the value of any variable to a new type.

```
gtnum = "lesser"    # now is a string
```

Numeric Constants

Python does not support the concept of named constants, as Java and C do. Any named entity is a variable; that variable takes on the type of the value you assign to it and changes type if you assign another value to it.

```
PI = 3.14159  # float
PI = "cherry" # string
```

However, it is conventional that variable names in all caps are considered to be constants.

Any number that you type into your program is automatically of type int if it has no fractional part or of type float if it does.

Python also has three reserved word constants: True, False, and None, where None means an object variable that does not yet refer to any object.

Strings

Strings in Python are groups of zero or more characters and are considered to be unchangeable, or *immutable*. All the methods that operate on strings produce a new string with the changes that method carries out.

You can represent strings by enclosing them in either single or double quotes. You can also use triple quotes, and such strings can go on for several lines. However, the line breaks become part of such strings.

```
# strings can be enclosed in single
# or double or triple quotes
fstring = "fred"
astring = 'sam'

longstring = """this can even go on for
         several lines"""
```

There are a number of useful operations you can perform on strings. Each string *method* returns a new string; the original is unchanged. For example:

```
newstring = oldstring.capitalize()
```

The most common string methods follow:

```
lower, upper
isalpha, isdigit
replace
split (returns a List)
strip
removeprefix, removesuffix (in version 3.9 and later)
```

A complete list of string methods is given in Table 31-1 at the end of the chapter.

Python does not have a substring method, but you can use the `in` operator to achieve the same result.

```
if "sam" in "samuel":
    print ("sam is there")
```

You can also cut out parts of a string using *slicing*. For example:

```
text = "Learning Python"
# first 3 characters
print(text[0:3]) #Lea
```

For more detail on slicing, check out the beginning of Chapter 34, "Python Collections and Files."

In addition, the `len` function works on strings as well as lists (or arrays):

```
num = len(newstring)
```

Character Constants

Python follows the C convention that whitespace characters can be represented by preceding special characters with a backslash. The backslash itself is a special character, so it can be represented by using a double backslash.

'\n'	Newline (line feed)
'\r'	Carriage return
'\t'	Tab character
'\b'	Backspace
'\f'	Form feed
'\0'	Null character
'\"'	Double quote
'\''	Single quote
'\\'	Backslash

Here we enclosed the characters in single quotes, but you could just as easily use double quotes.

Variables

Variable names in Python can be of any length and can be of any combination of upper- and lowercase letters and numbers; however, the first character must be a letter. Pythonistas like to use only lower case in Python variable and function names, but you can sometimes improve readability by placing an underscore between the words:

```
sum_of_pairs
```

Note that because case is significant in Python, the following variable names all refer to different variables:

```
temperature
Temperature
TEMPERATURE
```

However, it is customary to use mostly lower case for variable names. Class names usually begin with a capital letter, and it is customary (but not required) that names of constants are written all in caps.

Python deduces the type of variable by the value you assign to it. There is no requirement to declare variables before they are used.

```
j = 5                      # an integer
xyz = 273.16               # float type (double)
temp_name = "Celsius"      # a string
temperature = 92.8
hot = temperature > 80     # Boolean
```

Complex Numbers

Complex numbers are made up of a real and imaginary part in the form:

$a + bi$

Here, *i* is the imaginary number, the square root of –1. You can create a complex number using the `complex` method or by using `j` to indicate the imaginary part.

```
cmplx = complex(5.43, 2.22) # a complex number
cmplx2 = 5.5 + 2.2j         # also complex number
```

Complex numbers have a real and an imaginary part that you can access directly:

```
r = cmplx.real
ipart = cmplx.imag
```

You can carry out simple arithmetic on these numbers (add, subtract, multiply, and divide), but they usually come up as part of calculations such as the Fourier transform.

Integer Division

If you divide one integer by another one in Python, the result is not an integer, but a float, unlike in some other languages.

So the following

```
x = 4/2
print(x)
x = 5/2
print(x)
```

will print out both

```
2.0
```

and

```
2.5
```

If you want to get the actual integer result of division, where the remainder is discarded, you use the double slash or `floor` operator.

```
x= 5//2
print (x)
```

This produces the expected integer result of

```
2
```

Multiple Equal Signs for Initialization

As with C and Java, Python enables you to initialize a series of variables to the same value in a single statement:

```
i = j = k = 0
```

This can be confusing, so do not overuse this feature. The compiler generates the same amount of code for:

```
i = 0
j = 0
k = 0
```

You can also assign multiple values to multiple variables in a single statement:

```
a, b = 4.2, 5.6
```

This is of historical interest, but it does not generate different code. In fact, it takes *more* typing than this, and it is harder to read:

```
a = 4.2
b = 5.6
```

Try to come up with a sentence that cleanly describes that statement—maybe "a and b are assigned the values 4.2 and 5.6." These sorts of statements can sometimes lead to obfuscation rather than clarity.

However, you can use this syntax to swap the values of two variables in a single line:

```
a, b = b, a        # swap values
```

This will also work for three or more variables, although it is not clear why you would do this. Functions can return multiple values in a similar fashion:

```
x, y =calcFunc(z)
```

A Simple Python Program

Now let's look at a very simple Python program for adding two numbers together.

```
""" add 2 numbers together """
a = 1.75          # assign values
b = 3.46
c = a + b         # add together

# print out sum
print("sum = ", c)
```

If you type this code into any of the development environments and run it, the result is this:

```
sum = 5.21
```

Let's see what observations we can make about this simple program:

Comments start with # and terminate at the end of the line. You can also enclose comments in triple quotes. These can go on for several lines; you can use either single or double quotes, but there must be three of them in a row, all of the same type. It is conventional that you put a space after the # that starts the comment.

As in C, Java, and most other languages (except Pascal), the equal sign is used to represent assignment of data

The `print` function can be used to print values on the screen. In Python 3, the list of variables to print must be enclosed in parentheses. Earlier, Python 2 print statements did not require these parentheses.

Compiling and Running This Program

This simple program is called examples.py in the Chapter 31 folder of the Pythonpatterns directory of our GitHub site. You can compile and execute it by copying it to any convenient directory and loading it into your development environment.

Arithmetic Operators

The fundamental operators in Python are much the same as they are in most other modern languages.

+	Addition
-	Subtraction, unary minus
*	Multiplication
/	Division
%	Modulo (remainder after integer division)
//	Floor (remainder after division of two floats)

Bitwise operators

The bitwise operators are intended to do ANDs and ORs and complements on integers to add or mask out individual bits.

&	Bitwise AND
|	Bitwise OR
^	Bitwise exclusive OR
~	One's complement
>> *n*	Right shift *n* places
<< *n*	Left shift *n* places

You might be less familiar with bit manipulation, so here are a few examples. The whole purpose of setting specific bits in a byte or integer is really so you can use that number to set some sort of hardware register or other type of bitmap.

The bitwise AND is sometimes called a masking function. It returns a number that has bits set to 1 that are set in both of the input values. So if we start with

```
x = 7           # 0111, and
z = 10          # 1010, then
val = x & z     # 0010, since one bit is set in both
```

the OR operator sets bits in the result that are ones in *either* value.

```
val = x | z         # 1111 is the result
```

The complement operator switches all the ones and zeroes in the number.

```
val = ~z            # 11110101 - to 8 bits
                    # same as -z-1, or -1011
```

The left and right shift operators shift the bits to the left and right, filling with zeroes.

```
val = x << 1        # left shift 1 place 1110
val = x >> 1        # right shift 1 place 0011
```

Combined Arithmetic and Assignment Statements

Python allows you to combine addition, subtraction, multiplication, and division with the assignment of the result to a new variable.

```
x = x + 3       # can also be written as:
x += 3          # add 3 to x; store result in x

# also with the other basic operations:
temp *= 1.80    # mult temp by 1.80
z -= 7          # subtract 7 from z
y /= 1.3        # divide y by 1.3
```

This is used primarily to save typing; it is unlikely to generate any different code. These compound operators cannot have spaces between them.

Comparison Operators

Earlier, we used the > operator to mean "greater than." Note particularly that "is equal to" requires *two* equal signs and that "not equal" is "!=":

>	Greater than
<	Less than
==	Is equal to
!=	Is not equal to
>=	Greater than or equal to
<=	Less than or equal to

The input Statement

The previous examples show how to use various operators and print out results. But what if you want the user to enter some data for the program to work on. For this, Python provides the `input` statement, which can print out a prompting string and wait for keyboard input.

```
name = input("What is your name? ")
print("Hi "+name +" boy!")
```

This little program asks for your name and waits for you to type a string and press Enter. So, the resulting console test might look like this:

```
What is your name? Jim
Hi Jim boy!
```

Heinlein fans might recognize the reference.

Of course, you can enter numbers as well, but you *must be sure* to convert the entered string into an `int` or a `float`. The input statement always returns a string, no matter what kind of value you intended.

```
x = float(input("Enter x: "))
y = float(input("Enter y: "))
print("The sum is: ", x+y)
```

The resulting output is:

```
Enter x: 23.45
Enter y: 41.46
The sum is:  64.91
```

Of course, the naïve program expects only legal input. If you enter, say, `qq` instead of 22, you get a Python error:

```
File "C:\Users\James\PycharmProjects\input\inputdemo.py", line 7, in <module>
    y = float(input("Enter y: "))
ValueError: could not convert string to float: 'qq'
```

There are ways to check for this, of course, such as catching Exceptions, which we will explain in Chapter 34.

However, you will only find the `input` statement in rudimentary examples. Most programs that need user input get it from a windowing interface. We show these same examples at the beginning of Chapter 2, "Visual Programming in Python," using the tkinter GUI library.

PEP 8 Standards

Guido van Rossum and a few colleagues collected and documented some code readability standards in Python Enhancement Proposal number 8 (PEP 8). They pointed out that code is read more than it is written and suggested that people follow these standards. They are not hard-and-fast rules, but they are widely accepted.

You can easily find the complete PEP 8 document, as well as a number of summaries of it, online. To a large degree, the recommendations boil down to judicious use of more whitespace to make the code readable.

Variable and Function Names

Variable names should be all lower case. For readability of longer names, you use underscores to separate words within a variable name:

```
sum_of_pairs
```

This naming style is sometimes called *snake_case*. Functions within classes (sometimes called *methods)* follow the same convention.

It is more important that your style is consistent throughout a program than it is what variable naming style you choose. Mixed case is not disallowed, but it is less common. However, we have seen few programs utilizing snake case, because it is harder to type those variable names.

Be sure to choose readable, meaningful variable names instead of single character names such as a or x in your code.

```
apples =  boxes * capacity          # readable
a = b * c                           # confusing
```

You should also avoid using variable names like lowercase "L" or uppercase "O" because they are too easily confused with one and zero.

Constants

You should write names of constants in uppercase.

```
AVOGADRO = 6.02e23
```

This is only for your readers; it is not enforced by Python at all.

Class Names

Class names should begin with a capital letter, and they may have more capital letters to separate words but should not include underscores:

```
class Pairs:
```

```
class CsvFileReader:
```

This mixed-case naming style is called *CamelCase*.

Indentation and Spacing

Indentation within loops and classes should always be four spaces. Although you shouldn't use tabs, most development environments will translate a tab into four spaces for you.

You should put two blank lines before each new class and one blank line before each new function. (In printed coding examples, this is sometimes reduced to one blank line because of space restrictions.)

You should put spaces around equal signs and arithmetic operators:

```
y = m*x + b
```

However, when operators have different priorities, like the multiplication symbol above (*), you should only add spaces around the lower-priority operators (+).

Similarly, you should not put spaces into compound operators, such as here:

```
index += 1
```

You should add spaces after commas in lists and other sorts of arrays:

```
fruits = [apples, oranges, lemons]
```

Comments

You should put a space between the # and the first text character of a comment. While you can put the comment on a line by itself, you can also add comments on any line of code. The standard suggests that you should use in-line comments sparingly.

If your comments go on for several lines, you should align them with the current code indentation.

```
def addArrays(a, b):
    a[0] += b[0]        # add one element
        # The data in these arrays may be substantial
    # so we check the size next
```

Your initial reaction as you are learning a new language may be to ignore comments, but they are just as important at the outset as they are later. A program never gets commented at all unless you do it as you write it; if you ever want to use that code again, you will find it very helpful to have some comments to help you in deciphering what you meant for that code to do. Many programming instructors refuse to accept programs that are uncommented.

Docstrings

You can write a comment describing a function or class that goes on for several lines if you start with three quotation marks. If you place a comment just after a class or function declaration, it is called a Docstring. You can use such comments to describe these components in detail.

```
""" This module allows you to enter donations manually, or read them from a csv file
The donor table is a subset of all patrons who have at some time donated. """
```

String Methods

String methods are listed in Table 31-1.

Table 31-1 **String Methods**

Method	Description
`capitalize()`	Capitalizes the first character.
`casefold()` `lower()`	Changes all characters to lower case.
`center(length, char)`	Fills both ends of a string with spaces or with the optional `char` argument.
`count(arg)`	Returns the number of times the `arg` string appears in the string.
`endswith(char)`	Returns True if the string ends with the specified character.
`find(argstr)` `index(argstr)`	Returns the position of the argument string.
`isalnum()`	Returns `True` if all characters are alphanumeric.
`isalpha()`	Returns `True` if all characters are alphabetics.
`isdigit()` `isnumeric()`	Returns `True` if all characters are digits.
`isidentifier()`	Returns `True` if all characters are alphabetics, numeric, or underscores and do not start with a number.
`isprintable()`	Returns `True` if all characters are printable.
`isspace()`	Returns `True` if all characters are whitespaces.
`istitle()`	Returns `True` if all words in the string are in title case.
`isupper()`	Returns `True` if all characters are upper case.
`join()`	Joins the string with a tuple of other strings.
`lstrip()` `ljust()`	Returns a string with leading spaces removed.
`partition(argstr)`	Returns a tuple comprised of the string before the `arg` string, the `arg` string, and the string after the `arg` string.
`replace(oldarg, newarg)`	Returns a string where the string `oldarg` is replaced by `newarg`.
`removeprefix(argstr)`	Removes the prefix of the string (`vsn 3.9`).
`removesuffix(argstr)`	Removes the suffix of the string (`vsn 3.9`).
`rfind(argstring)`	Returns the index of the rightmost position of the `arg` string.
`rpartition(argstr)`	Returns a tuple broken by the last occurrence of the `arg` string.
`rsplit(argstr, max)`	Returns a list of strings that are separated by the `arg` string. If `max` is specified, it limits the length of the list.

`rstrip()`	Returns a string with right spaces trimmed.
`split(sep)`	Returns a list separated by whitespace characters or by the sep character.
`splitlines()`	Returns a list of strings split at line breaks.
`strip()`	Returns a string trimmed at both ends.
`swapcase()`	Returns a string with upper- and lower case swapped.
`title()`	Returns a string in title case.

Examples on GitHub

- examples.py: All the examples in this chapter
- printbin.py: All the bitwise operators
- inputdemo.py: Illustrates input statement usage

32

Making Decisions in Python

The familiar if-else C and Java syntax has its analog in Python. However, it is important to note that any conditional statement ends with a colon and that all the statements that are to be executed must be *indented* by four spaces. Many Python development environments allow you to use tabs to create this indentation:

```
if y > 0:
    z = x / y
    print("z = ",  z)
```

If you want to carry out either one set of statements or another depending on a single condition, you should use the else clause along with the if statement:

```
if y > 0:
    z = x / y
else:
    z = 0
```

If the else clause contains multiple statements, they must be indented, as in the previous example. Note that the else clause also requires a colon to set it off.

Python does not require that if statement conditions be enclosed in parentheses, as Java and C do. However, it is not an error to use parentheses if you think it makes the statement clearer.

elif is "else if"

When you have a number of choices in a row, such as in the following ticket price example, it is helpful to use if and then elif (which stands for "else if"). The final case can be else, which covers all the remaining possibilities.

```
"""Demonstration of elif"""
if age < 6:
    price = 0    # child is free
elif age >= 6 and age < 60:
    price = 35   # adult price
elif age >= 60 and age < 80:
    price = 30   # senior
```

```
elif hasStudentId:
    price = 15   # student
else:
    price = 20   # super Senior 80 or higher
```

Combining Conditions

When you need to combine two or more conditions in a single `if` or other logical statement, you use the logical And, Or, and Not operators. These are totally different than in any other languages, except C/C++, and are confusingly like the bitwise operators shown in Chapter 31.

and	Logical And
or	Logical Or
!	Logical Not

In Python, we would write

```
x = 12
if 0 < x and x <= 24:
    print ("Time is up")
```

The Most Common Mistake

The "is equal to" operator is "==" and the assignment operator is "=", which look very similar and can easily be misused. If you write

```
if x = 0:
    print("x is zero")
```

instead of

```
if x == 0:
    print("x is zero")
```

you will get the odd-seeming compilation error, "Syntax error," because the result of the fragment

```
x = 0
```

is the double precision number `0` instead of a Boolean `True` or `False`. Of course, the result of the fragment

```
x == 0
```

is indeed a Boolean quantity, and the compiler does not print any error message.

Looping Statements in Python

Python has only two looping statements: `while` and `for`. The `while` is quite analogous to that in C and Java.

```
i = 0
while i < 100:
    x = x + i
    i += 1
print ("x=", x)
```

The loop is executed as long as the condition in parentheses is true. It is possible that such a loop may never be executed at all; of course, if you are not careful, a `while` loop will never be completed.

The for Loop and Lists

In Python, `for` loops are just as powerful as in other languages but are much simpler to write. Suppose we create an array of numbers:

```
array = [5,12,34,57,22,6]
```

In Python, this is actually called a *List*, but it is essentially an array. We could iterate through the six members of this array and print them out like this:

```
for x in array:
    print (x)
```

If we want to go only partway through the array, we use the `range` function to generate those indexes:

```
for i in range(0,5):
    print (i, array[i])
```

This `range` function starts at 0 and stops just *before* the upper limit:

```
0 5
1 12
2 34
3 57
4 22
```

You have to use this line to get all six elements:

```
range(0,6)
```

And if you want to get just the middle of the array, you use this:

```
range(1,5)
```

Using range in if statements

You can rewrite the ticket pricing program at the beginning of this chapter using the range function and the in keyword to check whether the variable is within the range:

```
# elif Demo using range method instead
if age < 6:
    price = 0     # child is free
elif age in range(6, 60):
    price = 35    # adult price
elif age in range(61,80):
    price = 30    # senior
elif hasStudentId:
    price = 15    # student
else:
    price = 20    # super Senior 80 or higher
```

Using break and continue

The break and continue statements provide ways to jump out of a loop. Consider the following:

```
xarray= [5,7,4,3,9,12,6]
sum = 0
for x in xarray:
    sum += x
    if sum > 16:
        break
    print (sum)
```

The break statement ends the for loop when the sum reaches 1 or more. Of course, you could write this same code several other ways to avoid jumping out of the loop. For example:

```
sum = i = 0
quit=False
while not quit:
    sum += xarray[i]
    print(sum)
    i += 1
    quit = sum >= 16
```

Or you could use an iterator:

```
xiter = iter(xarray)
sum=0
while sum < 16:
    sum += next(xiter)
    print(sum)
```

Some programmers feel that loops should have only one entry point and one exit point and should avoid using break. Loops containing a break can be hard to trace when you are looking for errors. Other programmers feel that using breaks is simpler and cleaner.

The continue Statement

The `continue` statement is similar, except that it goes to the bottom of the current loop without exiting from it. For example:

```
for i in range(10):
    if i==6:
        continue
    print(i)
```

This program prints the numbers from 0 through 9 but leaves out 6. This is a simple example, but it can easily be rewritten as follows:

```
for i in range(10):
    if i != 6:
        print (i)
```

Python Line Length

Early Python programmers were encouraged to keep program lines under 80 characters because of the limitations of early displays, but this is not a hard restriction. Although really wide lines of program code are hard to comprehend, you can write statements that go on for several lines when this is required.

Although you might write

```
a = b*c + d*e
```

you can just as easily write more meaningful variable names, such as

```
apples = boxes * capacity + storage_bins * bin_size
```

To take the example further, you might better write the previous line as

```
apples = (boxes * capacity) \
       + (storage_bins * bin_size)
```

which is certainly more readable, using the line continuation character.

You can also have a multiline expression without the continuation character, as long as it is contained in parentheses, braces, or brackets.

```
apples = (boxes * capacity
       +storage_bins * bin_size)
```

The print Function

We have been using the `print` function promiscuously without ever explaining it. It simply prints strings to the console. If there are several elements separated by commas, Python converts each one to a string and adds a space between elements. These two statements

```
age = 12
print("I am", age, "years old")
```

print the following:

```
I am 12 years old
```

You can replace the space separator with any other character by adding a `sep=` argument to your `print` statement:

```
print(5, 6, 7, 8, sep="-")
```

This produces

```
5-6-7-8
```

Normally, the `print` function terminates the string it prints with a newline character so that the cursor moves on to the next line. You can change that by specifying the end character yourself—usually a space or an empty string.

```
print ("Your name is: ", end="")
print ("Susan")
```

This results in a single line:

```
Your name is: Susan
```

Formatting Numbers

Suppose you write

```
x = 4.5 / 3.22
k = 12
print(k, x)
```

You will be perhaps surprised that the answer Python prints is

```
12 1.3975155279503104
```

Similarly, if you write

```
print(0.1 + 0.2)
```

Python (or almost any other language) prints

```
0.30000000000000004
```

In the first case, `4.5 / 3.22` produces a long irrational decimal that looks pretty inelegant and adds little new information.

The second case, where you would expect `(0.1 + 0.2)` to produce 0.30, you get that number and a little more. This is because computers can't represent most fractions exactly in binary. The result is somewhat approximate.

If you simply chop off some of that string, the actual number to three places is pretty much what you'd expect. What you need to be able to do is format such numbers down to fewer figures: The 15th or 16th places are hardly significant.

Python has actually evolved three different formatting schemes over the years, and we'll present them in order of decreasing complexity.

C and Java Style Formatting

In this style of formatting, the format strings are grouped together in quotes along with any desired text. The variables to be formatted are listed last.

```
print("Amount: %5d Price: %4.2f" % (k, x))
```

So, the integer k is formatted as a decimal integer five characters wide, and the floating-point variable x is formatted four characters wide with two decimal places after the decimal point. The result is:

```
Amount:    12 Price: 1.40
```

Although this formatting style resembles C and Java, be aware that the quoted format string is separated from the list of variables with a % sign instead of a comma, and the list of variables is enclosed in parentheses.

Other formatting strings are %s for strings, %x for hexadecimal, and %b for binary. Adding a + forces the number to be represented with a plus or minus sign.

The format string Function

Another approach Python uses is for you to create a formatting string where placeholders for the variables are enclosed in braces along with the formatting info.

```
print("Amount:{a:5d} Price:{b:4.2f}".format(a=k, b=x))
```

In this example, the labels a and b show where the two numbers go. Then the format function says which variables are represented by a and b are replaced by k and x. The output is exactly the same as for the first example.

f-string Formatting

The final approach was introduced beginning in Python 3.6 and is by far the simplest. It is also considered the most Pythonic. The variable names and their formatting information are enclosed in braces.

```
print(f'Amount: {k:5d} Price: {x:4.2f}\n')
```

In this style, no percent signs are used, and the variables are followed by the formatting information within the same pair of braces. Note, in particular, that the f-string is a quoted string preceded by the letter f just before the first quote. The output is identical to the first two methods.

Note that this formatting approach creates a formatted string that then gets printed. But this is a very useful approach when you are formatting data to appear in some window. It gives you complete control over what that window actually shows:

```
label = f'Amount: {k:5d} Price: {x:4.2f}'
print(label)
```

Comma-Separated Numbers

If you have large integers or floats that you want to make more readable, you can use the comma format operator to format a number:

```
num=100000
label = f'{num:,}'
print (label)
```

This prints

```
100,000
```

Similarly,

```
fnum=150234.56
label = f'{fnum:,.2f}'
print (label)
```

prints

```
150,234.56
```

Note that `.2f` was used here to add the two decimal digits.

Strings

Formatting strings is pretty simple. You can control the width of the field and the justification. Normally, numbers are right-justified and strings are left-justified, but you can use the < and > symbols as part of the string format.

Here's a list of names in their normal format:

```
names=["Amy", "Fred", "Samuel", "Xenophon", "Constantine"]
for n in names:
    print(f"{n:12s}")
```

This prints

```
Amy
Fred
Samuel
Xenophon
Constantine
```

To right-justify the strings, you simply add the greater than sign in the formatting string:

```
for n in names:
    print(f"{n:>12s}")
```

This gives you the right-justified strings:

```
         Amy
        Fred
      Samuel
    Xenophon
 Constantine
```

Formatting Dates

The built-in Python `date` class can represent year, month, and date, and the `datetime` class also contains hours, minutes, and seconds. This code gets the current date and then prints it formatted:

```
# get today's date
todate = date.today()

# and print it formatted
print (f'Todate= {todate:%m-%d-%Y}')
```

You can use the two confusingly named functions `strptime` and `strftime` to convert from strings to dates. The function `strptime` takes a string and puts it into date format, while the function `strftime` gets a string from a time.

One use of these two functions is to convert dates to a different format. For example, you might have a table of dates in the common U.S. format mm-dd-yyyy, and you need to convert them to the yyyy-mm-dd format used for date objects in most databases.

```
#convert a date string to a datetime object
da = datetime.strptime("02/07/1971", "%m/%d/%Y")
ystring = da.strftime("%Y-%m-%d")
print(ystring)
```

Using the Python match Function

You are probably familiar with the `switch` statement found in C-like languages such as C, C++, C#, and Java. The following Java version is typical:

```
int tval =12;

      switch (tval) {
          case 2: System.out.println("two");
              break;

          case 3:
          case 12:
              System.out.println("3 or 12");
              break;

          default:
              System.out.println("all the rest");
              break;
      }
```

Until recently, Python programmers had to write a lot of `if` statements or try to approximate the `switch` statement using a dictionary. But, beginning in Python 3.10 (released in October 2021), you can use Python's new `match` function to carry out switch-like functions and a lot more. The `match` function matches simple values, strings, and pretty complex patterns. Here's the previous program converted to Python.

```
tval = 12
match tval:
    case 2:              # if 2
        print("two")
    case 3 | 12:         # 3 or 12
        print("3 or 12")
    case _:              # anything else
        print('all the rest')
```

Note that, unlike in Java, no braces are used, and you don't need to end each case with a `break` statement. You can `OR` together several values in a single `case` statement, and you use the underscore in place of `default` to provide a case for any values that don't match anything else.

In the same way, but unlike in most other languages, you can also match strings:

```
name = 'fred'
match name:
    case 'sam':
        print('sam')
    case 'fred':
        print('fred')
    case 'sally':
        print('sally forth')
```

Pattern Matching

The `match` statement can match more complex patterns pretty easily. However, the descriptions of the patterns must be made up of fixed values, not variables.

Let's consider a simple `Point` class with internal `x` and `y` variables:

```
class Point:
    def __init__(self, x, y):
        self.x = x
        self.y = y
```

You can match `Point` value patterns using an expression that looks much like a constructor:

```
def location(point):
    match point:
        case Point(x=0, y=0):
            print("Point is at the origin.")
        case Point(x=0, y=y):
            print(f"Y={y} point is on the y-axis.")
        case Point(x=x, y=0):
            print(f"X={x} point is on the x-axis.")
        case Point():
            print("The point is somewhere else.")
        case _:
            print("Not a point")
```

So, we can create a point and see how it matches:

```
p = Point(100, 0)
location(p)
```

The resulting match is to the pattern `x=x, y=0` and the program prints

```
X=100 and the point is on the x-axis.
```

This example is drawn from the tutorial on the `match` statement in the Python 3.10 documentation. You can also look at the extended tutorial in the PEP 636 document.

Reference

1. Structural Pattern Matching Tutorial, www.python.org/dev/peps/pep-0636/.

Moving On

In this brief chapter, we have seen the fundamental syntax elements of the Python language. Now that we understand the tools, we need to see how to use them. In the chapters that follow, we will examine lists, functions, and objects to show how to use them and how powerful they can be.

Sample Code on GitHub

- decisions.py: `while`, `if`, `elif`
- breaks.py: Examples of using `break`
- continue.py: Examples of using `continue`
- matches.py: Examples of the `match` function

33

Development Environments

You can download and install the current version of Python from python.org in just a few seconds. Python installation includes IDLE, Python's Integrated Development and Learning Environment, which of course honors Monty Python performer Eric Idle.

IDLE

IDLE is an interactive window where you can type Python statements and see what they do. If you type a variable name by itself, IDLE displays its current value.

You can also create fully functional programs by opening a new edit window with File | New and then typing a complete program into it.

Then you can run the program by pressing F5 or by selecting Run | Run Module. The result appears in the shell window you started with.

IDLE asks you where to save the code before it runs it so that you have a copy of every program you write.

IDLE is a nice little trial environment, but it has a number of limitations. There is no way to step through a program or set breakpoints to debug it. And there is no way to examine the values of variables while a program is executing. This may just be for beginners, but Python works differently enough than other languages that having these features can help you more easily grasp how Python works.

Thonny

Thonny is a free beginner's development environment that you can download from thonny.org. It is intuitive and has a program window, a variables window, and an output window.

You write code in the main window or import it from a file and then either click Run | Run Current Script or press F5. Thonny supports breakpoints, and you can step through the program with F6 and step into loops with F7. Along the way, you can observe the values of the variables changing.

It is quite possible to write fairly sophisticated programs using Thonny and even combine your program with existing Python packages. You can also access keyword and statement completion by pressing Ctrl / Spacebar. However, it only provides syntax completion if you stick with Python 3.6, which Thonny ships with. If you switch to a newer version, syntax completion is disabled.

PyCharm

Probably the most popular free development environment, PyCharm gives you a lot of help with syntax and debugging. Roughly equivalent in features is VSCODE, which we discuss next. These two are used by nearly all Python programmers.

PyCharm is a free downloadable Python development environment that enables you to create large, complex Python projects out of multiple files. It features syntax highlighting and checking and allows you to look up methods of any Python object by just typing the object name followed by a dot. The possible methods pop up in a convenient box.

PyCharm has a full debugger that enables you to insert breakpoints and examine variables. PyCharm's Community Edition is free, as noted, but to get the version that supports connection to databases and the Django web framework from Python, you pay around $200 per year. That version also provides direct use of GitHub.

However, we had no trouble connecting to MySQL from the Community edition.

Visual Studio

Microsoft Visual Studio Community Edition has all the features of Visual Studio for other Microsoft languages. With a little fussing around, you can install the Python plug-in and use VSCODE as a pretty slick development environment.

To locate the plug-in, type **Python** into the search bar at the top of the window. This should point you directly to the installation of the Microsoft Python plug-in.

The user interface of the IDE is really slick and features a lot of help with syntax completion. However, when you run your Python code, it launches another console window where it runs Python.exe to run your code. You can prevent this by going to the Project | Properties menu and clicking the Windows Application check box. The pythonw.exe is then launched instead. This is the only IDE that appears to run Python as a separate process, which does slow down development sometimes. VSCODE seems to launch considerably more slowly than PyCharm.

Other Development Environments

Several other development environments also should be mentioned.

LiClipse

The LiClipse development environment is a lightweight implementation of the Eclipse environment that supports development in a large number of languages, including Python. LiClipse is not free (it costs around $80), but it offers some helpful pop-up windows giving the manual page descriptions of each function it displays. PyCharm is more popular because of its mostly zero cost, but LiClipse does provide some real benefits.

Jupyter Notebook

Jupyter Notebook is a development environment that runs as a web browser page after you install all the underlying code. To install it, you using the `pip` Python installer and type the following:

```
pip install jupyter lab
```

When all the code is installed, you can start it from the command line by typing:

```
jupyter lab
```

This launches a web browser tab or window where you can enter small Python programs in line groups called *cells*. You can run any cell from the menu. The window actually is running against a server that you started with the command line and runs at http://localhost:8888/lab.

This Jupyter Notebook window has syntax completion if you press the Tab key but has no breakpoints or examination of variables. It uses the iPython interpreter and seems to run about 10% slower than the usual CPython interpreter. However, Jupyter Notebook is helpful for planning and testing little code segments without writing out the entire program.

The iPython compiler supports additional convenience functions that are not part of the Python language, for manipulation of system and file commands and configuration parameters. These are referred to as magic functions or magics, and are preceded with a `%` sign. For example, `%cd` can be used to change the current working directory. Obviously, using these functions restricts your Python program to the iPython system.

You can create GUI programs in this environment, but the resulting window appears *under* the notebook window; you have to discover it in the Windows task bar.

Google Colaboratory

Under Google Docs, you can create a Google Colab document. As with Jupyter Notebooks, you can write small programs in code cells and execute them. The execution takes place on the Google server and can be very slow. Google Colab also does not allow you to try out GUI code because it is running on Google's remote computer, not on yours. As such, it is not very useful for actual programming.

Anaconda

Anaconda is essentially a package manager for a large number of Python tools that you might eventually find useful. Installing Anaconda adds links to Jupyter Notebook, PyCharm, and data visualization and mining tools. It also includes the Spyder development environment, which looks a lot like the others, but we have found it to be pretty buggy. Anaconda is supposed to keep these tools updated, but in the case of Spyder, this did not succeed.

Wing

Wing is a very nice IDE that ranks with the best of them in many ways.

Wing has good syntax completion, but its debugger is a little harder to use: The display of variable values is hidden under stack data. Wing enables you to create code for the Django web framework, but it seems to lack intuitive support for virtual environments and, unlike PyCharm, does not allow you to connect automatically to GitHub for source code control. Wing is not free, but personal licenses cost only $67 a year; the current version costs $95 permanently for the current version. Upgrades have a small charge.

Command-Line Execution

You can also use any text editor you like (the Lime editor is popular and has syntax highlighting) and then run your programs from a command window by typing:

```
py yourprog.py
```

You might have to modify your `PATH` variable to include the path to your Python executable.

CPython, IPython, and Jython

All Python systems translate the source code into *byte codes*, which are instructions for a hypothetical computer. Then during execution, these byte codes are executed to cause the Python program to run. The first-pass compilers have been written in Python itself but could be in any language. The byte codes are generally executed by code written in C, generally called CPython. The JPython program, now called Jython, translates Python into Java byte codes, to be used in conjunction with Java programs. IPython is its own version of both the compiler and the byte code interpreter developed for interactive systems such as Jupyter, which is more versatile but runs about 10% slower than Python 3.8 on the same code.

34

Python Collections and Files

Python has a number of different collection objects: lists (essentially arrays), tuples, dictionaries, and sets. We look at all of them in this chapter, along with how we can read data into them from files.

We have already seen some simple examples of using Lists, the Python equivalent of arrays. You can create lists programmatically by simply declaring the contents inside square brackets.

```
nlist = [2, 4, 8, 16]   # create list
```

Then you can access elements of the list by position: All lists start at index zero.

```
print (nlist[0])         # first element 2
```

You can access the final element by using an index of -1.

```
print (nlist[-1])        # last element 16
```

Slicing

You can refer to *slices* of a list by the first index and the final index.

```
print(nlist[0:3]) # first 3 elements 0, 1 and 2
```

Note that the slice starts at the first index and stops just *before* the second index. You can also write this more succinctly (and perhaps more confusingly) by leaving out the first index when it is zero:

```
print(nlist[:3])   # first 3 elements
```

You can also leave out the last index in cases where it must be the final array index, but this is unnecessarily confusing.

```
print(nlist[-3:]) # last 3 elements
```

The form of the slicing statement is

```
nlist[first, last, stride]
```

Slicing Strings

Perhaps the most common use of slicing is in cutting out sections of a string. You can refer to the characters by position from the left end, where the first character is numbered 0, or from the right end, where the first character is -1.

L	e	a	r	n		P	y	t	h	o	n
0	1	2	3	4	5	6	7	8	9	10	11
-12	-11	-10	-9	-8	-7	-6	-5	-4	-3	-2	-1

You can select the first three characters by starting at 0 and ending at 3. The end index is the first character not selected, just as in the range function:

```
text = "Learn Python"
# first 3 characters
print(text[0:3]) #Lea
```

If you omit the first index, you mean to start at the beginning; if you omit the last index, you mean to go to the end.

```
#first four (0-4)
print(text[:4])  #Lear

# last 4
print(text[-4:]) #thon

#9 to end
print(text[9:]) #hon

print(text[ln-6:ln+1]) #Python
```

The third argument is the stride, or number to add to the index to get the next character. A stride of 2 skips every other character.

```
print(text[0:6:2])  #Lan
```

You can also use slicing to reverse a string:

```
# reverse a string
name = "I love Python"
newname = name[-1::-1]  # nohtyP evol I
```

However, accessing the string elements one at a time is just about as simple:

```
nn=""
for i in range(len(name)-1, -1, -1):
    nn += name[i]
print(nn)              # nohtyP evol I
```

Negative Indexes

Strings, arrays (lists), and tuples all support negative indexes, where index -1 means the last element of the object. However, you cannot get a negative "index out of bounds." All negative indexes are treated as modulo array length. Therefore, in the earlier 12-member string, `text[-13]` would evaluate to `text[-13 % 12]` or `text[-1]` or `n`.

String Prefix and Suffix Removal

In Python 3.9 and later, you have the option of using convenient methods for removing a prefix or suffix. Note that this operation is case sensitive.

```
town = "Fairfield"
newtown = town.removesuffix("field")
print(newtown)   #Fair
farm = town.removeprefix("Fair")
print(farm)   #field
```

Changing List Contents

Because arrays can be changed (they are not immutable), you can change one or more elements within your program:

```
nlist = [2, 4, 8, 16]   # create list
nlist[2] = 300
print(nlist)
```

which gives you

```
[2, 4, 300, 16]
```

Remember that indexes start at zero and go up to the length minus one.

But, more to the point, you can create such lists programmatically by starting with an empty list and appending to it.

```
# create a list of squares in a loop
newlist=[]          # empty list
x = 2
while x < 10:
    newlist.append(x*x)
    x += 1
print (newlist)
```

The result is

```
[4, 9, 16, 25, 36, 49, 64, 81]
```

You can also use the list as a stack, where the append method and the pop method push and pop the last element in the list. You can also insert and delete elements in the same way.

`lname.append(element)`	Adds to the end of the list
`elem = list.pop()`	Returns the last item in the list
`elem = list.pop(index)`	Removes and returns the indexed item
`lname.remove(index)`	Removes an element at the index
`lname.insert(index, elem)`	Inserts an element at the index
`Lname.sort()`	Sorts a list in place
`lname.reverse()`	Reverses a list in place

Note that even though you can access elements of a string by index, as if they were an array,

```
s="Python program"
for i in range(0, len(s)):
    print(s[i])
```

you cannot change a string character by using its index:

```
s[5]="k"  #will FAIL
```

This is because strings are *immutable.*

Copying a List

If you attempt to copy a list by simply writing

```
alist = newlist    # both point to same list
```

you will find that both variables point to the same list. The only way to copy a list is an element at a time:

```
blist = []          # create empty list
for x in alist:
    blist.append(x) # and copy elements into it
```

Or, you can use the `list copy` method, which does the same element-by-element copy:

```
blist = alist.copy()
```

Reading Files

However, it is highly unusual that the contents of an array or list are coded as part of a program. It is more likely that programs read in data from files, and Python makes this very easy indeed, especially if the data are in text files. For example, this simple code reads in a file of U.S. state names, where there is one name on each line of a file.

To open a file, you use the open function, which takes as arguments the filename and `r` for reading, `w` for writing, and `r+` for reading and writing. The default assumption is that you are reading text files. For binary files, you append a `b` after the `r` or `w` arguments.

The simple for statement simply reads one line at a time from the file.

```
""" Read file into array """
DATAFILE="stateNames.txt"

f = open(DATAFILE, "r") # open the file
statenames=[]          # create the empty list


# read in the state names
for sname in f:
    statenames.append(sname)
f.close()

print(statenames[0:4])
print(len(statenames))

This program produces
['Alabama\n', 'Alaska\n', 'Arizona\n', 'Arkansas\n']
50
```

Note the endline character \n that is read in with from the file because each name is on a separate line in the file. You can strip off this whitespace character with

```
statenames.append(sname[0].rstrip())
```

which will then produce the expected output:

```
['Alabama', 'Alaska', 'Arizona', 'Arkansas']
50
```

Using the with Loop

The with keyword creates a statement that starts a loop and thus *must* end in a colon.

```
with open(DATAFILE, "r") as f:
    statenames=[]
    for sname in f:
        statenames.append(sname.rstrip())

print(statenames[0:3])
print(len(statenames))
```

The main distinction is that with automatically manages the closing of files, so you need not worry about it.

You can also use the readline method to read a single line or use the readlines method to read an entire file into an array:

```
statenames=[]
statenames = f.readlines()
```

The newline characters are also included in each array element.

You can write text files in exactly the same way, using the w argument:

```
with open(DATAFILE, "w") as f:
    for sname in statenames:
        f.write(sname + "\n")
```

Handling Exceptions

If an error occurs during the execution of your Python program, Python creates an *Exception* object. Probably the most common of these is when the program can't find the file to open; then it generates a `FileNotFoundError`. You can easily write code to keep the program from crashing, although what you do next is more or less up to you. The easiest way around this is to use the `filedialog` in the tkinter library.

```
try:
    f = open("shrubbery", "r")
except FileNotFoundError:
    print("Can''t find that file")
```

Another fairly common error is dividing by zero. Here we also show the `else` clause to indicate what to do if the exception does not occur.

```
x = 5.63
y = 0

try:
    z = x/y
except ZeroDivisionError:
    print("Division by zero!")
else:
    print("result=", z)
```

Using Dictionaries

A dictionary is a group of key-value pairs grouped inside curly brackets.

```
statedict = {"abbrev":"CA", "name":"California"}
```

The first item is the key, which must be followed by a colon, and the second item is the value. There can be any number of such pairs in a single dictionary. You retrieve the value you want using the `get` method:

```
s = statedict.get("abbrev")
```

Or you can provide a default return value, in case that key doesn't exist:

```
s = statedict.get("abbrev", "none")
```

You can create a list of dictionaries like this:

```
# create a list of dictionaries
slist = [
    {"abbrev":"CA", "name":"California"},
    {"abbrev":"KS", "name":"Kansas"}
]
```

Then, you can list the state names in a simple loop:

```
# list out the values of "abbrev" in each dict
for st in slist:
    s = st.get("abbrev") # check to see it exists
    if s != None:
        print (st.get("name"))  # print out the name
```

This is somewhat cumbersome, however, and using a series of objects would work better. You can better use the dictionary as a hash table and put all the state and abbreviation pairs in it. Fetching the result is very fast, even for a very long list of entries. We illustrate here with a few entries:

```
# one single state dictionary, used as a hash table
states =\
{"AK": "Arkansas",
 "CA": "California",
 "CT": "Connecticut",
 "MO": "Missouri",
 "KS": "Kansas"
}
# a single statement gets the name we want
print(states.get("CT"))
```

But suppose that we want more than two entries, maybe including state capitals or populations. One simple and elegant solution is to put all these additional values in a little nested dictionary, one for each state:

```
# a dictionary with a nested dictionary or properties
fullstates =\
{"AK": {"name": "Arkansas", "capital": "Little Rock"},
 "CA": {"name":"California", "capital": "Sacramento"},
 "CT": {"name": "Connecticut", "capital": "Hartford"},
 "MO": {"name": "Missouri", "capital": "Jefferson City"},
 "KS": {"name": "Kansas", "capital": "Topeka"}
}
data = fullstates.get("CT")   #get nested dictionary

# and print out the state name and capital from it
print ("CT " + data.get("name")+" "+data.get("capital"))
```

In general, using them as a hash table opens up the possibility of rapidly processing various options in a program.

Combining Dictionaries

In Python 3.9 and later, you can OR together two dictionaries and obtain a new dictionary, with each entry appearing only once.

```
morestates =\
{"DE": "Delaware",
 "GA": "Georgia",
 "CT": "Connecticut",
 "MT": "Montana",
 "ND": "North Dakota"
}

mixedstates = states | morestates
for st in  mixedstates:
    print(st, end=" ")
```

This produces a single dictionary, with CT appearing only once:

```
AK CA CT MO KS DE GA MT ND
```

Using Tuples

One unusual feature of Python is the tuple, a comma-separated list of values or variables surrounded by parentheses:

```
tup1 = (1, 5, "fred")
dim = (200, 500)
```

Tuples can be treated like lists. However, unlike lists, tuples cannot be changed (they are *immutable*).

Effectively, tuples are arrays that you can't change but are otherwise identical. You can iterate through them and access them by index, but you can't put a new value in.

Python uses tuples internally in several ways. One common way is in representing the result of a database query. Each row is returned as a tuple, and you can access the elements with an iterator or an index.

While objects might sometimes be a better way to handle these things, tuples persist throughout Python because they are very efficient: Some functions return two or more variables or values as a tuple. And you can also write functions that return tuples yourself. For example, you could write a function that counts upper- and lowercase characters and returns the count of both in a tuple. We illustrate this in the next chapter.

In addition, if you have a very large array of data that you don't expect to modify, tuples work much faster because they don't require the additional memory needed to read and write values by index.

Using Sets

A set is an unordered collection of values, usually strings or numbers. You can create a set using curly braces:

```
fruit = {'apples', 'pears', 'lemons'}
fruitPie = {'apples', 'pears'}
```

Then you can check to see if one set is a member of another using either the `issubset` method or the less than operator.

```
fruit = {'apples', 'pears', 'lemons'}
fruitPie = {'apples', 'pears'}
print (fruitPie.issubset(fruit))
print (fruitPie < fruit)
```

You can combine sets using the | operator:

```
# combine sets
nuts = {'walnuts', 'pecans'}
granola = fruit | nuts
print(granola)
```

Sets can be made up of strings or numbers or both, but duplicate values are ignored. You can create an empty set and add values to it, but you cannot edit or delete these values. Note that the duplicate value `2.3` is ignored here. Be sure to use the add method, not the append method you used with lists.

```
data = set()     # create an empty set
data.add (2.3)  # and add vales
data.add (4.6)
data.add (7.0)
data.add (2.3)
print (data)
```

The resulting output does not contain the duplicate value.

```
{2.3, 4.6, 7.0}
```

You can use this feature to create a unique list of values, such as club names, by adding all of them to a set. This is shown in Chapter 23, "The Iterator Pattern."

Using the map Function

You can use the `map` function to perform the same operation on every element of an array—a list, a tuple, or even a string—as long as it can be iterated. The function returns a new iterable map object containing the data that the function has operated on. You can convert it to a list, tuple, or set using the `list()`, `tuple()`, or `set()` functions.

Suppose you want to square every element of a numerical array. You could write a `sq` function

```
def sq(x):
    return x*x
```

and then use the map function to carry out the operation on the whole array:

```
ara = [2,3,6,8,5,4]
amap = map(sq, ara)
ara1 = list(amap)  # convert back to List

print(ara1)
Here this produces the new list
[4, 9, 36, 64, 25, 16]
```

Using the map function can run somewhat faster than looping through the array yourself. Our experiments suggest that it can be as about 18% faster, depending on the function you call.

Writing a Complete Program

Let's finish this chapter by writing a program to generate a Fibonacci series:

1, 1, 2, 3, 5, 8, 13, 21

and so forth. Each new value is the sum of the previous two. You will find this sequence appearing in the petals of flowers, which may have 5, 8, or 13 petals, for example.

```
""" Print out Fibonacci series """
current=0
prev=1
secondLast=0

while current < 1000:
    print (current, end=" ") # without newlines
    secLast = prev            # copy n-1st to secLast
    prev = current            # copy nth to prev
    current = prev + secLast # compute next x as sum
```

The result is

```
0 1 1 2 3 5 8 13 21 34 55 89 144 233 377 610 987
```

Impenetrable Coding

You can also write the same program using multiple assignments on the same line. This hard-to-understand program does the same thing but is very difficult to explain or read aloud:

```
a, b = 0, 1        # assign a=0 and b=1
while a < 1000:
    print(a)
    a,b = b, a + b
```

This program is called fibohard.py in the examples on GitHub.

Using List Comprehension

Python has a unique shortcut for creating arrays in a single statement. This is called *list comprehension* and has the form

```
vlist = [expression for item in list]
```

For example, you can write

```
squares = [value**2 for value in range (1,21)]
print(squares)
```

and get an array of

```
[1, 4, 9, 16, 25, 36, 49, 64, 81, 100, 121, 144, 169, 196, 225, 256, 289, 324, 361,
400]
```

This is entirely equivalent to writing this somewhat longer but perhaps clearer code:

```
squares = []
for value in range(1,21):
    squares.append(value**2)
print (squares)
```

You can also append a conditional to that statement and generate only some of the values:

```
nlist = [x for x in range(20) if x%2 == 0]
print (nlist)
```

This produces only the even numbers, where `x modulo 2` is zero:

```
[0, 2, 4, 6, 8, 10, 12, 14, 16, 18]
```

You can also use comprehensions in sets and dictionaries if it looks like it might be helpful.

Some programmers have asserted that list comprehension generates more efficient code; however, our measurements show that list comprehension is compiled to 30 byte codes, while the `for` loop version is compiled to 66 byte codes. They are closer in execution time, with the comprehension taking 4.49 seconds and the `for` loop taking 5.43 seconds for 1 million executions of the code, making comprehension only about 10% faster. Table 34-1 includes the statistics for iPython.

Table 34-1 **Performance of List Comprehensions**

	Comprehension	List
CPython byte codes	30	66
1 million executions	4.49 seconds	5.43 seconds
IPython byte codes	38	52
IPython 1 million executions	5.55 seconds	5.82 seconds

Use it where you find it useful. Because of its compactness, list comprehension is considered easier to read and more Pythonic.

Sample Programs on GitHub

- slicing.py: String slicing illustration
- fibo.py: Basic Fibonacci series
- fibohard.py: The compressed version
- statearray.py: An array of states read in using statenames.txt
- sets.py: Examples of set manipulation
- exceptions.py: Illustration of exception code
- statedict.py: States in a dictionary
- maptest.py: Map function illustration
- comprehend.py: Comprehension examples

35

Functions

Functions are a significant part of Python and most other languages. They are units of code that carry out a specific set of operations. And while functions can be called many times throughout a program, there are plenty of cases where a function is called just once but conveniently groups a set of operations that you need to call within a program.

Functions are usually called with one or more arguments and usually return some value when they exit. To declare a function, start with the `def` keyword and end the declaration with parentheses and a colon. The actual code is indented four spaces, just as we saw for looping code. Let's write a really simple function first that calculates the square of a number:

```
# return a square of the input value
def sqr(x):
    y = x * x    # square the input
    return y     # and return it
```

Functions can create and use variables, as we illustrate here. These variables are internal to the function; and if you try to refer to that y variable outside the function, it will be flagged as an error. In this simple case, this is just illustrative. You could just as easily have written:

```
# return a square of the input value
def sqr(x):
    return = x * x    # return the square
```

Of course, functions can call other functions. We could create a cube function that calls the sqr function:

```
def cube(a):
    b = sqr(a) * a  # compute the cube using the square
    return b
```

Then we call the functions from our main program:

```
print(xvar, sqr(xvar), cube(xvar))
```

Returning a Tuple

Although functions usually return a single value, they can return more than one value using a tuple. This simple function counts the number of upper- and lowercase characters and returns both counts in a tuple:

```
# count upper and lowercase letters
def upperLower(s):
    upper = 0
    lower = 0
    for c in s:
        if c.islower():
            lower += 1
        elif c.isupper():
            upper += 1
    return (upper,lower)   #return a tuple

# get counts as a tuple
up, low = upperLower("Hello")
print(up, low)
```

Where Does the Program Start?

As soon as you write a program with several functions, it becomes harder to spot where the program actually begins. Of course, the Python interpreter will start executing the first code it finds that is not inside a function (or class). But to make it clear to the reader and to make sure Python starts where you want, it is common to put that startup code inside a `main()` function, and then call that `main()` function as shown:

```
"""main program begins here"""
def main():
    xvar = 12
    print(xvar, sqr(xvar), cube(xvar))

###  This is the real entry point ####
if __name__ == "__main__":
    main()                  # call main() here
```

This gives the expected result:

```
12 144 1728
```

The complete program, then, is shown here:

```
""" Some simple functions """
# return a square of the input value
def sqr(x):
    y = x * x   # square the input
    return y    # and return it
```

```
def cube(a):
    b = sqr(a) * a  # compute the cube using the square
    return b

""" main program begins here """
def main():
    xvar = 12
    print(xvar, sqr(xvar), cube(xvar))

###  This is the real entry point ####
if __name__ == "__main__":
    main()                      # call main() here
```

Summary

- You can create functions in any Python program using the `def` keyword, followed by a function name and zero or more arguments in parentheses.
- You can call these functions from anywhere in your program, including from other functions.

Programs on GitHub

- Funcs.py: Examples of functions
- Upperlower.py: Function that returns two results

Appendix A

Running Python Programs

Now that you have created your Python program, how do you run it? Of course, you can run it in your development environment, but maybe you want to run it on other computers or share it with friends.

If You Have Python Installed

If all the computers you plan to use your program have Python installed, the solution is simple.

In Windows 10, open a cmd window and change to the directory where your Python program is located. Suppose you want to run the simple example hellobuttons.py. Then, just type

```
python hellobuttons.py
```

You can even use the py shortcut and type

```
py hellobuttons.py
```

In fact, you can just type the filename alone, and the program will launch:

```
hellobuttons.py
```

If you display your files using the Windows File Explorer, you can double-click any file with a .py extension to open it if it has a tkinter interface. If it just runs in a command window, nothing appears; you then have to run it in a command window with the py command.

Notice that if you double-click a Python program that does have a tkinter interface, it starts with a command prompt window behind it. To change that behavior, you can simply change the file extension to .pyw.

Double-clicking that filename brings up the windowing tkinter interface without the cmd window in the background.

Shortcuts

You can also create a Windows icon or shortcut by right-clicking the desktop background and selecting New | Shortcut. You can then fill out the path to the Python program (with a .pyw extension) and Windows will create a desktop icon (see Figure A-1). Figure A-2 shows the actual icon. You also have the option to select a different icon for the shortcut if you like.

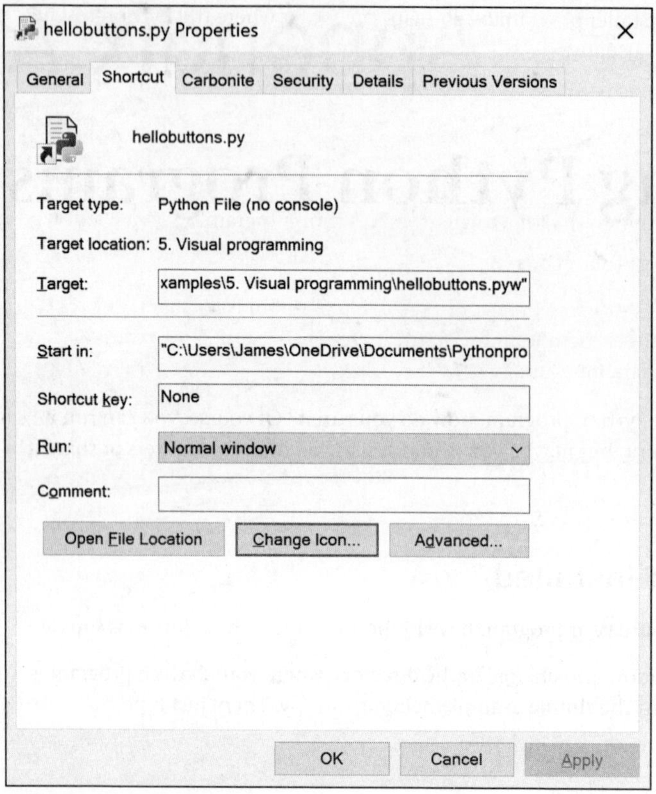

Figure A-1 Property dialog box for a shortcut

Figure A-2 Icon for a shortcut

Creating an Executable Python Program

The program pyinstaller puts together the libraries needed to execute a Python program in a Windows system. It is also available for Mac OS/X, GNU/Linux, and AIX.

You must first install the pyinstaller program by going to the folder where the Python install program pip is located. This is usually

```
"C:\Users\(yourname)\Appdata\Roaming\Python
```

Then just type

```
pip install pyinstaller
```

When installation is finished, go to the folder where your Python program is located and type

```
pyinstaller --onefile hellobuttons.py
```

This command will create a dist folder where your executable program is located. The program hellobuttons.exe is about 8MB, to include all the support files for Python. Note that it does not support the `quit` command; you must use `sys.exit()` instead.

Command-Line Arguments

You can pass arguments to Python programs on the command line. These arguments might include the name of a file that the program is to use or some special-purpose parameters. These commands are passed to the Python program as an array of strings in the `sys.argv` array.

For a simple example, suppose that we want to change the text of the two buttons and the color of the Quit button. We could type

```
Hellobutsargs Hi Leave green
```

The program then takes these arguments from the argv array. `Sys.argv[0]` contains the program name, so we get the three arguments from elements 1, 2, and 3.

```
leftText= sys.argv[1]
rightText = sys.argv[2]
bcolor = sys.argv[3]
```

We then put these values in the button creation statements

```
# create Hello button
slogan = tk.Button(root,
                   text=leftText,
                   command=self.write_slogan)
```

and

```
# create exit button with colored letters
button = tk.Button(root,
                   text=rightText,
                   fg=bcolor,
                   command=sys.exit)
```

Figure A-3 illustrates these buttons.

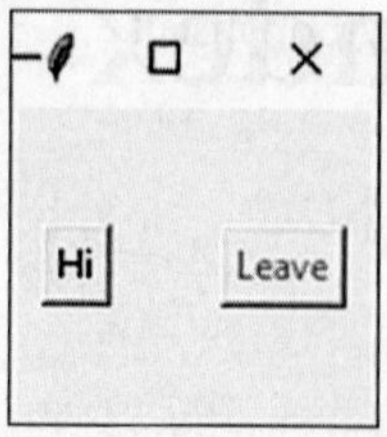

Figure A-3 Two-button program with button labels changed by the command line

You don't have to re-create the compiled .exe file to test the command-line arguments. In PyCharm, you can select Run | Edit configuration and enter the command-line argument in the Parameters line.

Index

Symbols

= (equal signs)
- assignment (=) operator, 264
- initialization, 254
- is equal to (==) operator, 264
- spacing, 259

A

Abstract Factory pattern, 75, 95
- consequences of, 77–78
- GardenMaker Factory, 75–77
- GitHub programs, 78
- purposes of, 77–78
- thought questions, 78
- user interfaces, 77

access (privileged), iterators, 192–193

accessor methods, 6

accounts (GitHub), setting up, 3

Adapter pattern, 99
- Class adapter, 103
- creating adapters, 101–102
- GitHub programs, 103
- moving data between lists, 99–101
- pluggable adapters, 103
- two-way adapters, 103

adapters
- Class adapter, 103
- creating, 101–102
- pluggable adapters, 103
- two-way adapters, 103

adding

menus, to windows, 35–38

two numbers, visual programming, 26

Anaconda, 277

AND operator, 256

arithmetic operators, 255, 259

arithmetic/assignment statements, combined, 256

arrays

lists, 265

range function, 265

assignment (=) operator, 264

attrgetter operator, sorting, 181–182

B

bar graphs, Line and Bar Graph strategies, 228–230

behavioral patterns, 55, 153

Chain of Responsibility pattern, 155–156

consequences of, 164–165

first cases, 162

GitHub programs, 165

help systems, programming, 160–161

help systems, tree structures, 163–164

listboxes, 159–160

receiving help command, 161–162

requests, 164

sample code, 156–159

using, 156

Command pattern, 167, 176

ButtonCommand objects, 175

buttons, creating, 175

buttons, Undo button, 175–176

Command objects, 168

Command objects, building, 171–172

Command objects, calling, 170–171

Command objects, containers, 172

Command objects, mediators, 199–200

consequences of, 172

GitHub programs, 176

keyboard example, 168–170

KeyModerator class, 169, 170

references, 176

Undo button, 175–176

Undo function, 172–175

Interpreter pattern, 177

attrgetter operator, sorting, 181–182

consequences of, 184–185

console interface, 182–183

GitHub programs, 185

languages, 179–180

parsing, 180–181

Print verb, 182

report generator example, 178–179

usefulness of, 177–178

user interfaces, 183–184

using, 177

Variable class, 181

Verb class, 181

Iterator pattern, 187

calling iterators, 189

composites and iterators, 193

consequences of, 192–193

creating iterators, 189

dunder methods, 188

external iterators, 193

Fibonacci iterators, 188–189, 191–192

filtered iterators, 189–191

generators in classes, 192

getting iterators, 189

GitHub programs, 193

internal iterators, 193

- iterable containers, 188
- iterator generator, 191
- for loops as iterators, 187–188
- modifying data, 192
- privileged access, 192–193
- using, 187

Mediator pattern, 195
- Command objects, 199–200
- consequences of, 200
- example system, 195–197
- GitHub programs, 201
- interactions between controls, 197
- sample code, 198–199
- single interface mediators, 200–201

Memento pattern, 203
- Caretaker class, 208–209
- consequences of, 209
- GitHub programs, 209
- graphics drawing program example, 204–209
- sample code, 204–209
- using, 203–204

Observer pattern, 211–212
- color changing program example, 212–214
- consequences of, 215
- GitHub programs, 215
- messages to the media, 215
- notifications, 215

State pattern, 217
- consequences of, 224
- GitHub programs, 224
- graphics drawing program example, 217–220
- sample code, 217–220
- StateManager, mediator interactions, 222–223
- StateManager, switching between states, 221
- switching between states, 221
- transitions, 224

Strategy pattern, 225
- consequences of, 230–231
- Context class, 227
- GitHub programs, 231
- Line and Bar Graph strategies, 228–230
- PlotStategy class, 226–227
- program commands, 227–228
- sample code, 226–227
- using, 225–226

Template pattern, 233
- callbacks, 238
- concrete methods, 234
- consequences of, 238
- empty methods, 234
- GitHub programs, 238
- hook methods, 234
- isosceles triangles, 236
- IsoscelesTriangle class, 236
- Point class, 234
- sample code, 234–235
- standard triangles, 235
- stdTriangle class, 235
- summary of, 238
- Template class, 234
- Triangle class, 234–235, 236
- Triangle Drawing program, 237
- using, 233

Visitor pattern, 239, 241
- Boss class, 242–243
- BVacationVisitor class, 243–244
- consequences of, 245
- double dispatching, 245
- GitHub programs, 245
- sample code, 241–242
- traversing a series of classes, 245

using, 239–240
visiting classes, 242
visiting several classes, 242–243
bitwise operators, 255–256
blank lines, classes/functions, 259
Blue button, creating, 175
Boolean variables, 250
Boss class
Composite pattern, 113
Visitor pattern, 242–243
break statements, 266
Bridge pattern, 105–107
consequences of, 109–110
creating user interfaces, 107
extending bridges, 107–109
GitHub programs, 110
Listbox builder, 105–106
Treeview widget, 105, 106, 107, 108–109
bridges, extending, 107–109
Builder pattern, 83–84, 95
calling builders, 86–87
Checkbox builder, 88
consequences of, 89
GitHub programs, 89
investment trackers, 84–86
Listbox builder, 87–88
selected securities, displaying, 89
thought questions, 89
ButtonCommand objects, Command pattern, 175
buttons
Blue button, creating, 175
checkbuttons, grid layouts, 32–34
creating
Command pattern, 175
object-oriented programming, 19–21
visual programming, 17–19
Decorator pattern, 121–122
Hello buttons, 17
Quit buttons, 17–18
radio buttons, 27–29
Red button, 175
Undo button, Command pattern, 175–176
BVacationVisitor class, Visitor pattern, 243–244
byte codes, 2, 278

C

C style formatting, 269
caching results, Composite pattern, 120
callbacks, Template pattern, 238
calling
builders, Builder pattern, 86–87
Command objects, 170–171
functions, 293
iterators, 189
CamelCase, 258
Caretaker class, Memento pattern, 208–209
case (upper/lower)
CamelCase, 258
classes, 258
constants, 258
functions, 258–259
variables, 249, 252
catching errors, 26–27
Chain of Responsibility pattern, 155–156
consequences of, 164–165
first cases, 162
GitHub programs, 165
help command, receiving, 161–162
help systems
programming, 160–161
tree structures, 163–164

listboxes, 159–160
requests, 164
sample code, 156–159
using, 156

character constants, 251–252

check boxes, disabling, 34

Checkbox builder, 88

checkbuttons, grid layouts, 32–34

CircleSeeding class, 71–72

Class adapter, 103

Class_init_Method, 6

classes, 5–6
blank lines, 259
Boss class
Composite pattern, 113
Visitor pattern, 242–243
BVacationVisitor class, Visitor pattern, 243–244
CamelCase, 258
Caretaker class, Memento pattern, 208–209
collections, 7
communicating between, 30
Context class, Strategy pattern, 227
creating, 7
Database class, Facade pattern, 132–133
Decorator class, 121–123
derived classes, 8
Docstrings, 259
Employee class, Composite pattern, 112–113
Facade classes, building, 131–135
Factory classes, operation of, 61–62
Factory Method pattern
CircleSeeding class, 71–72
Event classes, 69–70
Straight Seeding class, 70–71
Swimmer class, 68–69
generators, 192
indentation, 259
inheritance, 8–9
instances
creating, 6
Singleton pattern, 80–81
IsoscelesTriangle class, Template pattern, 236
KeyModerator class, Command pattern, 169, 170
naming conventions, 258
PlotStategy class, Strategy pattern, 226–227
Point class, Template pattern, 234
Query class, Facade pattern, 133–134
Results class, Facade pattern, 134
static classes, Singleton pattern, 81
stdTriangle class, Template pattern, 235
subclasses, Factory pattern, 62–63
Table class, Facade pattern, 133
Template class, methods, 234
traversing a series of classes, Visitor pattern, 245
Triangle class, Template pattern, 234–235, 236
Variable class, Interpreter pattern, 181
variables, 6–7, 30
Verb class, Interpreter pattern, 181
visiting, 242
Visitor class, 241–242

cloning, 91–92

coding, impenetrable, 288

collections
classes, 7
dictionaries
combining, 286
listing, 285
using, 284–285

GitHub programs, 290
lists
changing contents, 281–282
copying, 282
creating, 279
doubly linked lists, 117–118
moving data between, 99–101
slicing, 279
spacing, 259
sets, using, 287
tuples
returning, 292
using, 286
color
color changing program example, Observer pattern, 212–214
tkinter library, applying color with, 27
combining
arithmetic/assignment statements, 256
conditions, 264
dictionaries, 286
combo boxes, 46–47
Command pattern, 167, 176
ButtonCommand objects, 175
buttons
creating, 175
Undo button, 175–176
Command objects, 168
building, 171–172
calling, 170–171
containers, 172
mediators and, 199–200
consequences of, 172
GitHub programs, 176
keyboard example, 168–170
KeyModerator class, 169, 170
references, 176
Undo function, 172–175
command-line
arguments, 297–298
execution, 278
commands
Interp command, 180
program commands, Strategy pattern, 227–228
queuing, 168
comma-separated numbers, 270
comments
Docstrings, 259
indentation, 259
spacing, 259
common mistakes, Python decision making, 264
communicating between classes, 30
comparison operators, 256–257
compiling, simple Python program example, 255
complement operator, 250–256
complete Python programs, writing, 288
complex numbers, 253
Composite pattern, 111
Boss class, 113
caching results, 120
composite implementation, 112
consequences of, 118
doubly linked lists, 117–118
Employee class, 112–113
employee trees
building, 114
printing, 114–116
GitHub programs, 120
iterators, 193
leaf nodes, 112–113
recursive calls stet, 119
salary computation, 112
simple composites, 119
Treeviews of composites, 116–117

compound operators, spacing, 259
comprehension, lists, 289
concrete methods, 234
conditions, combining, 264
console interface, Interpreter pattern, 182–183
constants
case, upper/lower, 258
character constants, 251–252
named constants. *See* variables
naming conventions, 258
numeric constants, 250
containers
Command objects, 172
iterable containers, 188
Context class, Strategy pattern, 227
continue statements, 267
controls, interactions between, 197
copying, lists, 282
copy-on write objects
Flyweight pattern, 143
Proxy pattern, 149
CPython, 278
creational patterns, 55, 59
Abstract Factory pattern, 75, 95
consequences of, 77–78
GardenMaker Factory, 75–77
GitHub programs, 78
purposes of, 77–78
thought questions, 78
user interfaces, 77
Builder pattern, 83–84, 95
calling builders, 86–87
Checkbox builder, 88
consequences of, 89
displaying selected securities, 89
GitHub programs, 89
investment trackers, 84–86
Listbox builder, 87–88
thought questions, 89
Factory Method pattern, 67–68, 74
CircleSeeding class, 71–72
Event classes, 69–70
GitHub programs, 74
seeding program, 72–73
Straight Seeding class, 70–71
using, 74
Factory pattern, 61, 95
building, 63
Factory classes, 61–62
GitHub programs, 65
GUI, 64
math computations, 65
sample code, 62
subclasses, 62–63
thought questions, 66
using, 63–64
Prototype pattern, 91, 95
cloning, 91–92
consequences of, 94
GitHub programs, 94
using, 92–94
Singleton pattern, 79–80, 95
consequences of, 82
GitHub programs, 82
large programs, 81–82
static classes, 81
throwing exceptions, 80
summary of, 95

D

data modification, iterators, 192
data tables, 41–42
combo boxes, 46–47
listboxes, creating, 42–43
state data, displaying, 44–46

tree nodes, inserting in data tables, 50–51
Treeview widget, 47–49
data types, 250
Database class, Facade pattern, 132–133
database objects, Facade pattern, 129
databases, creating, 135–136
dataclass decorator, 125–126
dates, formatting, 271
DBObjects, Facade pattern, 134
decision making in Python
arrays, range function, 265
assignment (=) operator, 264
break statements, 266
combining conditions, 264
common mistakes, 264
continue statements, 267
elif (else if) statements, 263–264
format string function, 269
formatting
dates, 271
formatting, C style, 269
formatting, Java style, 269
f-string formatting, 269
numbers, 268, 270
strings, 270
GitHub programs, 273
if statements, 263
else clauses, 263
range function, 266
is equal to (==) operator, 264
line length, 267
lists, 265
looping statements, 265
for loops, 265
match function, 271–272
pattern matching, 272–273
print function, 267–268
declaring variables, 252
Decorator pattern, 121, 126
buttons, 121–122
consequences of, 126–127
dataclass decorator, 125–126
decorated code, 124–125
Decorator class, 121–123
GitHub programs, 127
nonvisual decorators, 123–124
def keyword, functions, 291, 293
derived classes, 8
design patterns, 57. *See also* separate entries
defined, 53, 54–55
learning process, 55–56
Model-View-Controller framework for SmallTalk, 53–54
object-oriented strategies, 56
objects over inheritance, 57
popularity of, 54
programming to interfaces, 56
resources, 54
development environments
Anaconda, 277
command-line execution, 278
CPython, 278
Google Colaboratory, 277
IDLE, 275
IPython, 278
Jupyter Notebook, 277
Jython, 278
LiClipse, 276–277
PyCharm, 276
Thonny, 275–276
Visual Studio, 276
Wing, 278
dictionaries
combining, 286
listing, 285
using, 284–285

disabling check boxes, 34
dispatching, double, 245
displaying
  images with PIL, 146
  selected securities, Builder pattern, 89
  state data, 44–46
dividing integers, 253
Docstrings, 259
double dispatching, Visitor pattern, 245
doubly linked lists, Composite pattern, 117–118
downloading SQLite, 138
drawing
  drawing program example
    Memento pattern, 204–209
    State pattern, 217–220
  isosceles triangles, 236
  rectangles/squares, 10–11
  standard triangles, 235
  Triangle Drawing program, 237
dunder methods, 188

E

elif (else if) statements, 263–264
else clauses, if statements, 263
Employee class, Composite pattern, 112–113
employee trees
  building, 114
  printing, 114–116
empty methods, 234
equal signs (=)
  assignment (=) operator, 264
  initialization, 254
  is equal to (==) operator, 264
  spacing, 259
errors
  catching, 26–27
  handling, 284
  message boxes, creating, 21
Event classes, Factory Method pattern, 69–70
exceptions
  handling, 284
  throwing, Singleton pattern, 80
executable Python programs, creating, 296–297
extending bridges, 107–109
external iterators, 193

F

Facade pattern, 129–131
  classes, building, 131–135
  consequences of, 137
  Database class, 132–133
  database objects, 129
  databases, creating, 135–136
  DBObjects, 134
  GitHub programs, 137
  MySQL database, connections, 131
  MySQL Workbench, 130
  Query class, 133–134
  Results class, 134
  SQLite, 136
  Table class, 133
  tables
    creating, 135–136
    names, 134–135
Factory classes, operation of, 61–62
Factory Method pattern, 67–68, 74
  CircleSeeding class, 71–72
  Event classes, 69–70

- GitHub programs, 74
- seeding program, 72–73
- Straight Seeding class, 70–71
- using, 74

Factory pattern, 61, 95
- building, 63
- Factory classes, operation of, 61–62
- GitHub programs, 65
- GUI, 64
- math computations, 65
- sample code, 62
- subclasses, 62–63
- thought questions, 66
- using, 63–64

Fibonacci iterators, 188–189, 191–192

file dialogs, 22–23

files
- opening, 282
- reading, 282–283

filtered iterators, 189–191

first cases, Chain of Responsibility pattern, 162

Flyweight pattern, 139
- copy-on write objects, 143
- example code, 140–142
- flyweights, defined, 139
- folders
  - as flyweights, 140–142
  - selecting, 142–143
- GitHub programs, 143

folders
- as flyweights, 140–142
- selecting, Flyweight pattern, 142–143

for loops, 187–188, 265, 266

for statements, 283

format string function, 269

formatting
- C style formatting, 269
- f-string formatting, 269
- Java style formatting, 269
- numbers, 268, 270
- strings, 270

frames, LabelFrame widget, 39–40

f-string formatting, 269

functions, 291
- blank lines, 259
- calling, 293
- case, upper/lower, 258–259
- def keyword, 291, 293
- Docstrings, 259
- format string function, 269
- GitHub programs, 293
- len function, strings, 251
- map function, 287–288
- masking function. *See* AND operator
- match function, 271–272
- naming conventions, 258–259
- print function, 267–268
- range function, arrays, 265
- returning tuples, 292
- starting Python programs, 292–293
- Undo function, Command pattern, 172–175

G

GardenMaker Factory, 75–77

GitHub programs
- Abstract Factory pattern, 78
- account setup, 3
- Adapter pattern, 103
- Bridge pattern, 110
- Builder pattern, 89
- Chain of Responsibility pattern, 165
- collections, 290
- Command pattern, 176
- Composite pattern, 120
- Decorator pattern, 127
- Facade pattern, 137

Factory Method pattern, 74
Factory pattern, 65
Flyweight pattern, 143
functions, 293
Interpreter pattern, 185
Iterator pattern, 193
Mediator pattern, 201
Memento pattern, 209
Observer pattern, 215
programs, 15
Prototype pattern, 94
Proxy pattern, 150
Python, decision making, 273
Python syntax, 261
Singleton pattern, 82
State pattern, 224
Strategy pattern, 231
Template pattern, 238
Visitor pattern, 245
visual programming
data tables, 51–52
examples, 40

Google Colaboratory, 277
graphics drawing program example
Memento pattern, 204–209
State pattern, 217–220
grid layouts, 30–34
GUI (Graphical User Interfaces), Factory pattern, 64

H

Hello buttons, creating, 17
help command, receiving, 161–162
help systems
programming, 160–161
tree structures, 163–164
hints, type, 13
hook methods, 234

I

icons, creating, 295–296
IDLE (Integrated Development and Learning Environment), 275
if statements, 263
else clauses, 263
range function, 266
images
displaying with PIL, 146
loading with threads, 146–148
PIL
displaying images, 146
using, 145–146
impenetrable coding, 288
importing
names to tkinter library, 19
tkinter library tools, 17
indentation
comments, 259
loops/classes, 259
statements, 263
indexes, negative, 281
inheritance, 8
multiple inheritance, 8–9
objects over inheritance, 57
initialization, equal signs (=), 254
input statements, 257
input (user), responding to, 25–26
inserting tree nodes in data tables, 50–51
installing
MySQL, 137
Python, 275
instances
classes, Singleton pattern, 80–81
creating, 6
integer division, 253
interactions between controls, Mediator pattern, 197

interfaces
- programming to, 56
- single interface mediators, 200–201

internal iterators, 193

Interp command, 180

Interpreter pattern, 177
- attrgetter operator, sorting, 181–182
- consequences of, 184–185
- console interface, 182–183
- GitHub programs, 185
- languages, 179–180
- parsing, 180–181
- Print verb, 182
- report generator example, 178–179
- usefulness of, 177–178
- user interfaces, 183–184
- using, 177
- Variable class, 181
- Verb class, 181

investment trackers, 84–86

IPython, 278

is equal to (==) operator, 264

isosceles triangles, drawing, 236

IsoscelesTriangle class, Template pattern, 236

iterable containers, 188

Iterator pattern, 187
- calling iterators, 189
- composites and iterators, 193
- consequences of, 192–193
- creating iterators, 189
- dunder methods, 188
- external iterators, 193
- Fibonacci iterators, 188–189, 191–192
- filtered iterators, 189–191
- generators in classes, 192
- getting iterators, 189
- GitHub programs, 193
- internal iterators, 193
- iterable containers, 188
- iterator generator, 191
- for loops as iterators, 187–188
- modifying data, 192
- privileged access, 192–193
- using, 187

J

Java style formatting, 269

.jpg files, PIL
- displaying images, 146
- using, 145–146

Jupyter Notebook, 277

Jython, 278

K

keyboards, Command pattern, 168–170

KeyModerator class, Command pattern, 169, 170

L

LabelFrame widget, 39–40

languages, Interpreter pattern, 179–180

large programs, Singleton pattern, 81–82

layouts, 17
- grid layouts, 30–34
- pack layouts, 18–19, 23–24

leaf nodes, Composite pattern, 112–113

learning design patterns, 55–56

left/right shift operators, 256

len function, strings, 251

LiClipse, 276–277

Line and Bar Graph strategies, 228–230

line length in Python, 267

Listbox builder
- Bridge pattern, 105–106
- Builder pattern, 87–88

listboxes
- Chain of Responsibility pattern, 159–160
- creating, 42–43

lists, 265
- changing contents, 281–282
- comprehension, 289
- copying, 282
- creating, 279
- dictionaries, 285
- doubly linked lists, Composite pattern, 117–118
- moving data between, 99–101
- slicing, 279
- spacing, 259

loading images with threads, 146–148

local variables, 13

logging from threads, 149

looping statements, 265

loops
- break statements, 266
- continue statements, 267
- indentation, 259
- for loops, 187–188, 265, 266
- with loops, 283–284
- for loops, as iterators,

lower/upper case
- CamelCase, 258
- classes, 258
- constants, 258
- functions, 258–259
- variables, 249, 252

M

making decisions in Python
- arrays, range function, 265
- assignment (=) operator, 264
- break statements, 266
- combining conditions, 264
- common mistakes, 264
- continue statements, 267
- elif (else if) statements, 263–264
- format string function, 269
- formatting
  - dates, 271
  - formatting, C style, 269
  - formatting, Java style, 269
  - f-string formatting, 269
  - numbers, 268, 270
  - strings, 270
- GitHub programs, 273
- if statements, 263
  - else clauses, 263
  - range function, 266
- is equal to (==) operator, 264
- line length, 267
- lists, 265
- looping statements, 265
- for loops, 265
- match function, 271–272
- pattern matching, 272–273
- print function, 267–268

map function, 287–288

masking function. ***See*** **AND operator**

match function, 271–272

matching patterns, 272–273

math computations, Factory pattern, 65

Mediator pattern, 195
- Command objects, 199–200
- consequences of, 200
- example system, 195–197
- GitHub programs, 201
- interactions between controls, 197
- sample code, 198–199
- single interface mediators, 200–201

Memento pattern, 203
- Caretaker class, 208–209
- consequences of, 209
- GitHub programs, 209

graphics drawing program example, 204–209
sample code, 204–209
using, 203–204
menus, adding to windows, 35–38
message boxes, 17
creating, 21–22
error message boxes, 21
warning message boxes, 21
messages to the media, Observer pattern, 215
methods, 5
accessor methods, 6
concrete methods, 234
dunder methods, 188
empty methods, 234
hook methods, 234
revised methods, class creation, 8
strings, 251, 260–261
Template methods, 234
mistakes (common), Python decision making, 264
Model-View-Controller framework for SmallTalk, 53–54
modifying data, iterators, 192
moving, data between lists, 99–101
multiple inheritance, 8–9
MySQL, 137
database connections, 131
installing, 137
PyCharm, 137
pymysql library, 137
MySQL Workbench, 130

N

named constants. *See* variables
naming conventions, 249, 252
classes, 258
constants, 258
functions, 258–259
variables, 258–259
negative indexes, 281
nodes (leaf), Composite pattern, 112–113
nonvisual decorators, 123–124
notifications, Observer pattern, 215
numbers
adding, visual programming, 26
comma-separated numbers, 270
complex numbers, 253
dates, formatting, 271
formatting, 268, 270, 271
numeric constants, 250

O

object-oriented programming
buttons, creating, 19–21
classes, 5–6
collections, 7
creating, 7
derived classes, 8
inheritance, 8
inheritance, multiple inheritance, 8–9
instances, 6
variables, 6–7
defined, 5
inheritance, 8
methods, 5, 8
polymorphism, 14
rectangles/squares, drawing, 10–11
types, 13
declaring, 13–14
hints, 13
variables
local variables, 13
properties, 13
visibility, 12

objects
ButtonCommand objects, Command pattern, 175
Command objects, 168
building, 171–172
calling, 170–171
containers, 172
mediators and, 199–200
copy-on write objects
Flyweight pattern, 143
Proxy pattern, 149
database objects, Facade pattern, 129
over inheritance, 57
Observer pattern, 211–212
color changing program example, 212–214
consequences of, 215
GitHub programs, 215
messages to the media, 215
notifications, 215
ODBC (Open Database Connectivity), 129
opening, files, 282
OR operator, 256
operators
AND operator, 256
arithmetic operators, 255, 259
assignment (=) operator, 264
bitwise operators, 255–256
comparison operators, 256–257
complement operator, 250–256
compound operators, spacing, 259
is equal to (==) operator, 264
left/right shift operators, 256
OR operator, 256
in strings, 251

P

pack layouts, 18–19, 23–24
parsing, Interpreter pattern, 180–181
pattern matching, 272–273
PEP 8 standards, 258
PIL (Pillow Image Library)
displaying images, 146
using, 145–146
PlotStategy class, Strategy pattern, 226–227
pluggable adapters, 103
Point class, Template pattern, 234
polymorphism, 14, 243
prefix/suffix removal, strings, 281
print function, 267–268
Print verb, Interpreter pattern, 182
printing employee trees, 114–116
privileged access, iterators, 192–193
program commands, Strategy pattern, 227–228
programming, help systems, 160–161
properties, 13
Prototype pattern, 91, 95
cloning, 91–92
consequences of, 94
GitHub programs, 94
using, 92–94
Proxy pattern, 145
comparing related patterns, 149–150
copy-on write objects, 149
GitHub programs, 150
PIL
displaying images, 146
using, 145–146
threads
loading images, 146–148
logging from, 149
PyCharm, 137, 276
pymysql library, 137
Python
arrays, lists, 265
classes

- blank lines, 259
- Docstrings, 259
- indentation, 259
- naming conventions, 258

command-line arguments, 297–298

comments
- Docstrings, 259
- indentation, 259
- spacing, 259

complete programs, writing, 287–288

complex numbers, 253

constants
- character constants, 251–252
- named constants. *See* variables
- naming conventions, 258
- numeric constants, 250

data types, 250

decision making
- assignment (=) operator, 264
- break statements, 266
- combining conditions, 264
- common mistakes, 264
- continue statements, 267
- elif (else if) statements, 263–264
- format string function, 269
- formatting, C style, 269
- formatting, dates, 271
- formatting, f-string, 269
- formatting, Java style, 269
- formatting, numbers, 268, 270
- formatting, strings, 270
- GitHub programs, 273
- if statements, 263
- if statements, else clauses, 263
- if statements, range function, 266
- is equal to (==) operator, 264
- line length, 267
- lists, 265
- looping statements, 265
- for loops, 265
- match function, 271–272
- pattern matching, 272–273
- print function, 267–268
- range function, arrays, 265

development, 1–2

development environments
- Anaconda, 277
- command-line execution, 278
- CPython, 278
- Google Colaboratory, 277
- IDLE, 275
- IPython, 278
- Jupyter Notebook, 277
- Jython, 278
- LiClipse, 276–277
- PyCharm, 276
- Thonny, 275–276
- Visual Studio, 276
- Wing, 278

dictionaries
- listing, 285
- using, 284–285

equal signs (=)
- initialization with, 254
- spacing, 259

executable programs, creating, 296–297

formatting, dates, 271

f-string formatting, 269

functions, 291
- blank lines, 259
- calling, 293
- def keyword, 291, 293
- Docstrings, 259
- format string function, 269
- GitHub programs, 293
- map function, 287–288

match function, 271–272
naming conventions, 258–259
range function, arrays, 265
returning tuples, 292
starting Python programs, 292–293
GitHub programs
collections, 290
decision making, 273
syntax, 261
icons, creating, 295–296
installing, 275
integer division, 253
line length, 267
lists
changing contents, 281–282
comprehension, 289
copying, 282
slicing, 279
spacing, 259
loops
break statements, 266
continue statements, 267
for loops, 266
indentation, 259
with loops, 283–284
negative indexes, 281
operators, 250–256
AND operator, 256
arithmetic operators, 255, 259
bitwise operators, 255–256
comparison operators, 256–257
compound operators, 259
left/right shift operators, 256
OR operator, 256
pattern matching, 272–273
PEP 8 standards, 258
running programs, 295
sets, using, 287
shortcuts, creating, 295–296
simple program example, 254–255
starting programs, 292–293
statements
break statements, 266
combined arithmetic/assignment statements, 256
continue statements, 267
elif (else if) statements, 263–264
if statements, 263
if statements, else clauses, 263
if statements, range function, 266
indentation, 263
input statements, 257
looping statements, 265
for statements, 283
strings
formatting, 270
len function, 251
methods, 251, 260–261
in operators, 251
prefix/suffix removal, 281
representing, 250–251
slicing, 251, 280
tuples, using, 287
variables
Boolean variables, 250
declaring, 252
naming conventions, 249, 252, 258–259
reassigning values, 250
upper/lower case, 249, 252

Q

Query class, Facade pattern, 133–134
queuing commands, 168
Quit buttons, creating, 17–18

R

radio buttons, creating, 27–29

Radiobutton widget, 24–29

range function, arrays, 265

reading files, 282–283

reassigning variable values, 250

receiving help command, 161–162

rectangles/squares, drawing, 10–11

recursive calls stet, Composite pattern, 119

Red button, creating, 175

removing prefixes/suffixes from strings, 281

report generator example, Interpreter pattern, 178–179

requests, Chain of Responsibility pattern, 164

responding to user input, 25–26

Responsibility pattern, Chain of, 155–156

- consequences of, 164–165
- first cases, 162
- GitHub programs, 165
- help command, receiving, 161–162
- help systems
  - programming, 160–161
  - tree structures, 163–164
- listboxes, 159–160
- requests, 164
- sample code, 156–159
- using, 156

Results class, Facade pattern, 134

returning tuples, 292

revised methods, class creation, 8

S

salary computation, Composite pattern, 112

securities (selected), displaying, 89

seeding program, Factory Method pattern, 72–73

selected securities, displaying, 89

selecting folders, Flyweight pattern, 142–143

series of classes, traversing, 245

sets, using, 287

shortcuts, creating, 295–296

simple composites, 119

Simple Factory pattern, 61

- building, 63
- Factory classes, operation of, 61–62
- GitHub programs, 65
- GUI, 64
- math computations, 65
- sample code, 62
- subclasses, 62–63
- thought questions, 66
- using, 63–64

single interface mediators, 200–201

Singleton pattern, 79–80, 95

- consequences of, 82
- exceptions, throwing, 80
- GitHub programs, 82
- large programs, 81–82
- static classes, 81

slicing

- lists, 279
- strings, 251, 280

SmallTalk, Model-View-Controller framework, 53–54

sorting, attrgetter operator, 181–182

spacing

- arithmetic operators, 259
- comments, 259
- equal signs (=), 259
- lists, 259

SQLite

- downloading, 138
- Facade pattern, 136

squares/rectangles, drawing, 10–11
standard triangles, drawing, 235
starting Python programs, 292–293
state data, displaying, 44–46
State pattern, 217
consequences of, 224
GitHub programs, 224
graphics drawing program example, 217–220
sample code, 217–220
StateManager
mediator interactions, 222–223
switching between states, 221
switching between states, 221
transitions, 224
StateManager
mediator interactions, 222–223
switching between states, 221
statements
break statements, 266
combined arithmetic/assignment statements, 256
continue statements, 267
elif (else if) statements, 263–264
for statements, 283
if statements, 263
else clauses, 263
range function, 266
indentation, 263
input statements, 257
looping statements, 265
switch statements. *See* match function
static classes, Singleton pattern, 81
stdTriangle class, Template pattern, 235
Straight Seeding class, Factory Method pattern, 70–71
Strategy pattern, 225
consequences of, 230–231
Context class, 227
GitHub programs, 231
Line and Bar Graph strategies, 228–230
PlotStategy class, 226–227
program commands, 227–228
sample code, 226–227
using, 225–226
strings
Docstrings, 259
format string function, 269
formatting, 270
f-string formatting, 269
len function, 251
methods, 251, 260–261
prefix/suffix removal, 281
representing, 250–251
slicing, 251, 280
structural patterns, 55, 59–97
Adapter pattern, 99
Class adapter, 103
creating adapters, 101–102
GitHub programs, 103
moving data between lists, 99–101
pluggable adapters, 103
two-way adapters, 103
Bridge pattern, 105–107
consequences of, 109–110
creating user interfaces, 107
extending bridges, 107–109
GitHub programs, 110
Listbox builder, 105–106
Treeview widget, 105, 106, 107, 108–109
Composite pattern, 111
Boss class, 113
building employee trees, 114
caching results, 120
composite implementation, 112
consequences of, 118

doubly linked lists, 117–118
Employee class, 112–113
GitHub programs, 120
iterators, 193
leaf nodes, 112–113
printing employee trees, 114–116
recursive calls stet, 119
salary computation, 112
simple composites, 119
Treeviews of composites, 116–117
Decorator pattern, 121, 126
buttons, 121–122
consequences of, 126–127
dataclass decorator, 125–126
decorated code, 124–125
Decorator class, 121–123
GitHub programs, 127
nonvisual decorators, 123–124
Facade pattern, 129–131
building classes, 131–135
consequences of, 137
creating databases, 135–136
creating tables, 135–136
Database class, 132–133
database objects, 129
DBObjects, 134
GitHub programs, 137
MySQL database connections, 131
MySQL Workbench, 130
Query class, 133–134
Results class, 134
SQLite, 136
Table class, 133
tables names, 134–135
Flyweight pattern, 139
copy-on write objects, 143
example code, 140–142
flyweights, defined, 139
folders as flyweights, 140–142
GitHub programs, 143
selecting folders, 142–143
Proxy pattern, 145
comparing related patterns, 149–150
copy-on write objects, 149
GitHub programs, 150
PIL, displaying images, 146
PIL, using, 145–146
threads, loading images, 146–148
threads, logging from, 149
summary of, 151
subclasses, Factory pattern, 62–63
suffix/prefix removal, 281
Swimmer class, Factory Method pattern, 68–69
switch statements. *See* match function
switching between states, 221
syntax, Python
classes
blank lines, 259
Docstrings, 259
indentation, 259
naming conventions, 258
comments
Docstrings, 259
spacing, 259
complex numbers, 253
constants
character constants, 251–252
named constants. *See* variables
naming conventions, 258
numeric constants, 250
data types, 250
equal signs (=)
initialization with, 254
spacing, 259

functions
blank lines, 259
Docstrings, 259
naming conventions, 258–259
GitHub programs, 261
integer division, 253
lists, spacing, 259
loops, indentation, 259
operators
AND operator, 256
arithmetic operators, 255, 259
bitwise operators, 255–256
comparison operators, 256–257
complement operator, 250–256
compound operators, 259
left/right shift operators, 256
OR operator, 256
PEP 8 standards, 258
Python, indentation, 259
statements
combined arithmetic/assignment statements, 256
indentation, 263
input statements, 257
strings
len function, 251
methods, 251, 260–261
in operators, 251
representing, 250–251
slicing, 251
variables
Boolean variables, 250
declaring, 252
naming conventions, 249, 252, 258–259
reassigning values, 250
upper/lower case, 249, 252

T

Table class, Facade pattern, 133
tables
creating, Facade pattern, 135–136
data tables, 41–42
combo boxes, 46–47
listboxes, creating, 42–43
state data, displaying, 44–46
tree nodes, inserting in data tables, 50–51
Treeview widget, 47–49
names, Facade pattern, 134–135
Template class, methods, 234
Template methods, 234
Template pattern, 233
callbacks, 238
concrete methods, 234
consequences of, 238
empty methods, 234
GitHub programs, 238
hook methods, 234
isosceles triangles, 236
IsoscelesTriangle class, 236
Point class, 234
sample code, 234–235
standard triangles, 235
stdTriangle class, 235
summary of, 238
Template class, 234
Triangle class, 234–235, 236
Triangle Drawing program, 237
using, 233
Thonny, 275–276
thought questions
Abstract Factory pattern, 78
Builder pattern, 89
Factory pattern, 66

threads
image loading, 146–148
logging from, 149
throwing exceptions, Singleton pattern, 80
tkinter library, 2
colors, applying, 27
importing names, 19
importing tools, 17
window setup, 17
tracking investments, 84–86
transitions, State pattern, 224
traversing a series of classes, Visitor pattern, 245
tree nodes, inserting in data tables, 50–51
Treeview widget, 47–49
Bridge pattern, 105, 106, 107, 108–109
Composite pattern, 116–117
Triangle class, Template pattern, 234–235, 236
Triangle Drawing program, 237
triangles, drawing
isosceles triangles, 236
standard triangles, 235
ttk libraries, 24
tuples
returning, 292
using, 286
two-way adapters, 103
types, 13
declaring, 13
hints, 13

U

Undo button, Command pattern, 175–176
Undo function, Command pattern, 172–175
upper/lower case
CamelCase, 258
classes, 258
constants, 258
functions, 258–259
variables, 249, 252
user input, responding to, 25–26
user interfaces
Abstract Factory pattern, 77
creating, 107
GUI, Factory pattern, 64
Interpreter pattern, 183–184

V

Variable class, Interpreter pattern, 181
variables
Boolean variables, 250
case, upper/lower, 249, 252
declaring, 252
inside classes, 6–7, 30
local variables, 13
naming conventions, 258–259
properties, 13
visibility, 12
Verb class, Interpreter pattern, 181
visibility of variables, 12
Visitor pattern, 239, 241
Boss class, 242–243
BVacationVisitor class, 243–244
consequences of, 245
double dispatching, 245
GitHub programs, 245
sample code, 241–242
traversing a series of classes, 245
using, 239–240
visiting
classes, 242
several classes, 242–243
visual programming
buttons
Hello buttons, 17
Quit buttons, 17–18
radio buttons, 27–29

check boxes, disabling, 34
classes
  communicating between, 30
  variables, 30
data tables, 41-42
  combo boxes, 46-47
  listboxes, 42-43
  state data, displaying, 44-46
  tree nodes, inserting, 50-51
  Treeview widget, 47-49
errors, catching, 26-27
file dialogs, 22-23
Hello buttons, creating, 17
layouts, 17
  grid layouts, 30-34
  pack layouts, 18-19, 23-24
menus, adding to windows, 35-38
message boxes, 17
  creating, 21-22
  error message boxes, 21
  warning message boxes, 21
numbers, adding, 26
Quit buttons, creating, 17-18
radio buttons, creating, 27-29
tkinter library
  applying colors, 27
  importing names, 19
  importing tools, 17
  window setup, 17
ttk libraries, 24
user input, responding to, 25-26
variables, inside classes, 30
widgets
  grid layouts, 30-31
  LabelFrame widget, 39-40
  pack layout manager, options, 23-24
  Radiobutton widget, 24-29
  Treeview widget, 47-49
  ttk libraries, 24
windows, adding menus to, 35-38
Visual Studio, 276

W - X - Y - Z

warning message boxes, creating, 21
widgets
  grid layouts, 30-31
  LabelFrame widget, 39-40
  pack layout manager, options, 23-24
  Radiobutton widget, 24-29
  Treeview widget, 47-49
    Bridge pattern, 105, 106, 107, 108-109
    Composite pattern, 116-117
  ttk libraries, 24
windows, adding menus, 35-38
Wing, 278
with loops, 283-284